# The New Classic
# CHINESE
## Cookbook

## MAI LEUNG

Drawings by
CLAUDE MARTINOT

COUNCIL OAK PUBLISHING
Tulsa, Oklahoma

This book is dedicated to my late husband Nelson S. T. Thayer
with love and gratitude.

Packaged by Freundlich Communications, Inc.
Designed by Anthony Meisel
Origination by Regent Publishing Services, Ltd.

Library of Congress Cataloging-in-Publication Data
Thayer, Leung Mai.
    The new classic Chinese cookbook / Mai Leung Thayer; drawings by Claude
    Martinot.
        p.        cm.
    Includes index.
    ISBN 1-57187-052-1 (cloth)
    1. Cookery, Chinese.    I. Title
TX724 . 5 . C5T48        1998
641 . 5951—dc21                                                    98–11488
                                                                      CIP

# CONTENTS

# INTRODUCTION TO THE 1976 EDITION

To the people and culture of China, I acknowledge my enduring indebtedness. The collective experience of my people has been my teacher and my benefactor. I had the good fortune to be born among them, to participate in their learning and experience.

I am especially grateful to my grandmother and mother, who encouraged my early ventures in the kitchen. To their spirits I bow deeply. I must also thank my father, who arranged to place me in the kitchens of several restaurants owned by his friends in Hong Kong.

During my youth, the cooks of my grandparents and parents stirred up my interest and basic skill in cooking, patiently tolerated my intrusions, and indulgently cleaned up my experiments. Of their simple and unassuming lives, I remain in awe.

Many kowtows go to Chef Tong Shui Lin, Chef Mui, Chef Lin, of Hong Kong; Chef Ng and Chef Chon of New York. I profoundly appreciate their hours of assistance and their generosity in sharing their special knowledge and skill in Sichuan and Peking cooking.

This book is an undertaking of fourteen years of hovering over hot woks and sizzling oil, thousands of hours of research, as well as countless visits with chefs, cooks, and grocers. Yet when I look back at these pages, I hesitate to claim them as my own. For they are the expression of millions of cooks, stretching through thousands of years. Most of those I am indebted to have become faceless, nameless, and are gone; a few I have known and hold dear.

Few of them were celebrated or wealthy. Most have been humble, many poor, but they have been blessed with talent, creativity, and rich and exuberant spirits. Cooks in homes, food-hawkers on the streets, chefs in restaurants, it is these ordinary people who have raised our cuisine to its peak. In so doing, they have served, enriched, and expressed our life.

Past and present, these are my people, the ordinary people of China. It is they who have patiently taught me. It is their collective experience that enables me to express my own. In addition to these recipes, it is their spirit which I wish to convey in this book.

Here are over two hundred well-loved dishes from Sichuan, Hunan, and Beijing, and from the east and south of China as well. All of these recipes have been tested and enjoyed by many hundreds of students and guests for nearly a decade.

I hope that with each meal you will share and love not only the abundant food of my people but also their spirit.

# INTRODUCTION TO
# THE NEW CLASSIC CHINESE COOKBOOK

I remain deeply grateful to the thousand of appreciative cooks and enthusiastic readers who have enjoyed THE CLASSIC CHINESE COOKBOOK through its six editions and eighteen years in print. In that time, several favorable changes, such as a wider and fresher availability of ingredients and improvements in kitchen equipment, have affected Chinese cuisine. In that same time, many of us have found ourselves working more and with less time to cook, but still wanting to provide delicious Chinese dishes for ourselves and loved ones, some of whom are vegetarians or particularly health conscious eaters. The NEW CLASSIC CHINESE COOKBOOK embraces and responds to these developments.

Rest assured, however, that the core of this book is composed of the classic recipes that made the original volume such a success. Recipes such as Peking Duck, Dong Po Pork, Hunan Crisp Sea Bass, Crisp Lemon Chicken, Puff Butterfly Shrimp, My Mother's Lettuce Packages, Beef In Oyster Sauce, Lotus Leaf Rice, and many other well-loved recipes remain.

Nevertheless, in response to our now-familiar concerns of health and wellness, I have changed some recipes from deep-frying to steaming or water blanching in order to reduce oil use, but only if the taste and integrity of the dishes are not compromised.

For instance, String Beans With Garlic traditionally calls for deep-frying and then stir-frying the string beans with other ingredients; happily, I have found steaming the beans not only retains the character of the dish but also brings out its freshness and natural sweetness. I should note, however, that we revel in the delicious flavors of many of these time-honored dishes precisely because they contain a certain amount of fat. I believe that there is no sin in oil or marbled meat, nor that they are intrinsically bad and have to be feared. They become bad only when the golden rule of moderation and common sense is violated by excess.

You may also note that I have greatly expanded the chapter on vegetables and tofu to take advantage of a wider range of fresh Chinese produce in the States, in addition to an abundance of once uncommon ingredients from China and Taiwan. Today, these items, even the rare varieties, are readily available, not only in urban Chinatowns, but also in the local Asian markets sprouting throughout the suburbs. Abundant displays of Chinese produce such as water spinach, long beans, Chinese chives, snow pea shoots, Taiwan bean sprouts, Shanghai bok choy, and various kinds of tofu are the envy of our visitors from China. Some of these delicious and nutritious dishes were created as one-dish meals for vegetarian relatives and friends, and for those who prefer reducing their meat intake on occasion.

Finally, improvements in kitchen equipment have also enhanced Chinese cooking. In some recipes, non-stick pans and non-stick vegetable-based sprays, not only make cooking some dishes easier, but also reduce the amount of oil in them. Because the microwave oven is excellent for reheating many Chinese dishes without harming their flavors or textures, this new volume offers a number of extra large recipes, so that a busy cook can enjoy a few meals from one recipe. Accordingly, you will find that the dumplings can be made ahead of time and frozen. They, and several others, serve well for working people who do not have the time to cook every day.

Whatever the developments affecting Chinese cuisine may be, as a cook and a gastronomic devotee, I feel profoundly blessed each time I enter a food market. I never cease to marvel at the ingredients I hold and select, and which I have embraced in the following recipes. I hope they offer you and your family and friends as much comfort and joy as they do mine.

Mai Leung
1998

# Utensils, Cooking and Cutting Techniques

# BEFORE BEGINNING

1. Read the entire recipe carefully before preparing the ingredients and cooking.
2. Have all the ingredients prepared and organized as directed in the Preparation of Ingredients.
a. Ingredients such as meat, poultry, and seafood can be cut in advance. It is easier to cut meat and poultry if they are semi-frozen (put them in the freezer for about 30 minutes). After they are cut, be sure to keep them covered and refrigerated before use.
b. Always cover the sauce mixture if it is prepared in advance. The vegetables, ginger, and scallions can also be cut hours ahead. Put them on a plate and wrap them to prevent from drying.
3. All measurements should be exactly as in the recipe.
a. If the measure is by spoon, especially the sauce mixture, it should always be a level spoon. Level it with your finger or a knife.
b. Do not add more than the recipe asks for; adding a few more ounces of meat, poultry, or seafood to a stir-fried dish will make the dish bland and cause it to lose its taste. (If you need more than a recipe calls for, repeat the recipe.) To ensure making no mistake, weigh ingredients. Exact measurement is essential for the success of these recipes. A scale is an indispensable aid to satisfactory results.
4. Do not use double black soy sauce because the dishes will be a little too salty for you.
5. This book is based on cooking on a gas stove. Since an electric stove is usually hotter than a gas one, you might need to adjust the heat to medium-high or medium (see Stove, page 13).

# UTENSILS, COOKING AND CUTTING TECHNIQUES

## UTENSILS

### WOK WITH COVER AND COLLAR

The wok is a round-bottomed, Chinese cooking vessel. It has been used for centuries and was designed for stir-frying to shorten cooking time and to save fuel. A few tablespoons of oil just barely cover a flat-bottomed skillet, but in the wok the same amount of oil forms a little pool, in which each piece of meat or vegetable has a chance to be immersed. Besides, the wok is almost an all-purpose cooking utensil. It can be used in many ways: to deep-fry, to stir-fry, to steam, to stew, to smoke, and to poach.

Woks come in different sizes, with matching covers, from 10 to 20 inches in diameter. The ideal size for family cooking is a 14- or 16-inch wok. The 10- or 12-inch one is too small to do Chinese cooking. Woks that are bigger than 16 inches are too large to use on your family stove. They are used by restaurants that have specially built high-heat stoves.

Woks are made with carbon steel, aluminum, stainless steel, or some other material. For Chinese cooking, I prefer the cast iron or the carbon steel ones. They get hot easily but do not retain heat as long as the others, so that they serve well for the purpose of stir-frying.

In China, a wok sits comfortably on a specially built stove. But your gas or electric ranges are not built for a round-bottomed wok, and you need a metal collar for it to sit on or a flat-bottomed wok.

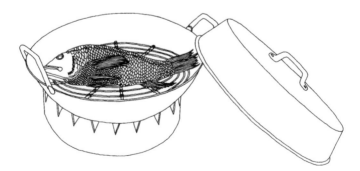

A new cast iron or carbon steel wok comes with a layer of machine grease to protect it from rusting. Clean it thoroughly with hot water and a mild detergent. Dry it, then season it by wiping it with a paper towel, slightly dampened with oil. Such treatment will not be necessary before each use. Your wok may become blackened after a few uses—it is supposed to be that way. Do not try to brighten it by scouring. No strong detergent should be used on the wok. The round bottom makes cleaning easy, for there is no corner in which the food can stick. Hot water and a dish brush are sufficient to clean it. If you keep it dry after each use, and oil it occasionally, it will last forever.

For convenience in cooking the Chinese way, I strongly recommend the purchase of a wok. If you do not have a wok, a big skillet can also be used for a lot of Chinese cooking.

## CLEAVER

The Chinese cleaver is quite a frightening piece of equipment. Its blade is broad and long, about 3 to 4 inches by 8 inches. The big, thick, heavy cleaver is for chopping meat with bones; it is called a "bone knife." The thin and light kind is for slicing meat and cutting vegetables. Cleavers are made of carbon or stainless steel and can be sharpened easily. It takes only a few seconds to sharpen a cleaver. There is nothing more dangerous than to have a dull knife skid on the meat than on to your fingers!

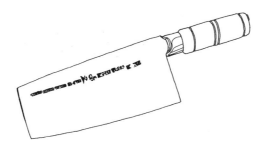

The cleaver is a very talented piece of equipment. It does an excellent job in slicing and mincing meat, cutting vegetables, or chopping bones, and the end of its wooden handle can mash salted black beans. The broad flat blade can scoop up and carry food from the chopping board to other places. Another impressive little trick a cleaver can do is to help peel off a garlic skin in a split second. Put the garlic on a hard surface, and give it a whack with the flat of the cleaver blade. Now, you find that the skin comes off the crushed garlic with just a gentle pull.

Each kind of cleaver has its own function, however. So don't force a meat cleaver to chop bones, or use a bone cleaver to ax wood! You will just break its sharp edges and end its service.

Having a cleaver is pleasurable and helpful, but not absolutely necessary. Any sharp knife in your kitchen, a carving knife, a boning knife, or even a steak knife is adequate to help in preparing the meat of the Chinese meal.

## LADLE

For Chinese stir-fry cooking, ideally, the spatula and the ladle should work together like your right hand and left hand. While the ladle in your left hand swirls in the oil, soy sauces, or wine, the spatula in your right hand tosses and stirs. Both coordinate in harmony. However, on the American stove the wok does not rest securely enough on the collar. Therefore, one hand is needed to hold on to one of the handles to ensure steadiness. Otherwise you could easily end up having a floor full of food.

A Chinese ladle is not essential; a big spoon or a serving spoon will do.

## SPATULA

The Chinese spatula is very useful for tossing, stirring, or turning food in the wok. It has a low rim around the heel to catch gravy. However, a pancake turner will serve equally well.

## STEAMERS

The traditional Chinese steamers are bamboo and handwoven. They are round baskets with a solidly woven lid on top. In order to save fuel and time, the baskets containing food are stacked and steamed over a wok full of boiling water. Sizes of bamboo steamers vary from 4-inch dim sum steamers to 16-inch seafood or poultry steamers. The most practical size is the 10-inch one in which you can steam a wide range of foods.

Aluminum and stainless steel steamers are very popular. They are not as handsome as the bamboo ones, but they last longer.

However, there are ways to steam food without a steamer (see Steaming).

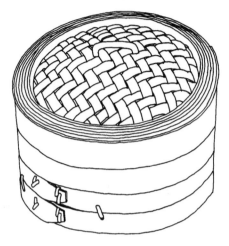

## DEEP-FRY DRAINER

The Chinese drainer is woven by hand with shiny brass wires, connected to a bamboo handle. The basket diameter ranges from 4 to 8 inches. For family cooking, the small drainer is more useful than the large one. It is used for draining fried food, blanched meat, vegetables, noodles, or spaghetti.

If you have a big slotted spoon, the drainer is optional.

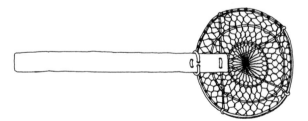

## STOVE

The American gas stove is perfect for Chinese cooking. The heat can be controlled instantly. If you have an electric range, controlling the heat is not as smooth as with the gas stove. But it will work out just as well if you turn on two burners at different temperatures. You simply switch the wok to the other burner if the heat is too high or too low.

Beware of the electric stove with an automatically controlled burner. Do not use this burner to deep-fry, for it will not heat the oil to deep-fry temperature.

You can now buy a specially built wok for an electric stove. It is circular and has sloping sides like a regular wok, but has a flat bottom so that it can rest directly on the burner. The highest possible temperature can then be reached due to direct contact with the burner. You can also use a round-bottomed wok with a collar, but it is more difficult to reach high temperature. Or, if you like, for stir-frying, you can remove the collar and rest the wok directly on the burner' using one hand to hold a handle of the wok to steady it. For deep-frying, I suggest that you use a pot instead. A wokful of hot oil without a collar to steady it is too dangerous.

CHOPSTICKS

In Chinese, chopsticks means "quick little ones." If you want to see the quick little ones in action, drop into Chinatown at lunch or supper hours and watch the shopkeepers eat. You will see chopsticks moving at great speed, diving, lifting, and shoveling among the few dishes and the rice bowls.

Chopsticks are used not only for eating but also for stirring ingredients, beating eggs, cutting food, or even as a thermometer to test the oil temperature (see Cooking Techniques).

In the old days, the nobles and the rich used silver, gold, or even jade chopsticks. Silver chopsticks were used by a number of emperors who feared foes might put poison in their food. It was said that the tips of the silver chopsticks would turn black when in contact with poisoned food.

Many Chinese families use lacquered or ivory chopsticks for eating. The ivory ones are given as wedding presents. Like silver flatware, they are well cared for and are expected to last at least a lifetime.

Nowadays, plastic chopsticks are very popular. They are made to look like ivory. Do not use them or the lacquered or ivory ones for cooking or deep-frying, for they will bend or melt with the heat. For cooking, use chopsticks that are made of bamboo or other wood.

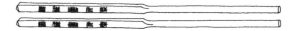

# COOKING TECHNIQUES

## STIR-FRYING

This unusual cooking method is uniquely Chinese. It is the most essential and frequently used technique in Chinese cooking. Experience, practice, and the training of your eyes, your nose, and even your ears are required for success in this cooking method. Preparation, organization, and concentration are also essential. Because it is very important for you to master this technique, I am going to explain it in detail.

To prepare for stir-frying, you should have all the vegetables or meat cut in advance. The shape and size of the ingredients are generally small and uniform. In most dishes, meat plays the leading role, and its size and shape determine the size and shape of the subordinate ingredients. For instance, in sweet and sour pork, the pork is cut into ¾-inch cubes, then the subordinate ingredients, such as bamboo shoots and green pepper, should be cut into the same size and shape as the pork. If it is a beef with noodles dish, and the beef is to be sliced, then the vegetables should be sliced like the beef. If it is a vegetable dish, such as stir-fry broccoli, the broccoli should be cut two times bigger than bite-size. A big piece of vegetable prevents overcooking and looks much prettier in the dish. All the recipes in this book have specific instructions about the sizes of the meat and vegetables.

After you have the meat and vegetables cut, organize all the ingredients and put them in bowls or on plates near the stove within reach. Now comes the most important part, the technique. Heat the dry wok until it is very hot. This takes from one to two minutes, depending on your stove and the weight of your wok. To know if the wok is hot enough, put your open palm about 3 inches above the bottom of the wok (not on it!). If your palm feels very warm, then the wok is hot enough for stir-frying. (Heating a dry wok before adding the oil prevents the food from sticking.) Swirl the oil in around the rim of the wok, as if you were drawing a circle. Because of the shape of the wok, the oil will naturally run down to grease most of the wok, and it will heat on the way down. (If you use a skillet, spread the oil with a spatula.) Wait a few seconds to allow the oil to get hot but not smoking. Throw in the salt, scallions, ginger, and garlic. Do you hear the sizzling sound? And do you see the scallions, ginger, and garlic spinning around? If so, you are getting there! if not, heat the wok and oil longer next time.

Salt, scallions, ginger, and garlic are almost always put into the wok right after the oil and before the other ingredients. The hot oil draws out the fragrance and the flavor of these seasonings. When the aroma flows from the wok to the air, Chinese chefs call it "wok aroma." Now it is time for you to put in the vegetables or the meat. They are never put in at the same time. Toss and stir the food constantly and vigorously. Use not just your wrist, but your whole arm. You should hear a nice sound and rhythm each time the spatula hits the wok. The intense heat of the oil instantly seals in the flavor and juice of the meat. The color of the vegetables is not only preserved by the hot oil, but is enhanced. All this happens in less than three minutes. Very few stir-fry dishes take longer than five minutes because all the vegetables and meat are cut into small pieces.

Remember that the heat is still high, and your spatula has to stir and toss constantly. Keep your eyes on the color change of the meat or the vegetables. Let your nose experience the fragrance released by the spices. Allow your ears to listen to the various sizzling sounds of the food. Sense it, feel it. If the phone rings, don't answer it. Let the world stop for you for a few minutes.

Be careful not to overcook food. Prolonged cooking will toughen meat and destroy the beautiful green color and the crunchiness of vegetables.

What happens if you fail a few times at the beginning? Stir-frying is learned from experience. Remember the old Chinese saying, "Beijing was not built in a day!"

## DEEP-FRYING

It is very important to have the oil at the right temperature for deep-frying. If the oil is not hot enough, residues from meat and poultry will cloud it; also the food will absorb more oil and thus become soggy and greasy.

If it is too hot, the food will burn or get brown outside and not be cooked enough inside. On the other hand, if the oil temperature is just right, the food will be crisp and will use less oil. Also, the oil should be deep enough to float the ingredients.

Since the Chinese do not care about the exact temperature of the oil, a cooking thermometer is not used. We judge the oil by experienced eyes or test it by dropping in a piece of scallion. If the oil is right for deep-frying, the scallion will spin vigorously and sizzle noisily. If it sizzles gently and does not spin, the oil should be a little hotter.

Another easy testing method is to dip a dry bamboo chopsticks into the oil. If a great many sizzling bubbles quickly gather around the chopstick, then the oil is ready for frying. If the bubbles surround the chopstick slowly, the oil is not quite ready. Be sure that the chopstick is dry. A wet chopstick does not work! If the oil is smoking, do not put in anything. Turn off the heat and let it cool.

Sometimes oil splatters. I found some students of mine uneasy about the hot oil. They throw in the food and run! But you don't need to be afraid. If you gently slide in the food, the oil will not splatter. To ensure that the oil will not fire single shots at you from time to time, be sure to dry the food thoroughly before slipping it in.

The oil left over from frying can be saved and reused.

## BLANCHING IN WATER
*(For Chicken and Vegetables)*
For Chicken: Use 1 quart of boiling water for each cup of sliced, shredded, or diced raw chicken. Immerse chicken in boiling water. Turn off heat at once. Stir to separate pieces. Let chicken blanch in water for 1 minute. Pour into a colander. Rinse thoroughly in cold water to prevent further cooking. Drain. Use as required in recipes.

For Vegetables: Use 2 quarts of boiling water for each ½ pound of fresh vegetables. Immerse vegetables in boiling water. Turn off heat. Let vegetables stay in water for about 10 seconds. Pour into a colander. Rinse thoroughly in cold water to prevent further cooking. Drain. Use as required in recipes.

## BLANCHING IN OIL
*(For Meat, Poultry, and Seafood)*
One of the unique Chinese cooking methods is to blanch food in oil. In Chinese it is called *yu-pao*. This method is different from deep-frying. The food is not fried for a long period to golden brown, but is removed from the oil immediately when it is just done. Usually the food is sliced or shredded into thin pieces before cooking. This method is mostly used by Chinese chefs. The purpose is to achieve the maximum tenderness, smoothness, and lightness of the food.
    Use 2 cups of oil for each cup of food.
For Meat: Heat oil to deep-fry temperature (test it with a piece of scallion; it should spin and sizzle noisily) over medium heat. Add the meat. Quickly stir to separate pieces. As soon as the meat loses its redness (it takes less than a minute), remove it with a drainer. Drain, put aside, and use as required in the recipe. Save oil for blanching and cooking again.

For Poultry or Seafood: Over medium heat, heat oil to hot (test it with a piece of scallion; it should just sizzle quickly). Add poultry or seafood. Quickly stir to separate pieces. In about 30 seconds, the poultry should turn milky-white, the seafood whitish or pink. Remove with a drainer. Drain and use as required in the recipe. The oil may be saved for blanching and cooking again.

## STEAMING
Steaming in bamboo or perforated metal steamer tray: Put food (buns, dumplings, poultry, meat, seafood, rice, eggs, etc.) on tray. If using rice, line steamer tray

*Utensils, Cooking and Cutting Techniques • 17*

with cheesecloth, so that the rice will not fall through.

Use a wok or a pot that will contain the steamer tray, and pour in enough boiling water to reach about 1 inch below the tray. Return water to rapid boil, place tray over water, cover, and steam over high heat according to the time given in the recipe. *(Important:* Never start steaming food if water is not boiling rapidly.) If you have a large amount of food and two steamer trays, you may place food on both trays; place one tray on top of the other, cover the top tray, and steam. Add boiling water to maintain the water level as necessary during steaming.

Steaming on a wire rack: A cake rack will do the job. Place one layer of cheesecloth on rack; place food on cheesecloth. Use a wok or a pot that will hold the rack. Pour in about 1 inch of boiling water. Place 1 or 2 small, heavy, heatproof bowls right side up in wok or pot. (Lightweight bowls such as thin aluminum containers may float and swim around.) When the water is boiling vigorously, gently place the loaded rack on the bowls. Cover the wok or pot and steam over high heat according to the time given in the recipe. Add boiling water to maintain the water level as necessary during steaming.

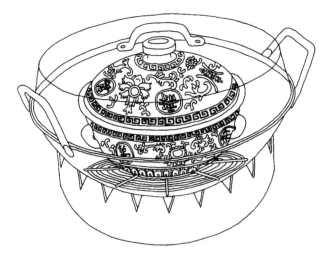

## DRY STEAMING
Dry steaming is somewhat like the Western way of cooking food in a double boiler, in which the food is cooked but not touched by the steam.

The method of dry steaming is to put food into a tightly covered heatproof container. A china bowl, a clay pot, or a casserole will do, but a tight lid is essential. Put casserole into a big wok or pot which has a tight lid and can comfortably hold the covered casserole.

Put enough water into the wok or pot to come two-thirds up the side of the casserole. Put lid on wok or pot, and steam over medium-high heat. Add boiling water from time to time to maintain the water level.

This steaming process is usually slow; it takes from 2 to 4 hours or more. But the food will come out whole, very tender, and tasty.

## RED COOKING

Red Cooking refers to the process in which food is covered and cooked slowly over low heat for an extended period. The color of the food runs from brown to black, depending on how much black soy sauce is added. The Chinese prefer to call this method of preparation "red" cooking because, unlike black or brown, red is considered a happy color connoting celebration.

## HOW TO TAKE OUT PART OF AN EGG WHITE

Open a hole as big as a blueberry on one end of the egg. Then turn over the egg and let one glob of egg white run out. One glob is about a third of an egg white, and 2 globs are about half of an egg white. To get a whole egg white, open a bigger hole (but not big enough to let the yolk fall out), and let the egg white run out completely, shifting the egg to prevent the yolk from covering the hole. To save washing a bowl, refrigerate the yolk in the shell.

# CUTTING TECHNIQUES

Cutting and Slicing: Always cut meat, especially beef, against the grain, to achieve tenderness. Flank steak is the best beef to use, for its grain is clear. If you want to cut meat into paper-thin slices, it is easier to cut or slice it when it is half-frozen. The size of a slice varies according to the recipe.

Shredding: The size of a shred in general is the size of a matchstick, ⅛-inch wide, ⅛-inch thick, and 1 to 2 inches long. The only way to shred is to slice the meat or vegetable first, and then cut each slice into shreds.

Dicing and Mincing: Dicing means cutting ingredients into peanut-sized or pea-sized pieces. In mincing, ingredients are chopped into rice-sized pieces or cut so finely that they become a paste. The best way to dice or mince is to cut ingredients into slices (thickness according to the recipe), cut slices into strips, then dice or mince strips crosswise into desired size.

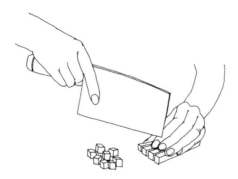

# Dim Sum
# and Appetizers

# DIM SUM

Dim sum figuratively denotes "those that delight your heart." They are small, stuffed dumplings, dainty pastries, little cakes and buns served in Chinese teahouses only in the morning.

Dim sum is the main attraction of the Chinese teahouse, which is the most popular and affordable eatery for the Chinese people. In China, some of them have tables among scented flowers and lotus ponds; a few are floating restaurants carved to look like dragons; many are immense halls, jammed with hundreds of buzzing masses. But most of them are just unornamented, regular restaurants.

Because of the increasing influx of Chinese in America, dim sum is no longer an exclusive commodity of the urban Chinatown. Today, more and more suburban Chinese restaurants are offering dim sum, though only on weekends.

One of the unique features of eating in teahouses is that you don't need to order your meal. All you do is relax over a pot of hot tea and wait for the vendor's dim sum carts and their singsong voices, calling out the dim sum's names of their carts. When you hear the names that entice your heart, a little signal from you will bring them to your table.

The art of eating in teahouses is not to eat your fill in a hurry. Nor should you pick everything from one cart, since each cart's dim sum is different and you will be too full for those that come later. Should you miss some dim sum, don't worry about chasing after the vendors. They will be back again and again even though they seem listless and slow. Allow yourself to eat at a leisurely pace, for as long as you add a few dim sum on your table now and then, no waiter will give you the evil eye to make you go. When your teapot is empty, it is not necessary to call the waiter, just uncover it, which is the signal for a refill.

But for many Chinese, coming to the teahouse is not just for sipping tea and savoring dim sum, but for other reasons. Some come to do business and to make deals; some come to share a grievance or to voice an injustice; some come to give opinion and sound advice; some come because coming becomes a tradition, a habit of the heart. But most come for the familiar faces and the conversations in which one can join in, listen to, or ignore as folly. This is how my father spends his mornings in Hong Kong. Retirement, Chinese style.

Since many dim sum can be prepared in advance to be frozen; therefore, the following recipes are big or can be doubled. They are excellent as appetizers or as a first course.

# HAH GAU, CANTONESE STYLE
## (STEAMED SHRIMP CRESCENTS)
Makes about 24

No one can resist a hah gau, a savory that pleases all hearts. Many Chinese consider it the most exquisite dim sum. It brings pleasure with every bite. It reflects the art and creativity of Chinese cuisine, transforming a few common ingredients to pure gastronomic delight.

"Hah" means shrimp and "gau" small crescent. A good hah gau must meet these requirements: the skin should be thin and translucent to show the shrimp wrapped within; the shrimp must be sonng—the Chinese standard of well-cooked shrimp, a combination of springiness, crunchiness and a little resilience felt between one's teeth; the size of the gau should be dainty, not larger than a chestnut, to show its maker's skill, for it is much easier to make it larger.

Hah gau skin is made of wheat starch instead of flour. Wheat starch contains no gluten and is, therefore, inelastic and fragile. This often dismays inexperienced hands. Don't be discouraged if your early efforts do not produce hah gau quite as dainty as you would like. Just keep practicing; be patient and remember the old saying: "Failure is the mother of success."

## PREPARATION OF INGREDIENTS

1 cup wheat starch (see page 336), sifted
¾ cup boiling water
1 tablespoon lard or shortening
Filling (mix in a bowl, keep refrigerated until used)

½ pound fresh shrimp: shell, devein, rinse in running cold water, drain, pat dry,
    cut into pea-sized pieces
6 water chestnuts, minced
2 tablespoons minced pork fat or bacon
½ teaspoon salt
½ teaspoon sugar
2 teaspoons sesame oil
2 teaspoons dry Sherry

Soy-Sesame Dip: put 4 tablespoons black soy sauce in a small serving dish, add
1 tablespoon of sesame oil, serve as dip

# DIRECTIONS FOR COOKING

1. Prepare the hah gau skins: Put wheat starch in a medium-sized bowl, and make a well in the center. Pour in boiling water, stirring quickly with a spoon. Add lard or shortening, and knead dough until it is homogenized. Then roll dough into a 1-inch diameter sausage. Cover with a warm, damp towel and let it rest for about 15 minutes. Cut dough into chestnut-sized pieces and roll them into round marbles. Cover with a towel.

2. Assemble the hah gau: oil one side of a cleaver or the blade of a broad knife. Press oiled blade on each marble of dough to make a thin circle. Put abut 1½ teaspoons of filling in the center of each circle. Make hah gau according to illustrations below.

3. Place hah gau on an oiled steamer basket. Cover and steam over high heat for 10 minutes. Serve hot with dip.

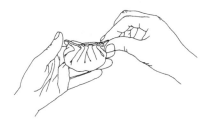

# SIU MAI
## (STEAMED PASTRY WITH SHRIMP AND PORK FILLING)
Makes about 48 siu mai

I n Chinese, siu mai means "cook to sell," and in fact they are one of the best-selling dim sum in teahouses. For Chinese gourmets, good siu mai should be filled with plenty of shrimp along with pork.

For the Chinese, siu mai is usually a breakfast dish. But they make a splendid appetizer or lunch. They are not only delicious but very attractive if served in their bamboo steamer.

Siu mai are easy to make. You can make them in advance, but be sure to keep them refrigerated until steaming, for shrimp goes bad quickly at room temperatures. Or you can quick freeze them uncooked and they will keep for two weeks. Steam them while they are still frozen. Of course, they taste best when fresh.

## PREPARATION OF INGREDIENTS

48 siu mai skins or wonton skins

FILLING (mix well, beat vigorously with a wooden spoon for about a minute, refrigerate until used)

1 pound fresh shrimp: shell, devein, clean with running cold water, pat dry, cut into chunks as big as cranberries
1 pound ground pork
½ cup Chinese dried mushrooms; soak in hot water until spongy, discard stems, mince caps
1 tablespoon cornstarch
1 teaspoon sugar
1 teaspoon salt
¼ teaspoon ground pepper
1 tablespoon dry Sherry
2 tablespoons thin soy sauce
2 tablespoons sesame oil

Soy-Sesame Dip (see page 315)

# DIRECTIONS FOR COOKING

1. If wonton skins are used, trim skins into circles. Spoon about 1 tablespoon of filling into the middle of a circle; pleat and press skin around filling. The siu mai now looks like a miniature cupcake. Gently squeeze siu mai in the middle crosswise to narrow its waist. Press down the top to firm up the filling. Lightly tap siu mai to flatten bottom so it can stand up. Make the others in the same manner. Cover and refrigerate them until steaming.

2. Grease a perforated tray or the bottom of a steamer with oil. Arrange siu mai on it. Cover and steam over boiling water and high heat for 12 minutes (20 minutes if frozen). Serve hot with dip.

NOTE: To freeze the uncooked siu mai, do not stack them directly on each other, but separate each layer with wax paper.

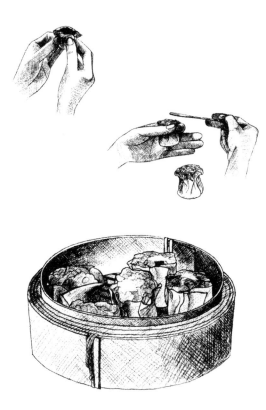

# BASIC JIAOZI
## (MEAT DUMPLINGS, NORTHERN STYLE)
Makes 50

Jiaozi, small meat-filled crescents, are one of the most popular foods in the regions of Beijing, Shanghai, Sichuan and Hunan. Like the sandwiches of the West, they are frequently prepared at home or eaten in restaurants as snacks as well as meals.

Jiaozi skins are a little thicker and sturdier than the skins of the Cantonese wanton. And their fillings are more meaty, robust with juicy minced pork and scallions, pork with chopped Chinese cabbage, beef or lamb. They are either steamed, boiled, or fried crispy on one side.

Jiaozi are served mostly by the dozen; the steamed ones are snuggled in bamboo steamer trays; the boiled ones gleam in tasty soup; and fried ones show off by lying in rows on the plate with their crispy sides up.

Accompany them with a cup of tea, a bowl of soup and a bottle of good Chinese beer (we have great beer), and no one can leave the table contented without consuming a dozen Jiaozis.

They are not only an excellent snack for before or after the theater, but also a hearty meal that does not strain one's purse. And they are even cheaper if prepared at home.

When I was growing up in China, most women, children, and even men learned to make jiaozis. It was always a festive activity in my family. Encircling the big, round dining table, we all sat, grandmother, mother, our amahs, Noble face and Obedience, and often a few distant relatives we called uncle and aunt but knew as "eating guests," who needed a place to eat and stay. Sometimes we were joined by Old Chan, my father's helper from Shantung Province, the best jiaozi maker we had ever known. Busy hands and bumping shoulders hovered over the large bowl of filling, while the gong-voices of Grandmother and Noble Face clashed with the deafening sound of Old Chan's cleaver pounding on the meat.

Old Chan was immense, and his shaved head and northern dialect, he was forever branded a stranger in the southern cities of Canton and Hong Kong. He was not old, but in his forties when my father first saw him, shivering and starving at the door of a Shanghai hotel where my father was staying just before the Japanese invasion. My father gave him a coat and a small amount of money, and when he brought Old Chan home, my mother was not surprised, for father never failed to believe a sad story of life even though he had heard it many times. Unlike some others, Old Chan was helpful in the household and fervently loyal to Father. And Mother could not bear to set him astray.

He was once an army cook—actually for a warlord—we believed. And when he was not traveling with Father on business he loved to make jiaozi and noodles. Grandmother was usually the one to prepare the dough, but we much preferred Old Chan. He twisted and stretched the dough in midair and sometimes snaked it around our necks.

He never used a rolling pin, because a good jiaozi maker was most proud of showing off his fast hands. First, he would pinch off a small piece of dough, the size of a walnut, and roll it between his palms to round it. Then he placed the round dough between his thumbs and all eight fingertips. Like a wheel spinning at high speed, his fingers rotated the dough clockwise until it became an even, thin round bowl to hold the filling. Then the jiaozi was filled and pleated, and its thin edges were pinched together to seal. And a delicate jiaozi resembling a dainty silk purse, was placed on a tray.

The children were all accepted at the preparation table, as long as our hands were not too dirty and our breaths were not too wet. When our jiaozi looked like some sleeping dinosaurs, Old Chan would announce, "A jiaozi reflects one's artistic nature!" Then our hands hurried to explore "artistic nature," creating more half-awake jiaozi dinosaurs.

When Old Chan was in the right mood—and he seldom was not when there was an audience—he would bellow his favorite songs of his home, the North. They tended to be about a maiden far away and her beautiful black eyes and a camel song that was full of the sound of Hey! Ah! Hey! Since the words made no sense to us then, we called them "the cow dung songs"; but we loved to echo loudly, Hey! Ah! Hey! Excited by the commotion, our little twin sisters would run gurgling around the table. Except for mother's composed face and the constrained politeness of the "eating guests," Old Chan might have been a genie reveling a goblin's lair.

The jiaozi-making process would be much delayed if Old Chan was wound up to his Beijing opera mood. In the middle of the room, he would sing in a shrilling lady's voice, and like a bear on tiptoe, imitate her willowy steps, a weeping heroine lamenting her bygone lover. And to the children's delight he would somersault and peer about, acting our famous monkey saint, Si Wu Kong. Then no one could make jiaozi. We doubled up, stomachs aching in uncontrollable laughter.

When, finally, the piping hot, juicy jiaozi were served, Old Chan would claim his share—three dozen and sometimes more. So when he was lazy, my father called him "Shantung Rice Bucket"; when he talked too much, "Shantung Cannon." Twenty-five years ago I said, "See you again," to Old Chan. Like to many others that I did not then realize, it was a last goodbye.

Now I make dainty jiaozi with flying fingers like Old Chan, and sing the songs of the camel and maiden that now I understand—a heart's longing for home, even after a willing goodbye.

## PREPARATION OF INGREDIENTS
Jiaozi can be made in advance and kept frozen.

2 pounds Chinese cabbage: separate leaves, steam for 30 minutes or until tender, mince, squeeze out excess water

### FILLING (Mix in a bowl)

1 pound lean ground lamb, beef or pork
½ teaspoon ground pepper
½ teaspoon salt
½ teaspoon sugar
1 tablespoon cornstarch
1 teaspoon sesame oil
1 tablespoon rice wine or dry Sherry
2 tablespoons black soy sauce
1 cup minced scallions, including some green part

### THE WRAPPER

4 cups all-purpose flour
flour for dusting
about 1 cup cold water
about 1¼ cups boiling water

### DIRECTIONS FOR MAKING JIAOZI

1. Combine steamed cabbage and lamb, beef, or pork mixture in a large bowl and stir vigorously for about a minute or until it becomes pasty. Refrigerate before use.
2. In a mixing bowl, add 2 cups flour. Gradually stir in 1 cup cold water to form a moist, soft dough. Knead dough on a floured surface until it is smooth and not sticky. Cover with wax paper.
3. In another mixing bowl, add the remaining flour and make a well at the center. Pour in boiling water and stir quickly with a wooden spoon to form a very soft and moist dough. Cover, allow dough to cool to touch. Knead dough

on a floured surface until it is soft, but not sticky. Form dough into a ball. Cover with wax paper.

4. Roll the cold dough into a pancake, large enough to wrap the hot dough. Place hot dough at the center of the pancake and wrap to form a ball. Knead on a floured surface for about 10 minutes until dough is soft, smooth, but not sticky. Cut dough into 2 portions. Cover with wax paper.

5. Take 1 portion of the dough and roll it into a sausage-like shape dough, 1 inch in diameter. Divide and cut dough into 25 equal pieces. Roll each one into a round ball. Cover with wax paper. Prepare the remaining portion of the dough in the same manner.

6. Take a small ball of dough and roll it into a thin pancake with a rolling pin. Spoon a heaping tablespoon of filling on the center of the pancake and fold in half. Pinch and pleat edges together as illustrated. Make the remaining jiaozi in the same manner. Cover jiaozi on floured surface. (At this point, you can freeze them on trays in a single layer. When they are firm to touch, stack them, but separate each layer with wax paper. Seal tightly. They can be frozen for weeks.

7. Steam or pan-fry jiaozi as directed in the following recipes.

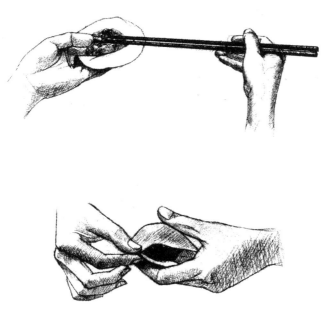

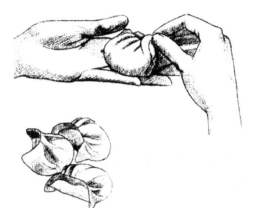

# STEAMED JIAOZI, NORTHERN STYLE
## (STEAMED, STUFFED DUMPLINGS)
Makes 50

PREPARATION OF INGREDIENTS

10 to 12 Chinese cabbage leaves
1 recipe of Basic Jiaozi: if frozen arrange dumplings on tray in single layer,
    thaw at room temperature for 30 minutes before use.

Soy-Sesame Dip(see page 315)
A small bowl of chili sauce (optional)

DIRECTIONS FOR COOKING

1. Line the steamer baskets or steamer trays with cabbage leaves to prevent dumplings from sticking to the steamers. Place dumplings on cabbage. Cover and steam over boiling water for 15 minutes or until they are cooked. Serve hot with dip and sauce. Don't forget to serve the cabbage. It is delicious.

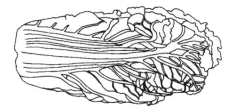

# GUOTIEH
## (PAN-FRIED MEAT DUMPLINGS, NORTHERN STYLE)
Makes 50

These popular and delicious dumplings are soft on the top and crispy on the bottom. They are also known as pot-stickers because they often stick to the pan if an impatient cook tries to lift them before their doughy undersides are brown and crispy. An experienced cook will allow enough time for the bottoms to crisp and thereby become firm and easy to lift. Today, this problem is eliminated by non-stick pans and non-stick oil spray, which allow you to lift up the dumplings to see if they are done, without tearing them apart.

## PREPARATION OF INGREDIENTS

oil for pan-frying
1 recipe of basic Jiaozi (see page 28): if frozen, thaw dumplings in a single layer at
    room temperature for about 30 minutes
Soy-Sesame Dip: (see page 315)

a small bowl of chili sauce (optional)

## DIRECTIONS FOR COOKING

1. Spray a large, heavy pan with non-stick oil spray. Add 3 tablespoons oil and roll pan to spread oil evenly. (Use 2 tablespoons oil for non-stick pan.) Place dumplings in pan, add cold water at the edge of the pan until water comes halfway up to the sides of the dumplings. Cover and cook over moderate heat for about 7 minutes or until dumplings turn opaque. Remove pan from heat. Drain liquid from pan, tilting the pan and opening the cover slightly. Add 3 tablespoons oil to pan (2 tablespoons for non-stick pan) and roll the pan gently to spread oil evenly. Cover and pan-fry over moderate heat until the undersides of the dumplings are brown and crispy. Transfer to serving platter. Serve hot with dip and chili sauce. Pan-fry the remaining dumplings in the same manner.

NOTE: You may use ⅓ to ½ of the recipe as appetizers or as a first course for dinner, and save the rest for other meals.

# VEGETARIAN GUOTIEH
## (PAN-FRIED VEGETABLE DUMPLINGS)
Makes 50

W hat do you do when more and more friends and relatives become vegetarians? Or when a guest tells you that he/she does not eat meat when
dinner is served? No problem. Make a lot of these dumplings and keep them in
the freezer. They are excellent for vegetarians and non-vegetarians. However,
prepare more for each person than you might expect, because they are not as
filling as the meat-filled ones.

PREPARATION OF INGREDIENTS

2 tablespoons oil
2 teaspoons minced garlic
1 cup minced scallions, including some green part
½ cup parsley
12 Chinese, medium-sized dried mushrooms (⅔ cup): soak in hot water until
    spongy, discard stems, mince caps into pea-sized pieces

FILLING (Mix in a bowl)

1 pound purple eggplants: quarter them lengthwise, steam for 15 minutes
    or until tender. Peel skins and discard, scrape seeds and discard, chop pulp
    into peanut-sized pieces.
1 pound Chinese cabbage: separate leaves and steam for 10 minutes or until soft,
    chop into peanut-sized pieces, squeeze out excess water.
1 cup water chestnuts, in pea-sized pieces
1 can (4 ounces) spicy, fried, gluten: drain and mince gluten
1 package (1¾ ounces) bean thread noodles: soak in hot water for about
    10 minutes or until soft, drain, cut into 1-inch lengths with scissors
3 eggs: beat with ¼ teaspoon salt, scramble them with 2 tablespoons oil,
    chop into small chunks

SAUCE MIXTURE (Mix in a bowl)

½ teaspoon ground pepper
1 tablespoon thin soy sauce
3 tablespoons black soy sauce
2 tablespoons oyster-flavored sauce

1 tablespoon rice wine or dry Sherry
2 teaspoons hoisin sauce
2 teaspoons sesame oil

1 recipe of wrappers (see Jiaoxis, page 28)
Soy-Sesame Dip (see page 315)
a small bowl of Chili sauce (optional)

DIRECTIONS FOR COOKING

1. Heat wok over high heat: when oil is hot, swirl in 2 tablespoons oil. Add garlic, scallions, and parsley and stir to cook until garlic turns golden. Add mushrooms and stir-fry until fragrant. Add fillings and stir to mix well. Swirl in sauce mixture and stir to cook over moderate heat for abut 1 minute. Put in a bowl and cool in refrigerator before use.
2. Wrap dumplings as directed in Jiaozi recipe (see page 34).
3. Pan-fry dumplings as directed in above recipe. Serve hot with soy-sesame dip and chili sauce.

# CRISP CURRY CHICKEN CRESCENTS
Makes about 16

These delicious crescents not only are easy to make, but can be prepared in advance. They are excellent as an appetizer or as lunch with a soup. You may also use cooked turkey, beef, pork, or ham to substitute for the chicken breasts.

PREPARATION OF INGREDIENTS

CHICKEN MIXTURE (mix in a bowl)

1½ boned skinless chicken breasts: cut into pea-sized pieces (to make 1 cup)
about ⅓ egg white
2 teaspoons cornstarch

3 tablespoons lard or shortening for stir-frying
⅓ cup chopped onion
2 scallions: cut into pea-sized pieces, including some green
2 tablespoons flour
⅓ cup water

SAUCE MIXTURE (mix in a bowl)

⅓ teaspoon five-fragrance powder
2 teaspoons curry powder
½ teaspoon sugar
¼ teaspoon salt
⅛ teaspoon ground pepper
2 teaspoon thin soy sauce
2 teaspoons dry Sherry

¼ cup snipped parsley

about 16 slices soft white bread: cut off crusts, roll bread with rolling pin until thin, cover with a damp towel
1 to 2 egg yolks; put in a bowl
oil for deep-frying
Soy-Vinegar Dip (see page 315)

1. Blanch chicken mixture in water (see page 17). Set aside.
2. Heat wok over medium heat, add lard or shortening, and spread to grease wok. Drop in onion and scallions. Stir and cook for several seconds; remove from wok and let oil drip back into wok.
3. Keeping wok hot over medium heat, drop in flour and stir immediately, splash in the water, and stir quickly to mix well (it forms a thick mass). Turn off heat. Add sauce mixture and mix well. Add blanched chicken, onions, scallions, and parsley. Mix filling and put in a bowl to cool in refrigerator.
4. Put a heaping tablespoon of filling in the center of a piece of bread; brush egg yolk around edges; fold bread in half; pinch to seal tightly. Trim edges with scissors to form crescents, and put between linen towels. Make the others in the same manner.
5. Heat oil to deep-fry temperature (375 degrees). Deep-fry crescents to golden brown. Drain on paper towels. Serve hot with dip or without.

Note: Crescents can be made a day or two in advance up through step 4; refrigerate or freeze (separate each with wax paper) before deep-frying. Fried crescents also can be kept in low or warm oven for at least 30 minutes.

# FESTIVE COUNTRY CRESCENTS
Makes about 20

T he skin of these country crescents is slightly crisp outside, deliciously soft and glutinous inside. They are a favorite traditional food, make only during the fall and winter when harvest is finished.

On my family's land, there was much to be done before making these crescents: the grains were harvested by the hired hands, then husked in a seesaw-shaped stone grinder, driven by their feet. While we children looked for field mice, the bond maids—who were really slaves, but also beloved and authoritative members of the family—dug and husked the turnips, taros, and yams. Trays of river shrimp, trapped by our uncles, were dried in the sun, and so were beans of red, black, green, and yellow: Grandmother sorted and stored them in clay jars. Since we had no marshland to grow water chestnuts, we traded a basket of our yams for them with our neighbor, called Deaf Man.

We also bought from him each year a barrel of delicious fat rice worms to be salted and spiced and eaten as a treat throughout the winter months. When the green vegetables and melons were picked, the maids pickled the mustard greens, blanched the bok choy, and hung them on bamboo poles to dry. Then we all watched and cheered the men chasing the squealing pigs, yelling our advice on how to squeeze them into the sausage-like pig baskets, and feeling slightly sorry when they were carried away. They were shouldered back as pork to be barbecued and made into sausages, ham, and bacon. This was done by the women in the house, commanded by Grandmother's boisterous voice. Grandmother loved commotion, running feet, active hands; even the children were called in to string the sausages and hang the bacon.

When the labor was over, the cold-storage bin full, a silent contentment prevailed over both old and young. To boast of our prosperity would tempt the dark and jealous spirits, who were always as near as the blessings of the gods.

In quiet happiness, then, we prepared these crescents to celebrate the first day of winter and again the Lunar New Year. To give thanks for the harvest, the benefits of the old year and the promise of the new, we offered them to the gods and the spirits of our ancestors. We exchanged them with friends and relatives to wish each other good harvest and good luck. We also took care to have plenty for ourselves to feast of all day long. These crescents can be made a day or two in advance, before they are deep-fried. Keep in refrigerator until use.

## PREPARATION OF INGREDIENTS

2 tablespoons oil

FILLING (Group them on a plate)

1 tablespoon dried shrimp: soften in hot water 15 minutes, mince
5 Chinese dried mushrooms: soak in hot water until spongy, discard stems, mince caps
about ½ pound Cantonese Barbecued Pork (see page 126): cut into pea-sized pieces (to make 1 cup)
⅓ cup bamboo shoots cut in rice-sized pieces
⅓ cup water chestnuts cut in rice-sized pieces

SAUCE MIXTURE (Mix in a bowl)

2 teaspoons thin soy sauce
¼ teaspoon salt
¼ teaspoon sugar
¼ teaspoon five-fragrance powder

## WRAPPERS

2 cups unsifted, glutinous rice powder
¾ cup plus 2 tablespoons boiling water
2 tablespoons lard or shortening
2 ½ tablespoons sugar

oil for deep frying

## DIRECTIONS FOR COOKING

1. Heat wok over high heat. Add 2 tablespoons oil. When oil is hot, add shrimp, mushrooms, and pork; stir-fry for about 10 seconds. Drop in bamboo shoots and water chestnuts. Stir in sauce mixture and cook for about 15 seconds. Put on plate, cover, and cool in refrigerator.
2. Sift rice powder in a mixing bowl; add boiling water and stir quickly. Knead into a ball. Add lard or shortening and sugar and knead until smooth. Cover with a towel and allow to rest for 10 minutes.
3. Roll dough into a 1-inch diameter sausage. Cut into 20 equal sections. Cover with a towel. Roll each section into a ball. Grease blade of cleaver (or use a broad-blade knife) with oil. Press blade on ball to make a thin circle, and fill it with 1 tablespoon filling. Fold circle into half. Pinch edges tightly together. Crimp edges. (See Illustration.) Put crescents between towels. Make the others in the same manner.
4. Heat oil in wok to deep-fry temperature (375 degrees). Deep-fry crescents, a few at a times, turning them often, until they are golden (they do not turn brown). Drain on paper towels. Serve hot or warm.

# CHINESE NEW YEAR SAVORY TURNIP PUDDING
Makes one 9-by 1½-inch pudding

Before every Chinese New Year, one of the holiday foods that many families busily prepared was this pudding. Everybody made plenty, and my grandmother made more than anybody else, so that it would not be exhausted during the holiday. It sits on every cupboard, on shelves, tables, bookcases, on empty bunk beds, and a few even were secluded in my bureau. My mother frowned and quietly objected.

Whoever came through our doors, if they ever wished to come back again, had to eat great quantities of my grandmother's turnip pudding—along with tea and sweets—even though they might already have a stomachful from the Wangs' the Chans', and the Lees' tables.

Besides prizing herself as the best turnip pudding maker in the neighborhood, Grandmother also had the gift for commanding others to eat, not by physical force, but by sheer eye power, staring food into others' throats.

After experiencing the agony of a nearly bursting stomach, relatives and friends learned to stop at the Leungs' first, before visiting the other households. When the pudding finally vanished from the territories occupied, my grandmother had again proved to my mother that her pudding was not only delicious, but was barely enough to supply the demand. Her happiness was complete, and so was mine when the last pan of turnip pudding was gone from my bureau. Turnip pudding can be prepared in advance and resteamed or reheated in a microwave oven. Also, you can cut cold pudding into ½-inch thick pieces and pan-fry them with a little oil until crisp and golden brown outside, but still soft inside.

## PREPARATION OF INGREDIENTS

2 teaspoons lard or shortening
½ strip Chinese bacon: discard skin, cut into pea-sized pieces
3 Chinese pork sausages: cut into pea-sized pieces
6 large Chinese dried mushrooms: soak in hot water until spongy, discard stems, cut caps in small pieces
⅓ cup Chinese dried shrimp: soak in hot water to soften, cut into small pieces
1½ to 2 pounds Chinese white turnip: peel, grate by hand or shred in food processor
½ cup water
½ cup clear, canned chicken broth
1½ cups rice powder

¼ teaspoon ground white pepper

1½ teaspoons salt

1 teaspoon sugar

1 tablespoon thin soy sauce

2 tablespoons white sesame seeds: roast in an ungreased pot over low heat
until golden-brown.

a small bowl of Chinese chili sauce or Tabasco sauce

## DIRECTIONS FOR COOKING

1. Heat wok over medium heat until it is hot. Add lard or shortening. When it is
hot, drop in bacon and sausages; stir-fry until they sizzle. Add mushrooms and
shrimp; stir-fry for about 30 seconds. Turn off heat, and put mixture in a bowl.
Do not wash the wok.

2. Add grated turnips and ½ cup water to wok, cook over low heat until turnip
becomes soft, then turn off heat, return sausages, bacon, mushrooms, and shrimp
mixture to wok; add the remaining ingredients except the sesame seeds and chili
or Tabasco sauce. Mix well.

3. Grease a 9-inch cake pan with vegetable oil, and pour in pudding mixture.
Spread and smooth it out with a spoon. Sprinkle sesame seeds on top.

4. Steam pudding mixture over boiling water for about 1 hour or until the tip of
a knife comes out clean. Allow to cool for about 5 minutes. Serve hot with
Chinese chili sauce or Tabasco sauce.

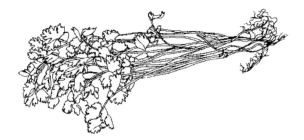

# FRIED WONTONS WITH SHRIMP OR PORK FILLING
Makes 40

This is an excellent appetizer and finger food for cocktail hours. But the Chinese always eat fried wontons with a sweet and sour dish, such as Sweet and Sour Pork (see page 122) rather than with plum sauce.

## PREPARATION OF INGREDIENTS

40 wonton skins

FILLING (Mix in a bowl. Refrigerate before use)

6 ounces fresh shrimp (or ground pork): shell, devein, rinse in running
    cold water, pat dry, cut into peanut-sized pieces
about ½ egg white
1 scallion: cut into pea-sized pieces, including some green part
¼ cup minced bamboo shoots or water chestnuts
½ teaspoon sesame oil
½ teaspoon dry Sherry
2 teaspoons thin soy sauce
1 large pinch ground pepper
¼ teaspoon salt

oil for deep-frying
Plum Sauce Dip (see page 314)

## DIRECTIONS FOR COOKING

1. Cover wonton skins with a damp cloth to keep them from drying.
2. Put about 1½ teaspoons of shrimp or pork filling in the middle of each skin. Make wontons as illustrated. Moisten edges with water to seal.
3. Heat oil to deep-fry temperature. Deep-fry wontons, several at a time, until golden brown. Drain on paper towels. Serve hot or warm with dip.

# SPRING ROLLS WITH SHRIMP
# AND CHICKEN FILLING
Makes 20

Egg rolls are similar to these spring rolls—except that spring rolls are purely Chinese, and egg rolls were created in the West by the Chinese for the Westerners. Once you taste spring rolls, you do not want egg rolls.

Spring rolls are filled with all sorts of delicious ingredients (not American cabbage), juicy and tasty. The skins are paper thin, like transparent crêpes. They are made from marshmallow-like dough, adhered to a hot iron surface, and then peeled off by hand. Each one is 9 inches in diameter. When fried, they are crisp, smooth, and delicate.

Egg roll skins are machine-made noodle sheets, cut into 8-inch squares. If they are thin, after frying, they become crisp, but not quite smooth, and are covered with tiny bubbles. The Chinese use egg roll skins only if spring roll skins are not available.

In many Chinese restaurants, especially the good ones, they prepare spring rolls as well as egg rolls. If you are Chinese, they give you spring rolls. The non-Chinese are presented with egg rolls.

## PREPARATION OF INGREDIENTS

3 tablespoons oil for stir-frying
2 teaspoons minced ginger
1 teaspoon minced garlic

SHRIMP MIXTURE (Mix in a bowl. Refrigerate before use.)

8 ounces fresh shrimp: shell, devein, rinse in running cold water, pat dry,
    cut into peanut-sized pieces
about ½ egg white
2 teaspoons dry Sherry
¼ teaspoon salt

8 Chinese dried mushrooms: soak in hot water until spongy, discard stems,
    cut caps into thin strips
6 water chestnuts: cut into thin strips
3 cups shredded Chinese cabbage
1 cup shredded bamboo shoots
2 scallions: cut into 1½-inch lengths, then shred

CHICKEN MIXTURE. (Blanch mixture in water [See Cooking Techniques page 17]. Drain. Put in a bowl. Refrigerate before use)

8 ounces boned, skinless chicken breast: shred into match stick strips
    (to make 1 cup)
1 teaspoon cornstarch
¼ teaspoon salt
⅛ teaspoon sugar
about ½ egg white

SAUCE MIXTURE (Mix in a bowl)

1 teaspoon cornstarch
¾ teaspoon salt
1 tablespoon black soy sauce
2 tablespoons thin soy sauce
1 tablespoon sesame oil
1 tablespoon water

20 Shanghai spring roll skins
1 egg yolk
oil for deep-frying
Plum Sauce Dip (see page 314) or Mustard-Oil Dip (see page 314) or
Soy-Vinegar Dip (page 315)

DIRECTIONS FOR COOKING

1. Heat wok over high heat. When it begins to smoke, swirl in 3 tablespoons oil. When oil is hot, slightly brown ginger and garlic .Add shrimp mixture. Stir-fry briefly until shrimp just turn whitish (less than 20 seconds). Remove with a drainer; press shrimp with a spoon to drain oil back into wok. Put shrimp in a bowl.
2. Reheat oil remaining in wok over medium heat, and add mushrooms. Stir-fry for about 15 seconds to draw out their flavor. Add water chestnuts, cabbage, bamboo shoots, and scallions. Stir-fry for about 20 seconds. Add chicken mixture. Mix well. Stir in sauce mixture and return shrimp to wok. Stir-fry for 15 seconds or until chicken is thoroughly hot. Put on plate to cool in refrigerator before wrapping. Clean and dry wok.
3. Put about 2 heaping tablespoons of fillings on a spring roll skin. Cover the remaining skins with a damp towel to keep them from drying. Wrap as illus-

trated, moisten edges of skin with egg yolk to seal.

4. Heat oil in wok to deep-fry temperature (375 degrees). Deep-fry spring, rolls until golden brown, turning from time to time. Drain on paper towels. Serve hot with dip.

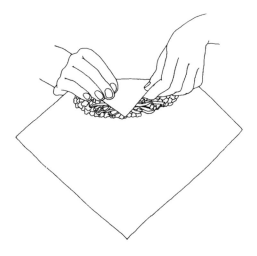

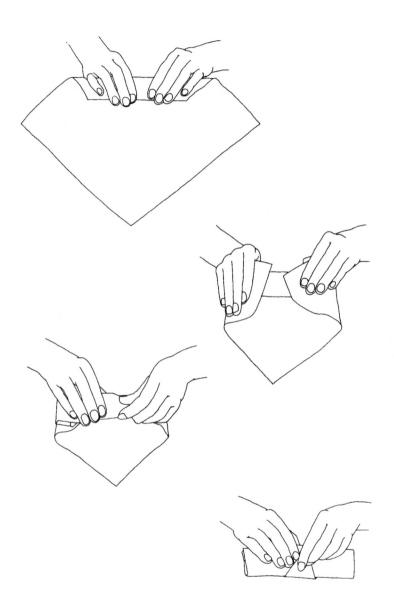

# VEGETARIAN SPRING ROLLS
Makes 20

Numbers of my nephews and nieces are vegetarians, and so are some of my friends. A few are dead serious, but the rest are part-timers; that means they make compromises on Thanksgiving, Christmas, and other special occasions. For them and for other vegetarians, this recipe, the following one, and others were put together. They not only contain protein, but also are full of wonderful flavor, to be enjoyed by carnivores as well and herbivores.

## PREPARATION OF INGREDIENTS

2 tablespoons oil or shortening to stir-fry
½ cup shredded leeks or scallions, about 1½ inch length, including some green
6 large Chinese dried mushrooms: soak in hot water until spongy, discard stems, shred caps

SHRIMP MIXTURE (Mix a bowl, refrigerate until use)

½ pound medium-sized fresh shrimp: devein, rinse in running cold water, pat dry, cut each in half lengthwise
1 teaspoon cornstarch
1 teaspoon dry Sherry
½ egg white

about ¾ pound zucchini: cut into ¼ inch-thick rounds, then cut rounds in match stick strips—but do not shred in food processor
1 cup bamboo shoots in match stick strips: rinse thoroughly in cold water, drain
2 ounces bean thread noodles: soak in hot tap water for about 5 minutes to soften, drain in colander, shorten a little, with a pair of scissors

SAUCE MIXTURE (Mix in bowl)

½ teaspoon five-fragrance powder
1 teaspoon salt
½ teaspoon sugar
2 teaspoons cornstarch
2 tablespoons mushroom soy or black soy sauce
2 tablespoons dry Sherry

20 spring roll skins
2 egg yolks for sealing rolls
oil for pan frying
Soy-Vinegar Dip (see page 315), Mustard-Oil Dip (see page 314), or Plum Sauce
    Dip (see page 314). Use more than one if you prefer.
a small dish of Chinese chili sauce or Tabasco sauce is optional

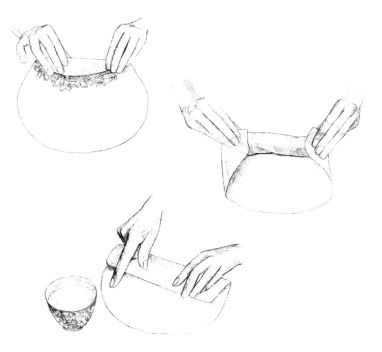

## DIRECTIONS FOR COOKING

1. Heat wok over high heat. When it begins to smoke, add oil or shortening and spread it with spatula. When oil is hot, drop in leeks or scallions and mushrooms, and stir-fry for about 15 seconds. Add shrimp mixture; stir and cook for several seconds (shrimp should be only half-cooked). Add zucchini, bamboo shoots, and noodles. Stir-fry for about 10 seconds. Stir in sauce mixture; toss to mix well; turn off heat. (Since this is a filling which will be wrapped and fried, it is preferable that the shrimp be undercooked and the zucchini half-cooked but still green.) Transfer the entire contents to a large uncovered tray and chill in refrigerator.

2. Put about 2 heaping tablespoons of filling on a spring roll skin. Cover the remaining skins with a linen towel to keep from drying out. Wrap as illustrated, and seal with egg yolk.

3. In a large heavy skillet, add enough oil to reach about halfway up the rolls. Heat oil over medium heat. When oil is hot, add enough rolls to cover bottom of skillet. Pan-fry rolls, turning from time to time, until golden brown. Roll them on paper towels to drain off oil. Serve hot with dips and chili sauce if desired.

NOTES: You may freeze spring rolls before frying. Put them on trays. Separate each layer with wax paper to prevent sticking if they are stacked. Cover with double layers of foil and seal tightly. Do not allow them to thaw, but pan-fry while they are still frozen. The oil temperature should be moderate, so that the filling can be heated thoroughly.

# BUDDHIST SPRING ROLLS
Makes 20

## PREPARATION OF INGREDIENTS

3 tablespoons oil
3 eggs: beat with ¼ teaspoon salt
½ cup shredded leeks or scallions in 1½-inch length, including some green
8 large Chinese dried mushrooms: soak in hot water until spongy, discard stems, cut caps in thin strips
2 pieces five-fragrance tofu (see page 334), cut in thin strips
2 cups packed Chinese cabbage, cut in thin crosswise strips
1 cup canned bamboo shoots cut in match stick strips: rinse thoroughly in cold water, drain
8 water chestnuts: shred
2 tablespoons dried cloud ears (tree mushrooms): soak in hot water until soft and fully expanded, tear each in 4 pieces, discard any tough parts
1 ounce bean thread noodles: soak in hot water for about 5 minutes to soften, drain in colander, shorten a little with a pair of scissors

## SAUCE MIXTURE (Mix in a bowl)

¼ teaspoon salt
1 teaspoon sugar
⅛ teaspoon ground pepper
2 tablespoons mushroom soy or black soy sauce
1 tablespoon dry Sherry
1 teaspoon sesame oil

20 spring roll skins
2 egg yolks for sealing spring roll skins
oil for pan-frying
Soy-Vinegar Dip (see page 315), Mustard-Oil Dip (see page 314), Chinese chili sauce, or Plum Sauce Dip (314). Choose one or more if you prefer.

1. Heat wok over medium-low heat. When it begins to smoke, add 2 tablespoons of the oil. When oil is hot, pour in the eggs. Spread eggs by tilting and rotating wok. When eggs begin to set around the edge, lift cooked edge and allow uncooked eggs to run under. Repeat until eggs are cooked but still moist. Put on a chopping board and cut into sugar-cube-sized chunks. Set aside.

2. Heat wok over medium-high heat. Heat the remaining I tablespoon oil and spread with spatula. When oil is hot, drop in leeks or scallions and mushrooms and stir-fry for about 10 seconds; add tofu, Chinese cabbage, bamboo shoots, water chestnuts, and cloud ears. Stir-fry for about a minute. Stir in sauce mixture and mix well. Add bean thread noodles and egg chunks. Toss and stir to mix well. Turn off heat. Transfer the entire contents to a large tray, uncovered and chilled in the refrigerator.

3. Put about 2 heaping tablespoons of filling on a spring roll skin. Cover the remaining remaining skins with linen towel to keep from drying out. Wrap and seal with egg yolks.

4.. In a large heavy skillet, add enough oil to reach about halfway up the spring rolls. Heat oil over medium heat. When oil is hot, add enough spring rolls to cover bottom of skillet. Pan-fry spring rolls, turning from time to time, until golden-brown. Roll on paper towels to drain off oil. Serve hot with one or two of the dips you choose.


# CHUNG YAO BING
## (CRISP SCALLION CAKES)
Makes six 10-inch round crêpes

These crisp savory cakes are one of the most loved foods among the Chinese; and no Westerner can forget them once they have tasted them. It is almost magical when a few humble ingredients—flour, scallions and lard—can create such a treat.

### PREPARATION OF INGREDIENTS

4 cups all-purpose flour
2 cups water
1 tablespoon salt
6 tablespoons lard or shortening
1½ cups chopped scallions, in pea-sized pieces, including some green
oil for pan-frying

1. In a mixing bowl, combine flour and water. Turn dough onto a floured surface, and knead until smooth. Cut dough into two portions and roll each portion into a thick sausage. cut each sausage into three equal parts. (Now altogether you have six pieces of dough.) Roll each piece of dough into a round ball, and put all of them under a damp kitchen towel to prevent them from drying.

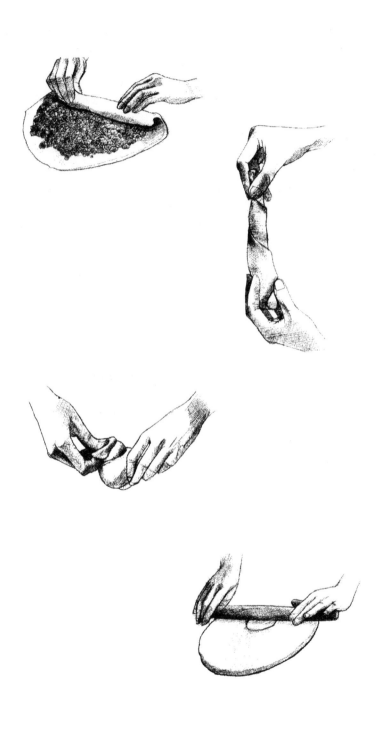

2. Dust rolling pin and working surface with flour. Roll a ball of dough into a big, thin pancake (about 11 to 12 inches in diameter.) Sprinkle ½ teaspoon salt evenly on pancake, and with your fingers, spread 1 tablespoon of lard or shortening on each pancake evenly; then sprinkle each with about 3 tablespoons of scallions. Roll each pancake into a sausage as you would roll up a jelly roll. Pick up the dough sausage and twist it like a rope, then hold it upright with one end on the table and press the top end straight down to the bottom end to form a round cake. Dust cake with a little flour and roll it into a thin cake about 10 inches across.

3. Head a large skillet and pour in enough oil to cover the bottom generously. When oil is hot, put in a scallion cake. Pan-fry each cake over medium heat until both side are golden brown. Drain on paper towels. They can be kept hot in a 200-degree oven. Cut cakes into big slices. Serve hot.

NOTE: Scallion cakes can be frozen uncooked; pan-fry them while they are still frozen.

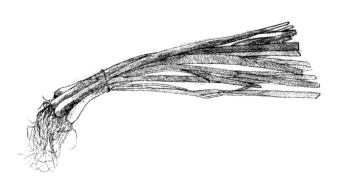

# SAVORY TARO TURNOVERS
Makes 20 to 24

Taro, a starchy tuber with dusty rough brown skin, comes in many sizes and varieties. The best kind is large, big as a coconut; the flesh inside is dry, white, and lined with feathery purple strands. The flesh is fragrant after it is cooked, fluffy if mashed. The Chinese call this kind "the fragrant taro." Most Chinese grocery stores have one or two taros cut open, so that the customers can see the flesh inside.

## PREPARATION OF INGREDIENTS

2½ pounds taro: peel, cut into ¼-inch slices, steam for 20 minutes or until tender
½ cup wheat starch
½ cup boiling water
9 tablespoons lard or shortening
2 tablespoons sugar
½ teaspoon salt

## FILLING

8 Chinese mushrooms: soak in hot water until soft, discard stems,
    cut caps in small pieces
½ pound lean pork, cut in pea-sized pieces
½ cup minced bamboo shoots (rinse in cold water before mincing)
6 ounces fresh shrimp: shell, devein, rinse in cold water, dry,
    cut into pea-sized pieces

## SAUCE MIXTURE (mix in a bowl)

¾ teaspoon salt
½ teaspoon sugar
⅛ teaspoon ground pepper
2 teaspoons cornstarch
1 tablespoon black soy sauce
2 tablespoons dry Sherry

2 hard-boiled eggs: peel and mince
¼ cup scallions in pea-sized pieces, including some green
about ½ cup wheat starch for dusting and coating turnovers

oil for deep-frying

## DIRECTIONS FOR COOKING

1. Put steamed taro in a large mixing bowl and mash by hand as you would mash potatoes; discard hard pieces. (You may mash it in a food processor.)
2. In a medium-sized mixing bowl, place ½ cup wheat starch and make a well. Pour in boiling water and stir quickly, then knead into a soft dough.
3. Combine mashed taro, dough, 6 tablespoons of the lard or shortening, sugar, and salt together, and knead by hand until thoroughly mixed. Cover and put taro dough aside for further use.
4. Heat and spread the remaining 3 tablespoons lard or shortening in wok. Drop in mushrooms, stir and cook for about 10 seconds. Add pork, and stir-fry until no longer pink. Add bamboo shoots and shrimp; stir-fry until shrimp is half cooked. Stir in sauce mixture. When sauce is thickened, turn off heat; add minced eggs and scallions; mix well. Put filling in a bowl to cool in refrigerator.
5. Dust working surface with wheat starch. Take a handful of taro dough, about as big as a lemon, and roll into a ball. With a rolling pin, gently roll ball out into a circle about ¼ inch thick. (If dough is rolled too thin, it will burst while deep-frying.) Put 1 to 2 tablespoons filling in the center of the circle. Fold circle in half and pinch edges tightly together. Coat turnover with wheat starch and put aside. Make the remaining turnovers in the same manner.
6. Heat oil in wok. The oil temperature should not be too hot; otherwise turnovers will burst open. Test oil by dipping a wooden chopstick or wooden spoon in oil; it should just sizzle slightly. Slide turnovers into oil, a few at a time, and deep-fry at moderate temperature until golden brown. Gently remove from oil (do not use tongs or anything that would squeeze or puncture turnovers) to drain on paper towels. They can be kept in a 150-degree oven for about 30 minutes.

NOTE: Taro turnovers can be cooked in advance. Reheat in 350-degree oven for 15 minutes or until crisp and hot.

# CRISP FRAGRANT TARO FRITTERS
Makes about 20

## PREPARATION OF INGREDIENTS

about 1¼ pounds taro
⅓ cup wheat starch
¼ cup boiling water
6 ounces shrimp: shell, devein, rinse in cold water, pat, dry,
    cut into pea-sized pieces
4 ounces Cantonese Barbecued Pork ( see page 126) : cut into small pieces
6 Chinese dried mushrooms: soak in hot water until spongy, discard stems,
    cut caps into small pieces
⅓ cup chopped scallions, including some green
⅛ teaspoon ground pepper
½ teaspoon salt
1 teaspoon sugar
¼ teaspoon five-fragrance powder
1 tablespoon thin soy sauce
1 tablespoon sesame oil
about ⅓ cup oil for pan-frying

## DIRECTIONS FOR COOKING

1. Peel taro, cut into ½-inch slices; steam until soft, mash, and put aside.
4. Put wheat starch in a mixing bowl and make a well; pour in all
the boiling water and stir quickly with a spoon. Knead and form into a soft
dough.
3. Combine dough, mashed taro, and the remaining ingredients except oil for
pan-frying. Knead to mix well. (You may prepare it up to this point a day or two
in advance. Cover and refrigerate until use.)
4. Form mixture into small fritters. Pan-fry in small amount of oil until both
sides are golden brown. Drain on paper towels. Serve hot. Taro fritters can be
kept in a warm oven for about 30 minutes or more.

# CRUNCHY JELLYFISH SKIN IN SOY-VINEGAR OIL

Serves 4 as appetizer

T his dish is for gourmets only, not for those who squeal at anything unfamiliar. However, most of my American friends have had jellyfish skin in our house without knowing it. For after it is prepared and cut into strips, it becomes "those crunchy things." Like most treasured delicacies of the Chinese, such as shark fin and sea slug, jellyfish skin has very little taste of its own. It has to borrow flavors from other ingredients. The Chinese enjoy it tossed with red vinegar, soy, and sesame oil as an appetizer or as a snack. We also use it to add texture to salad, cold noodle dishes, or congee.

## PREPARATION OF INGREDIENTS

½ pound dried jellyfish skin: rinse off salt, soak in plenty of cold water for at least
   4 hours, rinse thoroughly before use
1 small cucumber: peel, cut in half lengthwise, seeded, cut into thin slices.
½ teaspoon salt
¼ cup scallions cut into thin strips, including some green
several thin strips of red bell pepper or shaved carrot for garnish

## DRESSING (Mix in a bowl)

½ teaspoon sugar
¼ teaspoon salt
1 tablespoon red vinegar
2 teaspoons thin soy sauce
1 tablespoon sesame oil

## DIRECTIONS FOR COOKING

1. Bring a large pot of water to a boil. Immerse soaked jellyfish skin in water, then quickly remove it from pot and rinse in cold running water. (By now it has shrunk to half of it original size.) Pat dry. Cut into thin strips. Set aside.
2. Mix sliced cucumber and salt in a bowl; allow it to stand for 30 minutes. Rinse in cold water. Drain and pat dry.
3. Put cucumber slices on a serving plate and top with the jellyfish skin. Sprinkle with scallions and red pepper or carrot. (This may be prepared hours in advance and refrigerated until use.) Add dressing just before serving. Toss at the table. Serve cold or at room temperature.

# Chicken

# CHICKEN

I am told that years ago "a chicken in every pot" was an American dream. Now the dream seems to have come true, and chicken is the least expensive meat in this country. For the Chinese, "a chicken in every pot" is still a dream. Chicken does not come to their table every day. Rather, it is for special occasions such as birthdays, festivals, ancestor worshippings, and offerings.

In China, many families raise their own chickens. Even the boat people, living with their families on a 6-by-12-foot sampan, still have room for a few. In fact, the boat people's chickens are highly prized by many Chinese. Sometimes my family's cook, Ah Sahm, made a special trip to purchase these chickens. As a child, I used to go along with her.

The boat people raised and kept their chickens in small bamboo cages hung above the water along the boat's sides. The chickens were fed well with good grain, but they hardly had room to move. As a result, they grew fat and tender; even the bones, were soft and fragile. This practice might sound inhumane to the non-Chinese, but to us, humans come first. When the tender, juicy, fragrant chicken came to the table, we enjoyed it with all our hearts and souls and clear consciences.

For the American, buying a chicken is a casual thing. You simply pick up a package and throw it in your shopping cart. But for many Chinese like Ah Sahm, buying a chicken was a display of skill, experience, and expertise. She thoroughly examined every part of the bird, as if she were choosing a best-in-show champion. The feathers had to be shining and dark colored. She felt the chicken's breast and blew the feathers on it, so that she could make sure that the skin was yellow. Then, she gently squeezed the bird's body and felt its bottom to be certain it was a full-grown female that had not yet laid eggs. It had to weigh around 4½ pounds. If all its qualities pleased her, then it was chosen.

In order to obtain the chicken's best flavor, she would not have it killed in the marketplace. Instead, she took it home, alive and with feathers. Then she would kill it herself, just before cooking it. Chickens lose their flavor quickly. Therefore, the difference in taste between a fresh-killed chicken and a supermarket one is great. In America, chickens spend a great length of time waiting to be plucked and then rinsed. Then there is a long wait in the cold compartment before they are trucked to the markets, and then another wait to be packed and sold. By the time the chicken reaches your mouth, it has come a long way and the flavor is tired.

So what can we do? There are so few chickens alive with feathers near our neighborhood. If you have an idea like mine of raising you own chickens, be sure to check with your local police. "No chicken coop allowed in the backyard!" our local police and my neighbors told me firmly. So, we just have to take what we can get and show our skill. I was taught that a good cook should be able to make a banana peel fit for a king. And here I present many recipes which will make chicken fit not only for kings but also for gods in heaven and mortals on earth.

# IMPERIAL CONCUBINE CHICKEN
Makes 4 to 6 servings

Imperial Concubine refers to Yang Huei Fei, the favorite concubine of Emperor Ming of the Tang Dynasty, AD 618-907. It was said that she was plumply beautiful, a woman of extravagance, imperious. Living behind the palace wall, she was one of the emperor's three thousand concubines. Her beauty dazzled the old king; he no longer attended to state affairs, but wined and dined, enjoying Yang Huei Fei's songs and dances.

Then An Lu Shan, who governed the Northern Frontier, revolted. The king's army blamed Yang Huei Fei for weakening the country; they refused to advance unless she was executed. The old king, helpless, could only grieve as she was led away.

It was said that she was also fond of wine. When this dish, containing a good amount of wine, was created decades ago, it was named to honor this imperial lady.

## PREPARATION OF INGREDIENTS

2 to 2½ pounds chicken wings (or legs and thighs): disjoint
3 tablespoons oil
2 slices fresh ginger root, each as big and thick as a quarter
2 scallions: cut into 1½-inch lengths, including some green part
10 Chinese dried mushrooms: soak in hot water until spongy, discard stems
½ cup bamboo shoots cut into paper-thin slices

SAUCE MIXTURE (Mix in a bowl)
½ teaspoon sugar
¼ teaspoon salt
2 tablespoons thin soy sauce
2 tablespoons black soy sauce
⅓ cup Chinese rice wine or dry Sherry

about 1 cup canned clear chicken broth or water

## DIRECTIONS FOR COOKING

1. Heat a big pot of water to a boil. Blanch chicken in water for 1 minute. Remove chicken, place in a colander, and rinse with cold running water. Drain. Pat dry with paper towels.

2. Heat a 4- to 5-quart pot over medium heat. Swirl in the oil. When oil is hot, add ginger and scallions and brown slightly. Add chicken and evenly brown pieces. Put in mushrooms, bamboo shoots, and sauce mixture. Mix well. Add half the broth. Cover and cook over medium-low heat for 30 to 40 minutes or until chicken is tender. During cooking, add remaining broth if needed. There should be about ¾ cup sauce. Serve hot.

NOTE: This dish may be cooked a day ahead. Reheat on stove over low heat.

# PONG-PONG CHICKEN, SICHUAN STYLE
## (HACKED CHICKEN, A COLD DISH)
Makes 4 to 6 servings

## PREPARATION OF INGREDIENTS

2 big chicken breasts, with skin and bones
⅓ cup uncooked skinless peanuts
1 cup oil to fry peanuts
1 cup sliced cucumber or shredded celery: keep refrigerated
⅓ cup shredded scallions, cut 1½ inches lengthwise, including green part
1 tablespoon finely minced fresh ginger
1 tablespoon minced garlic
¼ teaspoon flower peppercorn powder

## SAUCE MIXTURE (Mix together smoothly in a bowl)

3 tablespoons smooth peanut butter
2½ tablespoons black soy sauce
1½ tablespoons Chinese red vinegar
2 tablespoons sesame oil
1½ teaspoons sugar
1 to 2 teaspoons Chili Oil (see page 311) or ½ to 1 teaspoon cayenne pepper
1 tablespoon dry Sherry
2 tablespoons water

## DIRECTIONS FOR COOKING
1. Immerse chicken breasts in a large pot of cold water. Cover and bring water to a rolling boil. Turn heat down and simmer for about 10 minutes or until just done. Drain, bone, and cool. Discard water.

2. Deep-fry peanuts in 1 cup oil until golden brown. Drain and cool. Put in plastic bag and crush coarsely with rolling pin. Put aside for later use.

3. Arrange cucumber on serving platter and top with half the scallions.

4. Put chicken breasts on a chopping board. Cut them in half, then crosswise into ¼-inch pieces. Arrange chicken pieces on cucumber and scallions. Sprinkle with ginger, garlic, flower peppercorn powder, and crushed peanuts. Then evenly pour sauce mixture over them. Sprinkle remaining scallions on top. Toss before eating. Serve at room temperature.

# SWEET AND SOUR CHICKEN
Makes 4 to 6 servings

## PREPARATION OF INGREDIENTS

about ⅔ cup cornstarch for coating chicken
oil for deep frying

CHICKEN MIXTURE (mix and marinate for at least an hour, keep refrigerated)

1 pound skinless and boneless chicken breasts or thighs: cut into 1-inch cubes
    to make 2 cups
1 egg beat until slightly foamy
½ teaspoon ground pepper
¼ teaspoon baking soda
½ teaspoon salt
1 tablespoon rice wine or dry Sherry
1 tablespoon thin soy sauce
1 teaspoon sesame oil

1 tablespoon sesame oil
2 teaspoons minced ginger
2 teaspoons minced garlic
½ cup water chestnuts: cut each in half
1 cup canned pineapple: cut into ½-inch squares
¾ cup red or green bell pepper: cut into ½-inch squares

SAUCE MIXTURE (mix in a bowl at least an hour in advance)

¼ cup sugar
1 tablespoon thin soy sauce
1 tablespoon black soy sauce
1 ounce shan zha bing (see page 331)
¼ cup white vinegar
⅓ cup canned pineapple juice
½ cup water or canned, clear chicken broth

1 tablespoon cornstarch mixed with 2 tablespoons water

DIRECTIONS FOR COOKING

1. Coat chicken cubes with cornstarch thoroughly and generously, until pieces are not sticky. Set aside.
2. Heat oil to deep-fry temperature, deep-fry chicken in batches for about 2 minutes or until they are firm and light golden and float to the surface. (Do not wait for chicken to turn brown, because cornstarch, unlike flour, does not turn brown easily. When it does, it is overcooked.) Put on serving platter.
3. While the chicken is being fried, heat a small pot over moderate heat, add 1 tablespoon sesame oil and roll pot to spread oil evenly. Drop in ginger and garlic, and stir to cook until they turn golden. Add pineapple, water chestnuts and bell pepper. Stir in sauce mixture and cook over low heat until sauce begins to bubble. Stir in cornstarch water, stir and cook for 10 seconds or until sauce is clear and thickened. Remove from heat and pour over chicken. Serve hot at once. Do not let chicken pieces stand in sauce for too long; otherwise, they will be soggy.


# CHICKEN SHREDS AND CUCUMBER SALAD
Makes about 4 servings

PREPARATION OF INGREDIENTS

2 cups agar-agar: soak in cold water until soft, cut into 2-inch lengths
2 cups sliced cucumber
2 boned, skinless chicken breasts: cut into matchstick strips, blanch in water (see Cooking Techniques, page 17)

½ cup jellyfish skin (optional) soaked in cold water overnight, blanched in water as with the chicken, shredded in matchstick pieces
2 tablespoons oil

SAUCE MIXTURE (Mix in a small bowl no longer than 30 minutes before serving—otherwise mustard will lose its strength)

2 tablespoons Chinese red vinegar
2 tablespoons thin soy sauce
1 tablespoon sugar
1 teaspoon salt
2 teaspoons Colman's mustard powder
¼ teaspoon cayenne pepper
4 teaspoons sesame oil

DIRECTIONS FOR COOKING

1. Arrange agar-agar on serving platter. Then arrange cucumber, chicken, and jellyfish skin on top. Chill.

2. In a small saucepan heat 2 tablespoons oil and pour in sauce mixture. Cook over low heat until sauce comes to a boil. Turn off heat. Pour sauce on the salad. Toss before serving.

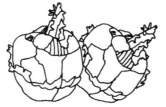

# CHICKEN AND WALNUTS IN MUSTARD SAUCE
## (A COLD DISH)
Serves 6 as an appetizer

¼ cup uncooked skinless peanuts or walnuts
1 cup oil for frying

CHICKEN MIXTURE (Mix in a bowl)

2 chicken breasts: bone, skin, cut into matchstick strips
1 egg white: beat slightly
4 teaspoons cornstarch

2 cups sliced cucumber or thin celery strips
6 scallions: shred into 1½-inch strips, including some green

SAUCE MIXTURE (mix into a smooth sauce no more than 15 minutes before
serving, otherwise mustard will lose its power: cover)

4 teaspoons Colman's mustard powder
4 teaspoons sugar
4 teaspoons water
2 tablespoons Chinese red vinegar
2 tablespoons plus 2 teaspoons black soy sauce
2 tablespoons sesame oil

several strips of red bell pepper or shaved carrot for garnish

DIRECTIONS FOR COOKING

1. Deep-fry peanuts or walnuts until golden brown. Drain on paper towels to
cool. Put nuts in plastic bag and crush them into small pieces with a rolling pin.
Put aside.
2. Blanch chicken mixture in water (see Cooking Techniques, page17).
3. Arrange cucumber slices or celery strips and half the scallions on a serving
platter, then top with the chicken shreds. Pour sauce mixture over chicken evenly
and garnish with remaining scallions, crushed nuts, and red pepper or carrot.
Serve at room temperature.

# DRUNKEN CHICKEN
## (A COLD DISH)
Makes 4 to 6 servings

## PREPARATION OF INGREDIENTS

2 whole chicken breasts (about 2 pounds) with skin and bones
2 teaspoons salt
½ teaspoon sugar
1 cup Chinese shaoshing wine (or your favorite white wine)

## DIRECTIONS FOR COOKING

1. Clean chicken breasts and pat dry. Cut breasts in half (you may bone the chicken, though the Chinese prefer it with bone). Rub breasts evenly with salt and keep in refrigerator overnight.
2. Place chicken breasts on rack over water, cover, and steam for about 15 minutes. Remove chicken and put in a dish.
3. Mix sugar with wine and pour it over chicken. Cover and soak chicken for one or two days or more before serving. Turn pieces from time to time to soak evenly. Drain chicken, place it on a chopping board, and chop crosswise, into ½-inch pieces. Arrange the pieces on a serving plate. Serve cold or at room temperature.

# SMOKED CHICKEN, NORTHERN STYLE
## (A COLD DISH)
Makes about 8 servings

## PREPARATION OF INGREDIENTS

RUBBING MIXTURE (Combine, then use to rub chicken inside and out. Marinate in refrigerator for 2 to 3 hours)

1 tablespoon dry Sherry
1 tablespoon salt
2 teaspoons flower peppercorn powder
1 teaspoon five-fragrance powder
½ teaspoon sugar

1 fresh chicken, 4 pounds

SPICED WATER (Combine in wok)

12 cups water
4 cinnamon sticks
8 whole star anise
1 chunk (big as a walnut) fresh ginger root: crush slightly
1 cup black soy sauce
2 tablespoons sugar
2 teaspoons salt

½ cup (loosely packed) light brown sugar
3 tablespoons dark-colored tea leaves, such as orange pekoe or lychee black tea
1 tablespoon sesame oil mixed with 1 tablespoon thin soy sauce

## DIRECTIONS FOR COOKING
1. Simmer spiced water in wok for about 15 minutes. Add chicken. Cover and simmer over low heat for about 40 minutes, turning once, or until chicken is just done.
2. Remove chicken from wok. Drain; put aside. (The spiced water can be frozen and reused for the next chicken; discard the anise, ginger, and cinnamon sticks.)
3. Line a big wok with heavy aluminum foil. Sprinkle bottom of wok with brown sugar and tea. Arrange four bamboo chopsticks or metal skewers overlapping each other to form a tick-tac-toe design. Rest chicken on chopsticks, breast side up. Cover wok tightly. (The cover should be high enough to allow the smoke to circulate, and the chicken should be at least 1 inch above the smoking ingredients.)
4. Turn heat to high. Smoke chicken for 20 minutes. Turn off heat, but do not uncover. Allow the smoke to subside (about 15 minutes).
5. Remove chicken to a cutting board. Carve and slice chicken and brush with sesame seed oil and soy sauce mixture. Serve chicken cold or warm.

NOTE: This chicken can be prepared a day in advance.

# CHICKEN WITH WALNUTS IN SPICY SAUCE
Makes 2 to 4 servings

## PREPARATION OF INGREDIENTS

oil for deep-frying
¼ cup raw walnuts: rinse in hot water, drain, and dry on paper towels
2 teaspoons minced fresh ginger
2 teaspoons minced garlic

## CHICKEN MIXTURE (Mix in a bowl)

1½ boned, skinless chicken breasts: cut into ½-inch cubes (to make 1 cup)
1 teaspoon dry Sherry
⅓ egg white
½ teaspoon thin soy sauce
1 teaspoon cornstarch

2 dried chili peppers: tear into small pieces, do not discard seeds
4 Chinese dried mushrooms: soak in hot water until spongy, discard stems,
    cut caps into small squares
½ cup quartered water chestnuts
½ cup bamboo shoots cut into ⅓-inch cubes
½ cup green or red bell pepper cut into ½-inch pieces
2 scallions cut into pea-sized pieces, including some green part

## SAUCE MIXTURE (Mix in a bowl)

2 tablespoons ground bean sauce
4 teaspoons hoisin sauce
4 teaspoons black soy sauce
4 teaspoons dry Sherry
½ teaspoon sugar

2 teaspoons sesame oil

## DIRECTIONS FOR COOKING

1. Heat oil for deep-frying in wok over high heat. Deep-fry walnuts until golden brown. Drain on paper towels.

2. Remove all but 4 tablespoons oil from wok. Heat oil, slightly brown ginger and garlic. Add chicken mixture. Stir-fry until chicken just turns white. Remove from wok to bowl.

3. Keep wok hot over high heat. Add chili peppers. Stir-fry for a few seconds. Drop in mushrooms and cook for about 10 seconds. Add water chestnuts, bamboo shoots, pepper, and scallion. Stir-fry for about 30 seconds. Stir in sauce mixture. Return chicken to wok, mix well and cook until sauce begins to bubble. Swirl in sesame seed oil. Put on a serving platter. Top with walnuts. Serve hot.

# CHICKEN WITH ALMONDS
Makes 4 servings

## PREPARATION OF INGREDIENTS

oil for deep-frying
⅓ cup uncooked, skinless almonds: rinse, dry on paper towels

## CHICKEN MIXTURE (Mix in a bowl)

1½ boned, skinless chicken breasts: cut into ½-inch cubes (to make 1 cup)
¼ teaspoon salt
½ egg white
1 pinch of white pepper
⅛ teaspoon sugar
1 teaspoon cornstarch

2 teaspoons minced fresh ginger
2 teaspoons minced garlic
4 Chinese dried mushrooms: soak in hot water until spongy, discard stems,
    cut caps into ½-inch squares
½ cup ⅓-inch pieces green or red bell pepper
½ cup ⅓-inch cubed pineapple
½ cup quartered water chestnuts
⅓ cup ⅓-inch cubed bamboo shoots
1 scallion cut into pea-sized pieces, including some green part

## SAUCE MIXTURE (Mix in a bowl)
1 teaspoon cornstarch

1 teaspoon sugar
4 tablespoons thin soy sauce
2 teaspoons black soy sauce
2 tablespoons dry Sherry
1 tablespoon sesame oil

## DIRECTIONS FOR COOKING

1. Heat oil in wok over high heat to deep-fry temperature. Deep-fry almonds until golden brown. Drain on paper towels.
2. Reheat oil in wok. Add chicken mixture and stir to separate pieces. Blanch chicken briskly until it just turns white. Remove with slotted spoon.
3. Remove all but 2 tablespoons of oil from wok. Heat oil, and add ginger, garlic, and mushrooms. Brown them slightly. Add pepper, pineapple, bamboo shoots, and water chestnuts. Stir-fry for about 1 minute. Return chicken to wok. Add the scallion and stir-fry for about 30 seconds. Stir in sauce mixture. Mix well and stir-fry for another 30 seconds. Put on a serving platter. Top with almonds. Serve hot.

# COCONUT CHICKEN
Makes 6 servings

This dish belongs to my aunt in Macao with whom I stayed for a year. Macao, an old Portuguese colony connected to mainland China, is an hour away from Hong Kong by boat. Ninety-five percent of the population is Chinese, and their cooking, culture, and customs remain purely Chinese. Only occasionally, a few Chinese restaurants would offer some dishes that had the flavor of the colonials, such as coconut chicken. My aunt learned to prepare this dish from a chef who was captivated by her charming smile; very few could resist giving her their secrets.

The Chinese fondness for coconut is similar to the Westerners' love for chocolate. It is the dominant flavor in candies and ice cream, and is so much a part of our lives that we hardly realize it is mainly imported.

## PREPARATION OF INGREDIENTS

1 large pot of water

CHICKEN MIXTURE (Mix in a bowl. Refrigerate before use)

3 boneless and skinless chicken breasts: pound with back of cleaver,
     cut into 1-inch-square pieces
1 egg white: beat slightly
⅛ teaspoon white pepper
2 teaspoons cornstarch
1 teaspoon sesame oil

SAUCE MIXTURE (Mix in a bowl)

1 cup unsweetened coconut milk
⅔ cup milk (or half-and-half )
1 teaspoon salt
1 teaspoon sugar
2 tablespoons cornstarch
2 tablespoons melted lard or butter

3 egg whites: beat until stiff

DIRECTIONS FOR COOKING

1. Bring water to a rolling boil. Add chicken mixture. Stir to separate pieces, and
blanch briskly until chicken just turns white. Remove with a drainer to a baking
dish.
2. Preheat oven to 375 degrees.
3. In a pot, heat sauce mixture over medium heat until sauce thickens. Pour sauce
over chicken and top with beaten egg whites.
4. Bake chicken in oven for 20 minutes or until egg whites turn golden brown.
Serve hot.

# CRISP LEMON CHICKEN
Makes 4 servings

## PREPARATION OF INGREDIENTS

2 large whole chicken breasts: bone but leave skin on, pound meat side with
    back of cleaver

MARINADE (Mix and marinate chicken in a bowl for an hour or longer)

1 egg: beat well
¼ teaspoon salt
¼ teaspoon sugar
1 teaspoon dry Sherry
juice from ½ lemon

½ cup cornstarch for coating
2 tablespoons oil for stir-frying
1 teaspoon finely minced fresh ginger
2 teaspoons minced garlic
¼ cup shredded scallions: 1½ inches long, including some green parts
8 very thin slices lemon without skin
¼ cup thinly shredded red or green bell pepper

SAUCE MIXTURE (Mix in a bowl and cover)

4 teaspoons sugar
¼ teaspoon salt
4 teaspoons white vinegar
2 tablespoons thin soy sauce
4 teaspoons dry Sherry
½ cup canned clear chicken broth

2 teaspoons cornstarch mixed with 2 teaspoons water
oil for deep-frying
Scallion Brushes (see page 198) or slices of lemon for garnish

## DIRECTIONS FOR COOKING

1. Put cornstarch for coating on a plate. Generously and evenly coat marinated chicken. Put chicken flat on a plate and set aside.

2. Heat a small pan over medium heat. Swirl in 2 tablespoons oil for stir-frying. When oil is hot, add ginger, garlic, and half the scallions. Stir to cook until garlic turns golden. Add lemon slices and shredded pepper. Immediately pour in sauce mixture. When sauce just starts to bubble, add cornstarch water, stirring constantly until sauce is thickened. Mix well. Cover to keep warm.

3. Heat oil in wok over high heat to deep-fry temperature. Slide breasts into hot oil and deep-fry until golden brown. Remove and drain.

4. Put chicken breasts on a chopping board and chop crosswise into half-inch pieces. Arrange pieces neatly on a serving platter. Sprinkle chicken with remaining shredded scallions.

5. Discard lemon slices from sauce. Pour sauce over chicken. Garnish platter with lemon slices, scallion brushes, parsley, or other greens. Serve hot.

# HAPPY UNION
Makes 2 to 4 servings

T he Chinese sometimes honor the shrimp by calling it "dragon" and the
chicken by calling it "phoenix." Chinese dragons symbolized manliness,
wisdom, strength, and kindness. It was said that because they were so wise, they
never truly revealed themselves, but appeared disguised as fish, shrimp, or other
creatures. The phoenix symbolized femininity, serenity, grace, and beauty. When
dragon and phoenix meet, it represents the happy union of men and women.

## PREPARATION OF INGREDIENTS

### CHICKEN MIXTURE (Mix in a bowl)

1 whole boned, skinless chicken breast: slice paper-thin
⅛ teaspoon salt
½ teaspoon thin soy sauce
½ egg white
1 tablespoon cornstarch

½ pound bok choy or broccoli: cut into bite-sized pieces
4 tablespoons oil
4 to 6 ounces fresh shrimp: shell, devein, split in half, clean under cold running
    water, pat dry
2 teaspoons minced ginger
1 teaspoon minced garlic
2 scallions: cut into 1½-inch lengths, including some green part
4 Chinese dried mushrooms: soak in hot water until spongy, discard stems

### SAUCE MIXTURE (Mix in a bowl)

⅛ teaspoon ground pepper
½ teaspoon salt
½ cup canned clear chicken broth
2 teaspoons oyster-flavored sauce
1 teaspoon sesame oil
1½ teaspoons thin soy sauce
1 teaspoon dry Sherry

1 tablespoon cornstarch mixed with 2 tablespoons water

# DIRECTIONS FOR COOKING

1.   Separately blanch chicken mixture and bok choy or broccoli in water (see Cooking Techniques). Drain and put on a plate.
2.   Heat wok over high heat until almost smoking. Add 2 tablespoons oil. When oil is hot, add shrimp. Stir-fry for a few seconds until shrimp turn white-pink. Remove with a drainer or slotted spoon to a bowl.
3.   Keep wok hot. Add remaining 2 tablespoons oil. When oil is hot, add ginger and garlic and cook until they are golden brown. Add scallions and mushrooms. Stir-fry for about 15 seconds and then stir in sauce mixture. When sauce begins to boil, return the chicken, bok choy, and shrimp to wok. Mix well and cook for about 30 seconds. Stir in cornstarch water. Stir for about 10 seconds or until sauce thickens. Serve hot.

# KWANGCHOW BUCKET CHICKEN

Serves 4 as a meal

T he people of Kwangtung province are renowned for preparing chicken. As you would travel through Kwangtung province by train, at each village stop, vendors would rush to the windows, offering pieces of chicken cooked according to the speciality of the village.

It is said that originally a vendor poached the chicken in a large amount of soy sauce, sugar, and many spices, then carried it in shoulder baskets, hawking it on the streets of Kwangchow (Canton).

A poached chicken is best because without fire underneath the chicken, the juice is not drawn out so that the chicken retains its natural sweetness. This chicken can be eaten cold and is excellent for picnics.

## PREPARATION OF INGREDIENTS

13 cups of water
12 ounces of rock or regular sugar
3 tablespoons sea salt
4 cups black soy sauce

SPICES (wrapped and tied in cheesecloth)

8 star anise
2 tablespoons flower peppercorns
2 tablespoons cloves
2 cinnamon sticks: break each in half
2 nutmegs
4 ounces fresh ginger: cut into large chunks

1 fresh chicken, 3½ –4 pounds
1 tablespoon sesame oil

## DIRECTIONS FOR COOKING

1. In a large pot, combine the water, sugar, salt, soy sauce and spices. Cover and simmer over low heat for about an hour. Add chicken, breast side down in sauce. As soon as the liquid comes to a full boil again, cover pot with a tight lid and remove from heat. Poach chicken for 1 hour. (Do not remove lid while poaching!)

2. Remove chicken from sauce, and brush with sesame oil. Allow chicken to cool before chopping or carving. Chop or carve chicken as desired. Serve hot or at room temperature.

Note: Chicken over 4 pounds are not suitable for this recipe. You can freeze the leftover sauce, including the bag of spices, and use it again—there should be enough to make two more chickens. (If there is not enough sauce for poaching a whole chicken, use it for cooking wings or livers.

# CHICKEN IN HOISIN SAUCE
Makes 8 servings

T his is one of the most delicious and stress-free dishes. I often cook it for large gatherings. It can be cooked hours in advance and reheated on the stove or in the microwave.

## PREPARATION OF INGREDIENTS

2 tablespoons oil
4 teaspoons finely minced fresh ginger
2 tablespoons minced garlic

## SAUCE MIXTURE (Mix in a bowl)

1 teaspoon salt
1 tablespoon sugar
⅔ cup hoisin sauce
3 tablespoons black soy sauce
3 tablespoons dry Sherry
1 tablespoon oyster-flavored sauce

1 fresh chicken, about 5-6 pounds: rinse, pat dry
about 1 cup boiling water
about 2 teaspoons sesame oil

## DIRECTIONS FOR COOKING

1. Heat wok over high heat. Swirl in oil. When oil is hot, slightly brown ginger and garlic. Stir in the sauce mixture. When sauce begins to boil, add chicken to

wok and roll it around to coat it with the sauce. Add gizzard. Pour in ⅔ cup of the water. Cover and simmer over low heat (sauce should be bubbling) for about 40 minutes. Turn chicken and add, if the sauce is too thick, the rest of the boiling water. Cover and simmer for another 40 minutes or until it is just done (about 172 degrees). Add chicken liver to sauce 20 minutes before chicken is done.

2. Place chicken on a chopping board and brush it with the sesame oil. Carve and slice chicken. Pour sauce over chicken. Serve hot.

# SALT ROAST CHICKEN
Makes 6 servings

Nobody could make this chicken better than our Elder Old Aunt. We never knew her by any name other than Elder Old Aunt. She was always there, and she was always old. My grandfather's elder sister, she had no family of her own. She sat in silence, with her lips tightly locked, and seldom spoke except when we were hailed before our parents for misbehavior; then she would add more crimes from her silent files. Among the children, she was called "the silent toad." My grandfather had taught her city manners, but she often forgot. The servants laughed because she made noise when she ate, and sometimes licked her bowl.

A few times a year, upon request, she would prepare this chicken for a special treat. She would ignore the compliments that followed and eat without a word. When she was ninety-two, somehow she knew that her time had come. She went back to her native village to lie next to her long-dead husband and her ancestors.

I learned how to cook this chicken from grandmother, who learned from Elder Old Aunt. I hope in heaven she knows that we savor her chicken, and regret, as we grow older, that we never searched her silence, which soundlessly still tolls.

## PREPARATION OF INGREDIENTS

6 pounds coarse sea salt
1 fresh chicken, 4 pounds: rinse, thoroughly dry inside and out with paper
    towels, rub outside with 2 teaspoons salt
cheesecloth, enough to wrap chicken
⅓ cup shredded scallions for garnishing
double recipe Ginger-Scallion Dip (see page 313)

## DIRECTIONS FOR COOKING

1. Pour the sea salt into a big wok. Cover and heat over medium-high heat for 30
minutes; stir and turn salt from time to time.
2. Wrap chicken in one layer of cheesecloth, overlapping cheesecloth slightly at
side of chicken. Tie knots at neck and tail.
3. Dig a well in the hot salt. Put in chicken, breast side down. There
should be a lot of salt between wok and chicken. Pile salt over chicken, covering
it completely. Cover the wok. Roast chicken over medium-high heat for 1½
hours.
4. Test chicken by piercing thigh with skewer or small knife. If juice runs clear, it
is done. Remove chicken from wok and put on a tray. Brush off salt with pastry
brush. Cut cheesecloth, then remove chicken and put on chopping board.
5. Carve and slice chicken. Arrange chicken pieces on a serving platter, garnish
with scallions and serve warm. Serve dip in individual dishes for each person.


# PURE CUT CHICKEN WITH GINGER-SCALLION DIP
Makes 4 to 6 servings

T his dish and the salt roast chicken in the preceding recipe are the most
famous dishes of Kwangtung Province. This good unadorned style of cooking and serving chicken is true art—simple and pure.

## PREPARATION OF INGREDIENTS

4 whole star anise
2 tablespoons salt
¼ cup Chinese rice wine or dry Sherry
2 chunks (each the size of a pecan) fresh ginger: crush slightly
2½ gallons water

1 fresh chicken, 4 pounds: rinse, pat dry
¼ cup shredded scallions for garnishing
double recipe Ginger-Scallion Dip (see page 313) or Oil-Oyster Sauce Dip
    (see page 315)

## DIRECTIONS FOR COOKING

1.   Add star anise, salt, wine, and ginger to the water in a large pot (a lobster or stock pot) and bring to a rapid boil. Immerse chicken in water to cover completely. Cover pot and bring water to a boil again. (It will take a few minutes.) As soon as the water boils rapidly, turn off the heat. Do not uncover for at least 2 hours. Do not peek, even once, at the chicken during the entire 2 hours because the heat and hot steam cooking the chicken must not be allowed to escape. The chicken can stay in the water for up to 3 hours.
2.   Fifteen minutes prior to serving the chicken, turn heat to medium and bring the water to a boil; simmer for 3 minutes. Turn off heat. Drain chicken and put it on a chopping board. Carve and slice chicken. Put on a serving platter. Garnish with scallions. Serve hot. Serve dip in individual dishes for each person.

# MOO GOO GAI PAN
Serves 4

Moo goo means "button mushrooms" and gai pan means "chicken slices."

## PREPARATION OF INGREDIENTS

½ cup canned straw mushrooms: rinse in cold water, drain
1 cup canned button mushrooms: rinse in cold water, drain
½ cup canned baby corn: cut each ear in half lengthwise
2 teaspoons Chinese rice wine or dry Sherry
2 cups canned, clear chicken broth
oil for deep-frying

## CHICKEN MIXTURE (Mix and marinate in a bowl)

2 whole boned, skinless chicken breasts: cut into paper-thin slices when
    still half-frozen
¼ teaspoon salt

¼ teaspoon sugar
1 tablespoon cornstarch
½ egg white
1 teaspoon dry Sherry

1 teaspoon minced garlic
1 scallion: cut into 1½-inch lengths, including some green part, then shred

SAUCE MIXTURE (Mix in a bowl)

½ teaspoon sugar
1 tablespoon thin soy sauce
2 teaspoons rice wine or dry Sherry
¾ cup canned clear chicken broth

1 tablespoon cornstarch mixed with 1 tablespoon water
1 teaspoon sesame oil

DIRECTIONS FOR COOKING

1. Put straw mushrooms, button mushrooms, corn, 2 teaspoons wine, and 2 cups chicken broth in a saucepan and bring to a boil. Remove from heat and let sit for half an hour. Drain vegetables. (Reserve ¾ cup broth for the Sauce Mixture).
2. Heat oil in wok to deep-fry temperature. Add chicken mixture. Stir to separate pieces. Blanch chicken briskly until pieces just turn white. Remove with a drainer or slotted spoon to a bowl.
3. Remove all but 2 tablespoons oil from wok. Heat oil over medium-high heat, and add garlic and scallion. When garlic turns a light golden color, add mushrooms and corn. Stir and cook for 15 seconds. Swirl in sauce mixture and bring to a boil. Pour in cornstarch water. Cook, stirring constantly, until sauce is clear and thickened. Return chicken to wok. Stir-fry briefly. Swirl in the sesame seed oil. Put on a serving platter. Serve hot.

# FAMILY WINTER CHICKEN
Serves 8 as a meal

T his large dish is a splendid dinner, especially on a wintry day after skiing or shoveling snow. It is delicious, hearty, and nourishing; and it requires very little preparation. You may serve it straight from the pot and eat it in front of a burning fire.

## PREPARATION OF INGREDIENTS

4½ to 5½ pounds whole chicken: rinse chicken, gizzard, liver, and heart; remove
   fat from cavity; cut gizzard and liver into bite-sized pieces; put liver aside.
In a bowl, mix and wash thoroughly the following:
⅓ cup dried lotus seeds
⅓ cup barley
⅓ cup black-eyed peas

10 shelled chestnuts, dried or fresh
4 Chinese dried red dates: slit each with a knife (you may use regular dates)
12 Chinese dried mushrooms: wash, discard stems
½ cup canned button mushrooms: rinse and drain
1 chunk fresh ginger, as big as a plum: crush it with a cleaver
1 teaspoon sugar
1 teaspoon ground pepper
2 cups canned clear chicken broth
¼ cup dry Sherry
salt to taste
Soy-Sesame Dip (see page 315)

## DIRECTIONS FOR COOKING

Put chicken (breast side up), heart, and gizzard in a 5-quart Chinese clay pot or metal pot. Add all the other ingredients, except chicken liver, salt and soy-oil dip. Pour in enough water to cover 90 percent of the chicken. Bring liquid to a rapid boil. Turn heat to low; cover and simmer chicken for about 2½ hours or until chicken is very tender. (Add water to maintain the water level while cooking if necessary.) Add liver about 10 minutes before the cooking is done. Skim off fat; salt to taste. Serve hot in individual bowls. Give each person a small dish of dip; use dip sparingly.

# PUFFED CRISP CHICKEN BALLS
Makes 6 to 8 servings

## PREPARATION OF INGREDIENTS

### BATTER

¼ teaspoon salt
1 tablespoon baking powder
1 cup all-purpose flour
5 tablespoons oil
about ⅔ cup cold water
2 tablespoons white sesame seeds
½ cup minced scallions

3 whole boned, skinless chicken breasts: pound with back of cleaver,
    cut into 1-by-2-inch pieces

### MARINADE (Mix and marinate chicken in a bowl for 30 minutes or more)

1 tablespoon cornstarch
½ teaspoon salt
¼ teaspoon sugar
½ teaspoon five-fragrance powder
1 big pinch of ground pepper
1 teaspoon dry Sherry
1 tablespoon thin soy sauce
1 egg white

oil for deep-frying
Soy-Vinegar Dip (see page 315)

## DIRECTIONS FOR COOKING

1. Add salt and the baking powder to flour. Mix well. Add 5 tablespoons oil, a little at a time, until flour becomes somewhat like pie dough. It should stick together. Add water, a little at a time to break up dough until it becomes a thick batter. Add sesame seeds and scallions. Mix well.

Important: To test the consistency of the batter, dip a piece of chicken in the batter and hold it up. The batter should drip off the chicken slowly.

2. Heat oil in wok over high heat to deep-fry temperature. Dip and roll a piece of chicken in batter to form a ball, and deep-fry until golden brown. A few pieces can be deep-fried at the same time. Drain and put in a warm oven. Deep-fry the rest of the chicken pieces in the same manner. Transfer to a serving platter. Serve hot with dip.

# CHINESE CURRY CHICKEN
Makes 6 to 8 servings

As they adopted Buddhism, the Chinese took Indian curry and made it their own. If you follow the directions below, your curry's fragrance can be sensed a block away. Close your bedroom doors and open a few windows, or you'll wake up tasting curry for days.

PREPARATION OF INGREDIENTS

3 tablespoons oil
3 whole chicken breasts with skin and bone: chop into 1½-inch pieces
1 tablespoon minced garlic
2 teaspoons finely minced fresh ginger
2 onions: cut lengthwise into narrow strips

SAUCE: MIXTURE (Mix in a bowl)

1 teaspoon sugar
¼ teaspoon salt
2 tablespoons yellow curry paste
1 teaspoon curry powder
¼ teaspoon cayenne pepper
2 tablespoons black soy sauce
2 tablespoons dry Sherry

2 medium-sized potatoes: peel, cut into walnut-sized pieces
½ cup water

DIRECTIONS FOR COOKING

1. Heat wok over high heat. Swirl in 2 tablespoons oil. When oil is hot, add chicken pieces. Brown chicken slightly. Remove chicken with drainer to a bowl.

2. Heat wok over medium heat; add the remaining 1 tablespoon oil. When oil is hot, drop in garlic, ginger, and onion. Stir-fry until garlic just turns golden. Swirl in sauce mixture. Stir and cook until sauce begins to bubble. Return chicken to wok. Add potatoes. Swirl in water. Mix well. Turn heat to low. Cover and cook for about 20 minutes, stirring and turning chicken pieces from time to time. When done, the chicken and the potatoes should be tender and the dish saucy. Serve hot.

# CHICKEN IN GINGER AND TOMATO SAUCE

Makes 4 to 6 servings

## PREPARATION OF INGREDIENTS

oil for blanching

CHICKEN MIXTURE. (In a bowl, stir vigorously to mix thoroughly; refrigerate for at least 2 hours beforehand)

1¼ pounds skinless, boneless chicken breasts or thighs: cut into ¾-inch cubes
    to make 2 cups
1 egg white: beat until slightly foamy
1 tablespoon cornstarch
1 tablespoon thin soy sauce
1 tablespoon rice wine or dry Sherry
2 tablespoons sesame oil
¼ teaspoon baking soda

2 tablespoons minced fresh ginger
5 scallions: cut into 1-inch pieces, including some green part
½ cup water chestnuts: cut in half
½ cup red or green bell peppers: cut into ½-inch squares
⅓ cup dried cloud ears: soak in hot water for 15 minutes or until soft:
    rinse, discard tough parts

SAUCE MIXTURE (Mix in a bowl)

¼ teaspoon ground pepper
2 tablespoons sugar
2 tablespoons black soy sauce

2 tablespoon rice wine or dry Sherry
1 tablespoon white vinegar
2 tablespoons tomato ketchup
2 teaspoons sesame oil

## DIRECTIONS FOR COOKING

1. Heat oil in wok over high heat to deep-fry temperature. Add chicken mixture and stir quickly to separate pieces. Blanch chicken briskly until it just turns white, almost, but not quite cooked through (about 10 seconds). Remove with a strainer to a bowl. (The chicken continues to cook in its own heat).
2. Remove all but 2 tablespoons of oil from wok. Heat oil over high heat for about 5 seconds. Add ginger and scallions and stir to cook, until ginger turns golden brown. Add water chestnuts, bell peppers and cloud ears; stir-fry for about 10 seconds. Return chicken to wok and stir in sauce mixture. Stir-fry over moderate heat until sauce bubbles gently. Swirl in sesame oil. Serve hot.

NOTE: leftovers can be reheated in microwave oven.

# GONG-BAO CHICKEN WITH PEANUTS

Makes 4 servings

Gong-Bao was a government official, "Guardian to the Heir Apparent." Kung-Bao was his title; Ding was his family name. It was said that he liked to serve this peppery dish when in Sichuan. If your palate does not match Ding Gong-Bao's, the hot pepper can be reduced.

## PREPARATION OF INGREDIENTS

oil for deep-frying
½ cup raw, skinless peanuts

### CHICKEN MIXTURE (Mix and marinate 2 hours or more, keep refrigerated)

1 pound boned, skinless chicken breasts or thighs: cut into ⅓-inch cubes
    (to make 2 cups)
2 tablespoons cornstarch
¼ teaspoon baking soda
½ teaspoon sugar
2 tablespoons water
1 tablespoon black soy sauce
1 tablespon rice wine or dry Sherry
1 egg white

4 dried chili peppers: tear into small pieces, do not discard seeds
2 tablespoons finely-minced, fresh ginger
2 scallions: cut into pea-sized pieces, including some green part

### SAUCE MIXTURE (Mix in a bowl)

¼ teaspoon salt
4 teaspoons sugar
1 teaspoon cornstarch
4 tablespoons black soy sauce
4 tablespoons Chinese rice wine or dry Sherry
2 tablespoons Chinese red vinegar or cider vinegar
1 tablespoon sesame oil

## DIRECTIONS FOR COOKING

1. Heat oil in wok and deep-fry peanuts until golden brown. Drain on paper towels.
2. Reheat oil in wok and add chicken mixture. Stir to separate pieces. Briskly blanch chicken pieces until they just turn white. Remove with a drainer or slotted spoon to a bowl.
3. Remove all but 2 tablespoons oil from wok. Heat oil. Slightly brown chili peppers. Add ginger and scallions, and stir-fry until they turn golden. Stir in sauce mixture. Cook and stir until sauce is thickened. Put chicken back into wok. Mix well. Stir-fry briefly to reheat. Add peanuts. Mix well and put on a serving platter. Serve hot.

# SICHUAN CHENG DU CHICKEN
Makes 4 to 8 servings

Cheng Du is the capital of Sichuan. This is one of its famous peppery dishes.

## PREPARATION OF INGREDIENTS

oil for deep-frying
3 whole chicken breasts: boned, but leave skin on, cut into 1-inch squares
1 to 2 dried chili peppers: tear into small pieces, do not discard seeds
1 teaspoon finely minced fresh ginger root
½ teaspoon flower peppercorn powder
1 tablespoon minced garlic
2 scallions: cut into pea-sized pieces, including some green part

## SAUCE MIXTURE (Mix in a bowl)

¼ teaspoon cayenne pepper
½ teaspoon sugar
1 tablespoon Sichuan sweet bean sauce or ground bean sauce
2 teaspoons Sichuan chili bean sauce
1 tablespoon Chinese red vinegar
1 tablespoon dry Sherry
1 tablespoon black soy sauce
½ cup canned clear chicken broth

1 medium green or red bell pepper: cut into 1-inch squares
1 teaspoon cornstarch mixed with 1 teaspoon water

DIRECTIONS FOR COOKING

1. Heat oil in wok to deep-fry temperature. Add chicken, stir, and blanch until half done (about 15 seconds). Remove with drainer to a bowl.
2. Remove all but 2 tablespoons oil from wok. Heat oil, then drop in chili peppers, ginger, peppercorn powder, garlic, and scallions. As soon as garlic turns golden, stir in sauce mixture. Add bell pepper. Mix well. Return chicken to wok. Cover and cook over medium heat for 10 minutes. Stir in cornstarch water. Stir and cook until sauce thickens. Put on a serving platter. Serve hot.

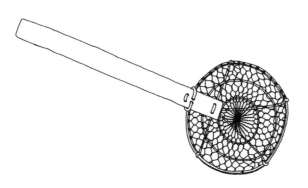

# CHICKEN AND CLOUD EARS WITH TANGERINE FLAVOR
Makes 4 servings

oil for deep-frying

CHICKEN MIXTURE (Mix in a bowl, keep refrigerated before use)

1 pound boneless and skinless chicken thighs or breasts: cut into 1-inch pieces
¼ teaspoon salt
1 egg white: beat until just foamy
3 tablespoons cornstarch
1 teaspoon rice wine or dry Sherry

SEASONINGS (Put on a plate)

4 quarter-sized Chinese dried tangerine skins
1 tablespoon minced fresh ginger
2 teaspoons minced garlic
3 scallions: cut into 1-inch pieces, including some green
½ cup shredded red bell pepper

SAUCE MIXTURE (Mix in a bowl)

2 tablespoons sugar
1 teaspoon cornstarch
¼ teaspoon cayenne pepper
1 teaspoon Chinese red vinegar
2 tablespoons black soy sauce
3 tablespoons dry Sherry
1 tablespoon hoisin sauce
2 tablespoons water

¼ cup cloud ears: soak in hot water until soft, discard tough parts, rinse, drain
2 teaspoons sesame oil

## DIRECTIONS FOR COOKING

1. Heat oil in wok to deep-fry temperature. Add chicken mixture. Stir to separate chicken pieces, and cook until chicken is light brown. Remove with a drainer to a bowl.

2. Remove all but 3 tablespoons oil from wok. Keep oil hot, add tangerine skins, and fry until they are dark brown. Add the seasonings and bell peppers and cook until garlic turns golden. Stir in sauce mixture and cook until it is thickened. Return chicken to wok, add cloud ears, and cook to reheat. Stir in sesame oil. Put on a serving platter. Serve hot.

# CHICKEN LIVERS WITH CASHEW NUTS
Makes 2 to 4 servings

## PREPARATION OF INGREDIENTS

oil for deep-frying cashew nuts
⅓ cup uncooked cashew nuts: rinse in hot water, dry on paper towels
1 scallion: cut into pea-sized pieces, including some green part
2 teaspoons minced fresh ginger
4 Chinese dried mushrooms: soak in hot water until spongy, discard stems,
 cut into ½-inch squares
½ cup ½-inch pieces red or green bell pepper
⅓ cup quartered water chestnuts
⅓ cup bamboo shoots: cut into small cubes
7 chicken livers: cut each into 8 pieces

## SAUCE MIXTURE (Mix in a bowl)

¼ teaspoon salt
¼ teaspoon sugar
1 tablespoon black soy sauce
1 teaspoon thin soy sauce
1 teaspoon Chinese rice wine or dry Sherry

1 teaspoon cornstarch mixed with 2 teaspoons water

## DIRECTIONS FOR COOKING

1. Heat oil in wok to deep-fry temperature. Deep-fry cashew nuts to golden brown. Drain on paper towels. Remove all but 4 tablespoons oil from wok.
2. Heat wok over high heat. When oil is hot, add scallion and ginger, and stir-fry to golden.
3. Keep heat on high. Add mushrooms and stir-fry for about 30 seconds. (Mushrooms need more heat than other vegetables to draw out the flavor.) Add remaining vegetables and stir-fry for about 20 seconds. Remove vegetables with a drainer or a slotted spoon. Let oil drain back into wok. Put vegetables in a bowl.
4. Reheat oil in wok until oil is very hot, but not smoking. Add chicken livers and stir-fry until they lose their red color and are almost cooked through. Stir in sauce mixture and thicken it with the cornstarch mixture. Mix well with the livers. Return vegetables to the wok and stir-fry briefly to reheat. Put on a serving platter and sprinkle cashew nuts on top. Serve hot.

# BROILED CHICKEN LIVERS WRAPPED IN CAUL
Makes 4 to 8 servings

## PREPARATION OF INGREDIENTS

2 sheets of caul (lace fat), about 7 by 8 inches

STUFFING (Mix in a bowl. Refrigerate before use)

8 chicken livers: cut into thin slices
8 ounces ground pork
2 scallions: cut into pea-sized pieces, including some green part
½ teaspoon five-fragrance powder
½ teaspoon sugar
½ teaspoon salt
2 tablespoons cornstarch
1 teaspoon sesame oil
1 tablespoon dry Sherry
1½ tablespoons black soy sauce

BATTER (Beat together with a beater until smooth)

2 tablespoons water chestnut powder
2 egg whites

Soy-Vinegar Dip (see page 315w)

DIRECTIONS FOR COOKING
1. Lay caul on a flat surface. Divide stuffing into two equal portions, and place one portion on a sheet of caul lengthwise, approximately 2 inches in diameter, near the edge of the sheet. Roll the stuffing in the caul and tuck in both ends to look like a thick sausage. Seal with the batter, then brush batter all over the sausage. Repeat with the other in the same manner.
2. Broil sausages on the upper rack under the broiler for about 12 minutes, turning once, or until sausages are golden brown and livers and pork are just cooked.
3. Cut sausages into 1-inch pieces crosswise. Put on a serving platter. Serve hot with dip.

# Duck

# DUCK

There are many kinds of ducks in China, the most famous of which is Peking duck (because Peking duck has such great fame, we will refer to it as "Peking Duck," rather than Beijing Duck"). Though I had been roasting Peking ducks regularly and knew that they were force-fed by hand in China, but, I had never seen how it was done. While visiting my family in Hong Kong, I called on Ah Lin, who, with her husband, Chou Ming, had a poultry farm in the New Territories near Hong Kong. They supplied Peking ducks as well as other kinds to various restaurants and barbecue stores in Hong Kong.

Ah Lin had been with my grandmother for thirteen years, for Grandmother had bought her when she was six years old, then married her to a fine man, Chou Ming, at the age of nineteen. She was now close to sixty, noisy as usual, but plumper and with more gold teeth each time I saw her. Her laughter rang through the valley, and her gold teeth shone in the hot Hong Kong sun. She gave me a big hearty welcome with a little good scolding. "Growing older, but not wiser! First messing yourself up in those restaurant kitchens, wasting the good life in all that cooking! Now, all the way from America to see the ducks! Here they are! Fifteen hundred of them!"

A mass of ducks was fenced in around a creek and a few shallow muddy ponds. Many of them were called mud ducks and rice ducks, I was told. Honestly, I could not tell the difference. But the dazzling swanlike ones were unmistakably Peking ducks—snow-white feathers, orange beaks, feet, and crests. They were big and heavy, but carried themselves with imperial dignity. Peking ducks are not only beautiful-looking, but their meat is fragrant and delicate, and their rich fatty skins are excellent for roasting. Besides, they grow easily, attaining 4 pounds in 2 months. But they can reach 6 to 8 pounds if they are force-fed with special food.

I saw that the Peking ducks prepared for restaurants were caged in 7 groups. The cages were just big enough for them to stretch a little because too much exercise reduces their fat and toughens their flesh. Each day they were force-fed twice and were allowed to have only a 20-minute swim. The rest of the time they stayed in the cages and grew fat.

I had missed the 6:00 A.M. feeding, and waited now for the afternoon feeding. Chou Ming and his 3 helpers had been busy preparing a lot of short and stout noodles, made of wheat, corn, and millet flours, a special diet for the caged ducks.

Each person squatted near a cage with a bucketful of noodles. Ah Lin swiftly pulled out a duck and held it gently between her legs. With her left hand holding the duck head, beak up, her right hand opened the duck's mouth and pushed in the noodles at the same time. Each duck got about 8 noodles.

Because the whole operation seemed smooth and simple enough, I volunteered to help. But the duck was so much stronger than I thought. She quacked loudly and kept flapping her wings while I was pulling her out, then decided to fly when I tried to put her between my knees. When I finally got her mouth opened, I was practically sitting on her. I was so scared and shaken that I just had no heart to stuff anything into that snakelike neck. Chou Ming kindly took over my duck while Ah Lin rocked back and forth gasping with laughter.

Ducks in America are good, especially the Long Island ducklings. They are plump, juicy and tender, perfect for Peking roasted duck and other kinds of roasted dishes.

Fresh ducks usually are available only in some poultry shops. Be sure to ask for a young duckling and have its oil sac removed.

If you prefer to pick your own on a duck farm, and you can't tell an old duck from a young one, here are some hints from Ah Lin: "Choose the ones that have sparkling eyes, warm feet, feathers full and tidy, breasts thick and round."

I must tell you, though, that somehow Ah Lin's hints did not work very well for me. Once I went to a small duck farm near Chicago. I felt dozens of breasts, held dozens of feet. I wound up with a pair of duck-dirt shoes, a body full of feathers, and 6 chewy, gamy old ducks.

Since ducks do not lose their flavor easily, the frozen ones in most markets are almost as good as the fresh-killed. Choosing a frozen duck is easy, because they are all guaranteed young ducklings. Just do not pick ones with the skin punctured during shipping and handling. Allow 10 to 12 hours to thaw out at room temperature or 24 hours in the refrigerator.

# SCALDING DUCK

In order to obtain a beautiful crisp skin, the duck has to be scalded in hot water with honey, ginger, wine, and vinegar. The honey will give the duck's skin a glossy, reddish-brown color; the wine, vinegar, and hot water draw out some fat from the skin to make a crispier skin, and the ginger helps to take away the gamy odor.

14 cups water
4 tablespoons honey
4 slices fresh ginger, each as big and thick as a quarter

½ cup white vinegar
½ cup rice wine or dry Sherry
1 duck

Put water, honey, ginger, vinegar, and wine in a wok or large pot and bring to a boil.

Tie the duck by the neck or by its wings and dip it in the boiling honey water. Ladle the water to scald the duck on both sides for about 15 seconds altogether. Drain and dry duck thoroughly with paper towels.

NOTE: The honey water can be frozen and reused for one more duck; discard ginger and skim off residues and fat before use.

# BONING DUCK

The end we want to achieve in this process is to remove the carcass and main bones from the fowl while leaving the skin and flesh whole and intact. It is not as difficult to do the boning as it is to describe it.

1. Cut off neck 2 inches from base. Slit neck skin to base. With a sharp boning knife, working close to the bone, carefully separate the flesh from the bone so as not to pierce the skin. When you reach the wing, disjoint the main wing bone from the shoulder; cutting close to the main bone, remove it, leaving the wing intact.

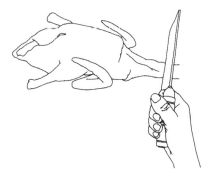

2. Keep the knife close to the bone and work down to the lower part of the body, leaving the carcass separated from the flesh and skin.
3. When you reach the legs, in the same fashion as for the wings, detach and remove the thigh bones, leaving the legs intact.

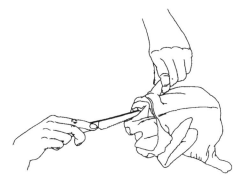

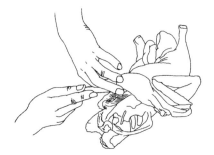

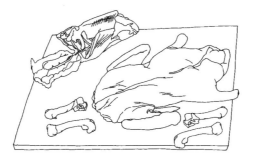

4. Remove carcass from body and save it to make soup or for some other use.

5. Lay out the boned fowl. If there are a few knife punctures, do not be discouraged. Just mend them with needle and thread. If you boned the fowl in less than 10 minutes, I bow to you.

## CUTTING COOKED DUCK FOR SERVING

1. Place fowl breast side up. With a heavy cleaver, chop off head and split it into halves lengthwise. Chop neck into bite-sized pieces, set aside.

2. Cut fowl into halves lengthwise from chest down to back. Disjoint wings and legs. Split fowl's halves lengthwise along the back bones. Chop back bones crosswise into bite-sized pieces; chop breast sides in the same manner.

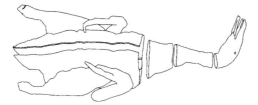

3. Reshape back bones in the center of a platter and arrange breast side pieces on them. Place head (optional), neck pieces, wings, legs, and tail at their original places to reshape the fowl. Garnish the platter with scallion brushes (see recipe), parsley, or greens.

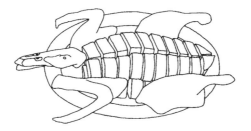

# CANTONESE ROAST DUCK
Makes 4-6 servings

This duck originated in a few small villages near Kwangchow, but the village that prepared it best was Guh Jeng, meaning Old Well, the home of my grandmother. It was there that my grandmother was engaged to my grandfather when she was 8 and was married to him when she was barely 16, never seeing him until the wedding day. She was born in the late Ching Dynasty, survived two revolutions and two world wars, but never learned to read or write. A tiny, uncomplicated woman with a kind and generous heart, she received everything that life brought her, good or bad. To all her grandchildren, she was a blanket of protection, embracing all our little woes and pains while we were growing up. During her 83 years, she never saw America or tasted a hot dog, but through her beloved Tarzan movies and my husband, she loved this faraway country.

Life comes and life goes, and quietly she went. She left me beautiful memories—and this delicious duck.

## PREPARATION OF INGREDIENTS

1 fresh 5-pound duckling: remove fat in cavity, rinse duck and pat dry
14 cups water
4 tablespoons honey
4 slices fresh ginger, each as big and thick as a quarter
½ cup white vinegar
½ cup dry Sherry

## STUFFING (Mix in a bowl)

2 teaspoons sugar
1½ teaspoons salt
½ teaspoon five-fragrance powder
1 tablespoon minced garlic
2 teaspoons minced, soaked dried tangerine peel (optional)
2 tablespoons rice wine or dry Sherry
2 tablespoons water
1 tablespoon ground bean sauce

about 1 tablespoon thin soy sauce
about 2 teaspoons sugar to taste

## DIRECTIONS FOR COOKING

1. Scald duck according to directions for scalding. Hang it in an airy, cool place to dry for at least 8 hours.
2. Stuff duck. Then sew up the cavity with skewer.
3. Place a big roasting pan, containing an inch of water, on the bottom of a gas oven or on the lowest rack of an electric oven to catch the drippings and prevent them from burning.
4. Preheat oven to 400 degrees.
5. Put duck directly on oven rack with breast side up. (If a gas oven, put duck on middle rack. If electric, put duck on upper rack.) Roast for 1½ hours. Remove duck and put on a chopping board.
6. Remove skewer and thread. Scoop out stuffing (mostly sauce) and put in a small saucepan. Measure ½ cup of the drippings (avoiding the grease) and mix with the stuffing. Add soy sauce and sugar to correct taste. Heat sauce over low heat until it comes to a boil. Cover and simmer over very low heat.
7. Carve and slice duck. Put on a platter. Pour sauce over duck. Serve hot.

# STUFFED BONELESS EIGHT-JEWEL DUCK

Makes 8 servings

## PREPARATION OF INGREDIENTS

1 duckling, 4 to 5 pounds (if frozen, allow 10 to 12 hours to thaw at
    room temperature): bone as illustrated, page 102
3 tablespoons oil
⅓ cup soaked Chinese dried mushrooms: discard stems, cut caps into ¼-inch
    squares
½ cup lean pork, cut in pea-sized pieces
1 Chinese pork sausage or ½ cup Cantonese barbecued pork: cut into pea-sized
    pieces
1 tablespoon dried shrimp: soak in very hot water to soften, mince
1 cup shelled chestnuts (dried or fresh): boil in water until soft
¼ cup water chestnuts: cut into pea-sized pieces
¼ cup shelled ginkgo nuts (canned may be used): split into halves
¼ cup dried lotus seeds: cook in water until tender

## SAUCE MIXTURE (Mix in a bowl)

⅛ teaspoon white pepper
½ teaspoon sugar
1 tablespoon black soy sauce
1 tablespoon thin soy sauce
1 tablespoon oyster-flavored sauce
2 tablespoons sesame oil
¼ teaspoon five-fragrance powder
1 tablespoon dry Sherry

¾ cup white, glutinous rice: soak overnight until plump, steam over water for 10
minutes or until done, loosen and put aside
2 teaspoons salt
Soy-Sesame Dip (see page 315)
Five-Fragrance Salt Dip (see page 312)

## DIRECTIONS FOR COOKING

1. Scald boned duck according to directions for scalding, page 101. Hang duck to
air-dry for at least 8 hours.

2. Heat wok until it is hot. Add 3 tablespoons oil. When oil is hot, add mushrooms and lean pork, and cook until pork is done. Add sausage or barbecued pork and shrimp; stir-fry for about 2 minutes. Put in chestnuts, water chestnuts, ginkgo nuts, and lotus seeds. Stir in sauce mixture. Add rice and mix until all of it is glazed with sauce. Put this stuffing in a bowl to cool in the refrigerator.

3. When duck is air-dried, rub it inside with 2 teaspoons of salt. If it is a frozen duck and the head has been removed, sew together neck skin with thread. Stuff duck with stuffing (do not pack it too tightly or it might burst). Close the cavity with thread or skewer .

4. Place a big roasting pan, containing an inch of water, on the bottom of a gas oven or the lowest rack of an electric oven to catch the drippings and prevent them from burning.

5. Preheat oven to 400 degrees.

6. Put duck directly on oven rack with breast side up. (If a gas oven, put duck on middle rack. If electric, put duck on upper rack.) Roast duck for 1½ hours. Remove from oven.

7. Put duck on a big oval serving platter. Remove thread and skewer. Cut off wings and legs. Cut duck into ½-inch pieces crosswise and then cut it down the middle lengthwise. (Cut carefully, disturbing the stuffing as little as possible.) Serve hot with dips.

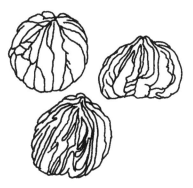

# SICHUAN CRISP SPICED DUCK

Makes 6 to 8 servings

From this duck's appearance, it would seem as if the cook has had a bad day or has played a joke on the diners. The duck's breast sinks into its body. The pale brown skin is dull and dry. But it is really a beauty in disguise: the skin is crisp and luscious, the meat is fragrant, and even the bones are crunchy and tasty. This duck is for the true gourmet!

## PREPARATION OF INGREDIENTS

1 duckling, 4½ to 5 pounds (if frozen, allow 12 hours to thaw)

MARINADE (Mix in a bowl)

1 tablespoon flower peppercorn powder
1 teaspoon five-fragrance powder
1 tablespoon finely minced fresh ginger
½ teaspoon sugar
1½ tablespoons salt
1 tablespoon pale dry Sherry
2 tablespoons thin soy sauce

oil for deep-frying
Lettuce, Scallion Brushes (see page 198), or parsley
Flower Peppercorn and Salt Dip (see page 312)

## DIRECTIONS FOR COOKING

1. Clean and dry duck. Remove fat from the cavity. With both hands, press down on duck's breast to flatten the breastbone.
2. Rub duck inside and out with the marinade. Cover and marinate in the refrigerator for 8 to 10 hours.
3. Steam duck in a steamer or on a rack over water for 2½ hours, adding boiling water from time to time to maintain the level. Drain and air-dry duck on rack for several hours.
4. In a wok, heat oil over high heat to deep-fry temperature. The oil should cover half the duck. Deep-fry duck over medium heat for about 30 minutes, turning twice. When done, the duck is stiff and the skin is dull light brown. Drain.

5. Chop duck (including the bones) as illustrated in this chapter. Garnish with lettuce, scallion brushes, or parsley. Serve hot or warm with dip.

NOTE: After you marinate and steam the duck, you may freeze it. Thaw at room temperature, then deep-fry it.

# PEKING DUCK
Makes 6 to 8 servings

Never has a dish had such publicity and a duck spread its wings so far! It all began around the year 1855 in Peking. Pen Yee Inn, a restaurant specializing in chicken and duck dishes, created the method which made Peking duck a star. The dish was purely for the very rich, and the primary interest was the crisp skin.

The traditional way to prepare Peking duck required a student of the Peking cuisine three months of training just to learn to kill and dress the duck correctly. A hole was opened under each wing to remove the innards so as to keep the duck's skin whole and unbroken. In order to make the skin crisp but not hard, rich but not oily, air was blown in from the duck's throat to separate the skin from the meat. Then the duck was dipped in hot water with honey, wine, vinegar, and ginger. The hot water and the wine helped to draw out some fat; the honey gave the skin a glossy, reddish-brown color when it was roasted; the vinegar stiffened the skin; and the ginger took away the gamy odor. Then the duck was hung to air-dry the skin. Finally, hanging by the neck, it was roasted in a huge drumlike clay oven with charcoal or coal burning below. An even skin was acquired by shifting the duck's position many times. Controlling the heat and the timing required an experienced cook.

Then the glistening, crisp brown skin, cut and arranged on a preheated platter, was served with warm pancakes, accompanied by scallion brushes and sauce. The tender meat, not the primary concern, was served as a separate side dish. And the carcass was used for soup.

Fortunately, living in the West has some advantages. With modern gas and electric ovens, and the young and plump Long Island ducklings, preparing Peking duck is quite easy. The following method is very simple. All you need is a duck about 5 pounds.

## PREPARATION OF INGREDIENTS

14 cups water
4 tablespoons honey
4 slices fresh ginger root, each as big and thick as a quarter
1 Long Island duckling, 5 pounds (if frozen, allow 12 hours to thaw
    at room temperature): remove fat from cavity
½ cup rice wine or dry Sherry
½ cup white vinegar
Mandarin Pancakes (see the following recipe)
24 Scallion Brushes (see page 198)
Hoisin Sauce Dip (see page 314) or Bean Sauce Dip (see page 311)

## DIRECTIONS FOR COOKING

1. Scald duck according to directions for scalding (see page 101).
2. Hang duck in a cool and airy place to dry for 8–12 hours.
3. Have the Mandarin pancakes covered and ready to be reheated. Prepare the scallion brushes and the dip.
4. Preheat oven to 400 degrees. Put duck, breast side up, directly on an oven rack. (If a gas oven, put duck on middle rack. If electric, put duck on upper rack.) Put a big roasting pan with about 1 inch of cold water on the bottom of gas oven or on the lowest rack of electric oven to catch drippings and prevent them from burning. Roast duck breast side up for 30 minutes. Turn oven to 375 degrees and roast duck for a final 1 hour.
5. Ten minutes before the duck is done, fold pancakes in quarters or in halves. Put them, slightly overlapping each other, on a steamer or a rack. Steam over boiling water for 3 minutes or until pancakes are hot. You may also wrap pancakes in a stack with aluminum foil and heat them in a 275-degree oven for 10 minutes or until all the pancakes are warm. Arrange pancakes on a platter just before serving.
6. When duck is done, drain off juice in its cavity, being careful not to let juice wet the crisp skin. Put duck on chopping board. Cut off legs and wings. Remove skin with a sharp knife or with scissors. Cut skin into 1-by 2-inch pieces and arrange them in one layer on a heated platter. Garnish with some of the scallion brushes. Slice duck meat and cut into pieces as big as the skin. Place them on another preheated platter, and arrange legs and wings beside the meat to look like a duck. Garnish with remaining scallion brushes.
7. Bring the dip, duck meat, duck skin, and pancakes to the table at the same time.

8. Give each person a plate. Unfold a pancake and put a piece of meat topped with a piece of skin in the middle of the pancake. Take a scallion brush and paint the skin with ¼ to ½ teaspoon sauce dip. Place the scallion brush on the pancake holding the sauced duck meat and skin, roll the edges of the pancake into a package, and eat.

NOTE: Be sure that you place a pan with an inch of water in the oven to catch the drippings. One of my students had a small fire in his oven because he used a shallow pan with very little water. No damage was done, except his duck and his guests all took on a little smoky flavor.

# MANDARIN PANCAKES
Makes about 20

Mandarin pancakes can be purchased in Chinese grocery stores in frozen packages. Thaw them at room temperature, then steam or reheat them in foil in a 275-degree oven for about 10 minutes. If you are going to use them for the Peking Duck recipe, trim the pancakes to about 6 inches in diameter; otherwise, you will not have enough duck to go around.

Making Mandarin pancakes is not as easy as making ordinary pancakes. But it is not hard either. They need just a little practice and patience. Don't make them when you are in a grouchy mood or in a hurry. Because the pancakes can be frozen and kept for months, the best thing to do is to make plenty of them. Wrap them in foil or in plastic bags by the dozen and freeze them. (It is not necessary to separate them.) Any time you prepare Peking duck or moo shu pork, you will then have Mandarin pancakes on hand.

Because the pancakes should be served warm and soft, it is important to steam them or reheat them in a low oven.

## PREPARATION OF INGREDIENTS

2 cups all-purpose flour, sifted
¼ teaspoon salt
about ¾ cup boiling water
about 3 tablespoons sesame oil

# DIRECTIONS FOR COOKING

1. Put flour and salt in a mixing bowl. Add boiling water gradually. Knead until mixture is soft and smooth. Cover and allow to rest for 15 minutes. Roll dough into a long sausage about 1 inch in diameter and cut into pieces as big as walnuts. Put a damp towel over them to keep them moist.

2. Slightly flour two pieces of dough and roll into small balls. Press each ball flat with your palm to make two small round pancakes, 1½ inches in diameter. Brush sesame oil on one side of a pancake, then place a second pancake on it to make a small sandwich. Roll the two together into a very thin round pancake about 6 to 7 inches in diameter.

3. Heat a flat ungreased frying pan over low heat. Cook both sides of pancake until it turns clear and puffs up slightly; do not brown. Remove from pan and separate it into two very thin pancakes. Trim pancakes with scissors to make them round, if necessary. Wrap in foil or put in a covered container while the others are being cooked. Repeat process for the rest of the dough.

4. Steam pancakes over medium-low heat for 3 minutes, or reheat them in foil in a 275-degree oven for about 10 minutes or until they are hot. Arrange them on a serving platter just before serving. Serve hot.

# Pork

# PORK

Chinese pigs look very different from their American cousins. They are darker and much softer-looking; their backs curve in a great deal, and their bellies nearly touch the ground. They are no great beauties, but they are good-natured. It does not take much good food or care for them to grow and get fat. Chinese country people treat pigs with much affection. If you visit the countryside or a Chinese village, you can see pigs wandering around the household almost like pets.

During the Second World War, food was scarce in many villages. Some families could not afford to raise a pig by themselves; a few families used to share in raising one or two. Each day, they took turns feeding the pigs, so one could see the animals being walked back and forth between families.

These pigs were usually slaughtered just before the Chinese New Year. The meat, the intestines, the feet, and even the bones were equally divided. It was a big occasion for many families. With great care, they treated their shares in endless ways—some for roasting, some for salting, some for smoking, some for sausages.

In an agricultural country such as China, meat is hardly a part of the daily diet. The desire for animal fat is accordingly great among many Chinese. For this, pork does wonders. It keeps many stomachs from getting rusty. Moreover, since cows are used to work in the fields, beef is of low quality. Therefore, pork is the most popular meat among the Chinese. When we say meat, we mean pork.

As I mentioned, pigs are good-natured. And so is their flesh. Pork gets along well with almost everything—all kinds of vegetables, meat, and even seafood. Above all, pork is tasty, tender, juicy, and sweet. No matter how you cut it or cook it, it is always good!

# MOO SHU PORK
Makes 4 servings

## PREPARATION OF INGREDIENTS

4 eggs beat with ½ teaspoon salt, until foamy
5 tablespoons oil

1 teaspoon minced fresh ginger
2 scallions: shred into 1½-inch lengths, including some green part
5 Chinese dried mushrooms: soak in hot water until spongy, discard stems,
    shred caps into matchstick strips

## PORK MIXTURE (Mix and marinate in a bowl)

8 ounces lean pork: shred into matchstick strips (to make 1 cup)
1 teaspoon cornstarch
¼ teaspoon sugar
⅛ teaspoon pepper
1 teaspoon dry Sherry
1 teaspoon thin soy sauce

1 tablespoon rice wine
⅓ cup dried cloud ears: soak 15 minutes or until soft, pinch off hard parts,
    tear remainder into halves
25 dried lily buds: soak in hot water for 15 minutes or until soft, break off tough
    parts, tear remainder into halves lengthwise
1 cup tightly packed, thinly shredded (crosswise) Chinese cabbage
½ cup shredded bamboo shoots into match stick strips

## SAUCE MIXTURE (Mix in a bowl)

½ teaspoon salt
½ teaspoon sugar
1 teaspoon cornstarch
2 tablespoons black soy sauce
1 tablespoon thin soy sauce
1 tablespoon rice wine or dry Sherry
4 tablespoons water

1 ounce bean thread noodles: soak in hot water until soft, cut about
4 inches long with scissors
1 tablespoon sesame oil
Mandarin Pancakes (see page 111); steam until hot or reheat in oven
wrapped in foil

## DIRECTIONS FOR COOKING

1. Heat wok until hot. Swirl in 2 tablespoons oil. When oil is hot, add eggs and cook them as you would scrambled eggs. Do not overcook—eggs should be smooth and moist. Cut eggs into chunks about the size of sugar cubes. Set aside.
2. Heat wok until hot. Swirl in 3 tablespoons oil. When oil is hot, slightly brown ginger. Throw in scallions and mushrooms, and brown them slightly. Splash in 1 tablespoon rice wine or Sherry and add pork mixture immediately. Stir-fry until meat is no longer pink. Add cloud ears and lily buds, then cabbage and bamboo shoots. Cook over medium-high heat until they are heated thoroughly. Stir in sauce mixture and cook for 15 seconds. Add cooked egg chunks and bean thread noodles. Toss to mix well. Add sesame seed oil. Mix. Put on serving platter and serve hot with Mandarin pancakes.

To eat, put 2 to 3 spoonfuls of Moo Shu pork in the center of a heated pancake, and fold pancake into a package.

NOTE: This dish can be cooked in advance without the eggs. Scramble eggs and add chunks just before you reheat.

# RED-COOKED FRESH HAM, SHANGHAI STYLE
Makes 4 to 6 servings

## PREPARATION OF INGREDIENTS

2 tablespoons oil
4 slices fresh ginger, each as big and thick as a quarter
2 cloves garlic: crush and peel
2 scallions: cut into 1½-inch lengths, including some green part
about 4 pounds fresh uncured ham

## SAUCE MIXTURE (Mix in a bowl)

4 tablespoons sugar
½ teaspoon salt
½ cup black soy sauce
2 tablespoons thin soy sauce
¼ cup rice wine or dry Sherry

about 5 cups boiling water
1 stick cinnamon
3 whole star anise
½ head iceberg lettuce: separate leaves and break into large pieces

## DIRECTIONS FOR COOKING

1. Heat wok or a Dutch oven and pour in oil. When oil is hot, add ginger, garlic, and scallions. Brown them slightly. Add the ham and sear it evenly.
2. Turn heat to medium-low. Pour in sauce mixture. Add 1 cup of boiling water, cinnamon stick, and star anise. Cover and simmer until ham is very tender (about 4 hours). Check ham from time to time during cooking, and add additional boiling water by the cupful as needed. There should be 1½ to 2 cups of sauce left in the pot at the end of the cooking time.
3. Discard ginger, garlic, cinnamon stick, and star anise. Skim off fat.
4. Heat a large pot of water to a rolling boil, add lettuce and let it stay for only 5 seconds. Remove with a strainer to a serving platter.
5. Slice the ham and arrange the pieces on lettuce. Spoon sauce over ham. Serve hot.

NOTE: This dish can be precooked and reheated on stove.

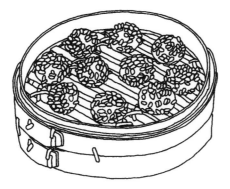

# SLICED PORK, CHICKEN, SHRIMP, AND SCALLIONS, BEIJING STYLE

Makes about 6 servings

PREPARATION OF INGREDIENTS

oil for blanching

CHICKEN AND PORK MIXTURE (Mix in a bowl)

8 ounces lean pork: cut into paper-thin slices while half-frozen
1 boned, skinless chicken breast: cut into pieces same as pork
2 tablespoons cornstarch
1 tablespoon brown sugar
1 tablespoon black soy sauce

SHRIMP MIXTURE (Mix in a bowl. Refrigerate before use)

4 ounces fresh shrimp: shell, devein, rinse in cold water, pat dry
⅓ egg white
¼ teaspoon salt
1 pinch white pepper

6 scallions: cut into 1½-inch pieces, including some green part
2 teaspoons minced garlic

SAUCE MIXTURE (Mix in a bowl)

2 teaspoons brown sugar
1 tablespoon ground bean sauce
1½ tablespoons black soy sauce
3 tablespoons rice wine or dry Sherry

DIRECTIONS FOR COOKING

1. Heat oil in wok to deep-fry temperature. Add chicken and pork mixture. Stir quickly to separate pieces. Blanch briskly until chicken turns white and pork loses its pink color. Remove with a drainer to a bowl.
2. In the same hot oil, briskly blanch shrimp mixture until shrimps just turn white-pink. Remove with a drainer to a bowl.
3. Remove all but 2 tablespoons oil from wok. Heat oil. When it is hot, then add scallions and garlic. When garlic turns golden, swirl in sauce mixture. Stir and cook until sauce begins to bubble. Return chicken, pork, and shrimp to wok. Mix and stir-fry for about 15 seconds. Put on a serving platter. Serve hot.

# RED-COOKED LION HEADS
Makes 6 servings

The hearts of the Chinese cabbage are the manes of the lions. Since it is too costly to use just the heart of the cabbage in the United States, you may use the other parts of the celery cabbage also.

This is a northern dish, very tasty, meaty, with a lot of gravy for rice.

PREPARATION OF INGREDIENTS

PORK MIXTURE (Mix in a bowl. Do not overmix or meatballs will be tough)

1 pound ground pork
5 Chinese mushrooms: soak in hot water until soft, drain, discard stems, and mince
2 tablespoons cloud ears: soak in hot water until soft, drain, mince
⅓ cup minced water chestnuts
¼ cup minced bamboo shoots

2 scallions: mince, including some green part
½ teaspoon sugar
⅛ teaspoon pepper
1½ tablespoons cornstarch
1 tablespoon dry Sherry
2 tablespoons black soy sauce

2 tablespoons oil
1½ pounds Chinese cabbage hearts: cut into big pieces

SAUCE MIXTURE (Mix in a bowl)

1 teaspoon sugar
1 tablespoon dry Sherry
1 tablespoon thin soy sauce
½ cup canned, clear chicken broth

1 tablespoon cornstarch mixed with 1 tablespoon water
¼ teaspoon salt or to taste

DIRECTIONS FOR COOKING

1. Form pork mixture into 6 big peach-sized meatballs.
2. Heat oil in wok. When oil is hot, add meatballs and turn heat to medium. Brown meatballs evenly, then remove them to a plate.
3. Leave oil in wok, and add the cabbage. Turn on heat, stir-fry for a minute. Transfer cabbage to a 3- to 4-quart pot. Stir in sauce mixture and mix well. Put meatballs on top of cabbage. Cover and simmer for 20 to 30 minutes or until cabbage is soft.
4. Transfer meatballs and cabbage to a serving bowl, placing cabbage at the bottom and meatballs on top. Leave liquid in the cooking pot. Stir cornstarch water into liquid and cook until thickened. Salt to taste. Pour sauce over meatballs and cabbage. Serve hot.

NOTE: This dish can be cooked in advance and reheated on stove.

# FIVE-FRAGRANCE PORK CHOPS
Makes 6 servings

## PREPARATION OF INGREDIENTS

6 pork chops: cut each in half and pound with back edge of cleaver
    (leave bone in)

MARINADE (Mix in a bowl and marinate pork chops for 30 minutes or longer.
Turn from time to time)

1 tablespoon brown sugar
½ teaspoon five-fragrance powder
½ teaspoon finely minced fresh ginger
¼ cup black soy sauce
1 tablespoon rice wine or dry Sherry
2 scallions: mince finely, including some green part

about ¼ cup cornstarch for coating
oil for pan-frying

## DIRECTIONS FOR COOKING

1. Put cornstarch on a plate and lightly dredge marinated pork chops in it.
2. Heat oil in a large skillet. Pan-fry pork chops, a few at a time, until they are
golden brown. Drain on paper towels. Serve hot.

# SWEET AND SOUR PORK
Makes 4 to 6 servings

The most elegant and delicious sweet and sour pork is prepared the way my
aunts, my grandmothers, and their cooks prepared theirs. They never put
ketchup in the sauce, but used shan zha bing. These little wafers give the sweet
and sour sauce a very delicate, fruity flavor and a natural clear red color; therefore, no red food coloring is needed. But if shan zha bing is not available, you
may substitute 2 tablespoons ketchup for it.

For this dish, choose pork marbled with some fat (such as pork butt), so it
will be crisp after frying. Lean pork will come out dry and tough.

PREPARATION OF INGREDIENTS

about ¾ cup cornstarch for coating pork

PORK MIXTURE (Mix in a bowl)

1 pound pork butt or shoulder: cut into ¾-inch cubes (to make 1½ cups),
    pound with back edge of cleaver or heavy knife
1 teaspoon dry Sherry
1 egg, beaten
½ teaspoon salt
1 big pinch pepper

2 tablespoons oil

⅓ cup water chestnuts, each cut in half
¼ cup bamboo shoots cut into small sugar-cube-sized pieces
¼ cup red or green bell pepper cut into ½-inch squares
⅓ cup canned pineapple chunks

SAUCE MIXTURE (Mix in a bowl. Allow to sit for an hour or more)

¼ cup sugar
1 teaspoon minced garlic
⅓ cup canned pineapple juice
1 tablespoon thin soy sauce
1 tablespoon black soy sauce
¼ cup white vinegar
1 ounce shan zha bing (see page 331): separate wafers so they will dissolve easily
½ cup water

1 tablespoon cornstarch mixed with 2 tablespoons water
oil for deep-frying

DIRECTIONS FOR COOKING

1. Put cornstarch on a plate and roll marinated pork mixture in it until cubes are
no longer sticky. Put pork on plate, and after it absorbs cornstarch, roll in cornstarch again.

2. Heat a small saucepan over low heat. Add 2 tablespoons oil, water chestnuts, bamboo shoots, pepper, and pineapple. Pour in sauce mixture. Cook, stirring constantly, over medium-low heat until sauce bubbles gently. Stir in cornstarch water. Stir and cook until sauce is thickened. Turn heat to very low to keep sauce hot.

3. Heat oil to deep-fry temperature. Deep-fry pork in batches until pieces float to the top and turn a light golden color (about 5 minutes). Remove pork with drainer or slotted spoon and put on a serving platter. Pour sauce over pork. Serve piping hot immediately. Do not let pork stand in sauce for long, otherwise it becomes soggy.

# DICED PORK WITH WALNUTS

Makes 4 to 6 servings

PREPARATION OF INGREDIENTS

oil for deep-frying
½ cup uncooked walnuts (or cashews or peanuts)

PORK MIXTURE (Mix and refrigerate for at least an hour before use)

1 pound lean pork, cut into ¾-inch cubes
¼ teaspoon salt
¼ teaspoon pepper
2 teaspoons sugar
2 tablespoons cornstarch
1 tablespoon black soy sauce

2 teaspoons minced fresh ginger
2 teaspoons minced garlic
½ cup scallions, in 1-inch pieces, including some green
¼ cup red bell peppers, in ½-inch squares
½ cup water chestnuts cut in half
1 tablespoon rice wine or dry Sherry

SAUCE MIXTURE (Mix in bowl)

2 tablespoons light brown sugar
3 tablespoon black soy sauce
3 tablespoons rice wine or dry Sherry

2 teaspoons sesame oil

DIRECTIONS FOR COOKING

1. Heat oil and deep-fry walnuts at moderate temperature until golden brown. Drain on paper towels.
2. Heat oil to deep-fry temperature. Deep-fry half of the pork until pieces are rich brown. Drain and put aside. Deep-fry the remaining half of the pork in the same manner.
3. Remove all but 2 tablespoons oil from wok. When oil is hot, add ginger and stir-fry for about 10 seconds; add garlic and scallions and stir-fry until garlic turns golden. Add bell pepper and water chestnuts. Stir-fry for about 20 seconds. Splash in 1 tablespoon wine, stir quickly. Add sauce, cook for about 5 seconds. Return pork to wok. Stir-fry until sauce bubbles and pork is reheated. Stir in sesame oil. Transfer to serving platter. Top with walnuts. Serve hot.

# SICHUAN SPICED PORK SHREDS
Makes 2 to 4 servings

PREPARATION OF INGREDIENTS

4 tablespoons oil
1 teaspoon minced fresh ginger
2 teaspoons minced garlic
3 scallions: cut into sticks, including some green part

PORK MIXTURE (Mix in bowl)

½ pound lean pork: cut into matchstick strips
2 teaspoons cornstarch
1 teaspoon sesame oil
2 teaspoons rice wine or dry Sherry

⅓ cup shredded bamboo shoots
⅓ cup dried cloud ears: soak in hot water until soft, rinse,
    drain and discard tough parts

SAUCE MIXTURE (Mix in a bowl)

¼ to ½ teaspoon ground red pepper
¼ teaspoon salt
1 teaspoon sugar
I teaspoon sesame oil
1 tablespoon black soy sauce
1 tablespoon rice wine or dry Sherry
1 tablespoon Sichuan sweet bean sauce or ground bean sauce
2 teaspoons Chinese red vinegar or rice vinegar
½ cup water

2 teaspoons cornstarch mixed with 1 tablespoon water

DIRECTIONS FOR COOKING

1. Heat wok over high heat. When it begins to smoke, swirl in 4 tablespoons oil.
When oil is hot, add ginger and stir-fry for several seconds. Add garlic and scallions and stir-fry until garlic becomes fragrant. Add pork mixture. Stir-fry until
pork is no longer pink. Add bamboo shoots and cloud ears. Stir-fry for about 10
seconds. Swirl in sauce mixture and stir to cook until sauce begins to bubble.
Add cornstarch-water, stir until sauce is clear and thickened. Put on a serving
platter. Serve hot.


# CANTONESE BARBECUED PORK
Serves 8

This famous barbecued pork is a Cantonese specialty. Eat it cold or hot as
you like. Since most Chinese families do not have ovens or grills, barbecued pork is prepared mostly in restaurants and some grocery stores. Some put
food coloring to make the pork red, the color of happiness and festive occasions.

To the Chinese, it is a dish for many occasions: for a special family treat, for
a picnic, for the drop-in guests who do not leave at dinner time.

For this recipe, it is best to use meat from the shoulder. If you use tenderloin, it will come out a little dry. Since barbecued pork freezes will, this recipe makes enough for dinner as well as for leftovers.

## PREPARATION OF INGREDIENTS

5 pounds boneless pork shoulder: cut into 1½-inch thick and 2-inch wide strips

### MARINADE (Mix in a bowl)

1 tablespoon minced garlic
6 tablespoons sugar
1 teaspoon salt
4 teaspoons five-fragrance powder
½ cup plus 2 tablespoons black soy sauce
½ cup rice wine or sake
2 tablespoons ground bean sauce
⅔ cup hoisin sauce

### GLAZE (Mix in a bowl)

1 tablespoon sesame oil
1 tablespoon thin soy sauce
4 tablespoons honey

## DIRECTIONS FOR COOKING

1. Put pork strips in a large pan. Spoon marinade over pork evenly and refrigerate for 8 hours or more. Turn pork from time to time.
2. Preheat oven to 500 degrees.
3. Spear pork strips lengthwise with metal skewers and put directly on an oven rack. (if it is a gas oven, put rack in middle of oven. If electric, put rack in upper part of oven). Place a big pan with ½ inch of water on bottom of gas oven or on lowest rack of electric oven to catch the drippings and to prevent oven from smoking, Roast pork for 15 minutes. Turn pork and roast for another 15 minutes or until pork is done.
4. Remove pork from oven and brush with glaze; remove pork skewers. Slice and serve.

NOTE: If you freeze any of the pork, do so before you slice it.

# CANTONESE BARBECUED SPARERIBS
Makes 4 to 6 servings

M r. Ng was a very good barbecue chef. He worked for a grocery store in New York's Chinatown. He was about fifty-five, noisy, and his face was full of expression when he talked. Fascinated by that face, I often did not hear what he said. He seemed to be forever arguing with his fellow workers, then a minute later he forgot. He laughed, he yelled, he joked, all in the same breath. Each week he barbecued about 150 ducks and at least 300 pounds of spareribs and pork. And yet he still found time to jest and quarrel. If he was not in a jubilant mood, he splashed the marinade and pushed the ducks around.

Since he did not speak English or write it, he seldom ventured out of Chinatown. His whole world was his family and his kin. He felt that he was my uncle simply because I had lived in the village where he was born. He thought that anybody who could write English was very smart; therefore, I was the scholar of his heart. I have met many cooks and chefs like Mr. Ng; many of them are not as noisy, and some are even shy. They all work long hours but never lose their steam. They own very little, but are extravagant spirits. Such persons humble one.

## PREPARATION OF INGREDIENTS

3 to 4 pounds uncut spareribs

SAUCE MIXTURE (Mix in a bowl)

2 teaspoons minced garlic
⅔ cup hoisin sauce
⅓ cup black soy sauce
6 tablespoons light corn syrup or honey
4 tablespoons rice wine or dry Sherry

GLAZE (Mix in a bowl)
1 tablespoon thin soy sauce
4 tablespoons honey

## DIRECTIONS FOR COOKING

1. Marinate ribs in sauce mixture at least 4 to 6 hours or overnight.
2. Heat oven to 375 degrees.

3. Put ribs directly on oven rack. (If it is a gas oven, put rack in the middle of the oven. If electric, put rack in upper part of the oven.) Put a big pan with ½ inch of cold water on the bottom of a gas oven or on the lowest rack of an electric oven to catch drippings and prevent them from burning. The ribs and the water should be 9 to 10 inches away from each other; otherwise the water will steam the ribs, causing them to lose their barbecued flavor.

4. Cook ribs for about 45 minutes. Generously brush upper side of ribs with the glaze, and catch the drippings with a plate. Cook ribs for another 2 minutes. Turn ribs and glaze the other side in the same manner. Cook for 2 more minutes.

5. Put ribs on chopping board, cut into strips, and serve hot or cold.

NOTE: This recipe can be doubled. You may freeze cooked ribs in aluminum foil. Thaw, then reheat in slow oven, wrapped in foil.

# STEAMED SPARERIBS OR PORK IN GARLIC AND BLACK BEAN SAUCE
Makes 4 servings

## PREPARATION OF INGREDIENTS

SPARERIB OR PORK MIXTURE (Mix together and marinate at least 1 hour in refrigerator)

1 pound pork spareribs: ask your butcher to cut them into bite-sized pieces
    and trim off excess fat; if pork is used, cut into bite-sized pieces
3 tablespoons salted black beans: put in a small drainer, rinse in running
    hot water, drain, mash to paste.
1 to 2 fresh chili peppers (optional): cut into small rounds; use seeds also
1 small piece of dried tangerine peel (optional): soak in hot water for 10 minutes,
    mince (to make 2 teaspoons)
1 tablespoon minced garlic
¼ teaspoon salt
½ teaspoon sugar
2 tablespoons thin soy sauce
2 teaspoons dry Sherry

2 teaspoons sesame oil
2 tablespoons chopped scallions, including some green

## DIRECTIONS FOR COOKING

1. Put sparerib or pork mixture in a 9-inch, heat proof plate (a pie plate will do).
2. Steam spareribs or pork over water for about 10 minutes. Pour in sesame oil and mix well. Transfer the whole contents to a heated serving platter, top with Scallions. Serve hot with rice.


# DONG PO PORK
Makes about 6 servings

For hundreds of years, Su Dong Po's name has evoked affectionate smiles and deep admiration among the Chinese people. He was considered a multifaceted genius and is best described by noted writer Lin Yutang as "a great humanitarian, a friend of the people, a prose master, an original painter, a great calligraphist, an experimenter in wine making, an engineer, a yogi, a Buddhist believer, a Confucian statesman, a secretary to the emperor...a human judge. a dissenter in politics, a prowler in the moonlight. a poet, and a wag." Still, these words cannot sum up this beloved soul, reminding us always of all that is good and noble in humanity.

Born in 1036, during the turbulent Sung dynasty, Su Dong Po fell victim to political intrigue in his late fifties. He was demoted and banished to live in exile for the remaining six years of his life. Two of those years he spent in Huichow, a county in southern China famous for its lichi trees, orange groves, sugar cane and tender pork. There, he wrote to his brother about cooking, making cinnamon wine, the friendly people, and the beauty of the region. He spent his time fishing, roaming the countryside, and dining with the local people who indulged him with food and wine. Without a care in the world or any official duties, he was happy and content.

When word reached the capital that Su Dong Po was having the best of times in exile, his enemies in court punished him by banishing him to Hainan, a primitive island off the southern coast of China. In this remote tropical jungle, he and his family were given a leaky hut and were often without food. Never losing his spirit or his humor, he wrote to friends that he filled his hunger by eating morning rays.

In 1101, his fortune changed with the political climate in the capital. The new emperor pardoned Su Dong Po and restored his honor. On his journey home, people flanked the river banks to greet him at every town. He was ill during the journey and died shortly after he arrived home.

In his writings, Su Dong Po wrote about how delicious pork was if it was cooked slowly for hours with soy sauce. This is a classic dish which has always borne his name. It has been a favorite for many, especially my father, a native of Huichow. My father prides himself on not knowing how to cook, except for this Dong Po pork. He never allowed anyone to prepare the dish for him. When he visited us from Hong Kong, he would always bring with him his own salted beans and insisted on choosing his own pork from a Chinese butcher. He examined each slab of pork as if he were buying a piece of antique jade. Then he would take over my kitchen and make a mess of all my pots and pans. So out of his character, my family looked on with amusement. The result was a dish of savory pork steeped in rich and haunting flavors that melted in our mouths.

My father, 88 years old and too frail to travel to America, no longer prepares his favorite pork. But I have learned from my sisters that he taught a chef at the club he belongs to how to cook it for him.

Today, juicy marbled pork, crispy duck skin, tender spring lamb and the glorious egg are avoided out of our intense concern for our health, body image and fat count. But I do believe in the wisdom of moderation and the forgiving of occasional gastronomic sin. After all, what is so good about a long life if one has to eat like a rabbit?

For the love of history and this heavenly pork, I faithfully reproduce this dish with the complete approval from my father. To him and our beloved Su Dong Po, I bow with affection and gratitude.

PREPARATION OF INGREDIENTS

1½ pounds boneless pork butt or pork belly: leave whole
2 tablespoons black soy sauce
oil for deep-frying

SAUCE MIXTURE

1 tablespoon sugar
2 tablespoons salted black beans: wash in hot water, drain
3 tablespoons rice wine or dry Sherry
4 tablespoons black soy sauce

2 tablespoons oil
½ pound watercress (pinch off tough stalks, wash, drain) or ½ head iceberg
    lettuce (separate leaves)
1 teaspoon cornstarch mixed with 1 teaspoon water

DIRECTIONS FOR COOKING

1. Bring a big pot of water to a boil. Immerse pork. Cover and cook over medium heat for 30 minutes. Rinse pork in cold water, pat dry, and cut into 2-inch cubes. Roll cubes in 2 tablespoons black soy sauce. Put on a cake rack to drain.
2. Heat oil to deep-fry temperature. Deep-fry pork for about a minute or until nicely browned. Immediately immerse browned pork in a big bowl of cold water to cool for about 30 minutes.
3. Remove pork from water and put in a medium-sized casserole with a cover. Pour sauce mixture over pork and cover.
4. Put a heatproof bowl in the middle of a wok or a big pot, then place a heat proof plate on the bowl. Place the covered casserole of pork on the plate. Pour boiling water into wok to reach the level of the plate, then cover wok. Dry-steam over medium heat for 4 hours until pork is very tender, adding boiling water to wok from time to time to maintain water level.
5. When pork is nearly done, heat another wok or skillet. Swirl in 2 tablespoons oil. When oil is hot, stir-fry watercress or lettuce until just softened. Drain and put on a serving platter.
6. Spoon pork cubes onto watercress or lettuce. Heat sauce in casserole and thicken it with cornstarch water. Pour sauce over pork. Serve hot.

# STEAMED EGGS WITH PORK OR DRIED SHRIMP
Makes 6 servings

T his is a classical family dish, well loved by all ages. It is always served at home all the time, because it is nutritious and easy to prepare. This dish never has leftovers. The children always fight over whatever little bit that has cleaved to the plate. The winner scours the plate with a few spoonfuls of rice, with the concentration of a miner shifting for gold; then relishes ever little speck of it in victorious satisfaction.

PREPARATION OF INGREDIENTS

1 pound lean, ground pork or ½ cup dried shrimp (soak shrimp in hot water until soft, rinse, drain)
½ teaspoon white, ground pepper
2 preserved eggs (optional): peel and cut into sugar-cube sized chunks

EGG MIXTURE (Mix in a bowl)

6 large eggs
2 salted duck eggs
½ teaspoon sea salt
¼ teaspoon sugar
1 tablespoon sesame oil
½ cup water

2 tablespoons thin soy sauce

DIRECTIONS FOR COOKING

1. Mix ground pork or dried shrimp with ground, white pepper, and spread in a
9- to 10-inch and 2-inch deep heatproof plate. Top with preserved eggs.
2. Beat egg mixture until it is slightly foamy. Pour over pork or shrimp and
preserved eggs. Cover and steam for about 15 minutes or until pork is no longer
pink. Swirl in 2 tablespoons thin soy sauce. Serve hot with plain rice.


# MY MOTHER'S LETTUCE PACKAGES
## (MINCED PORK AND SMOKED OYSTERS WITH
## WALNUTS AND NOODLES WRAPPED IN LETTUCE)
Makes 6 to 8 servings

This dish is beautiful and delicious. It has been a treasure to me and my
students. Unlike most persons who prepare lettuce packages with only
minced pork or chicken and water chestnuts, my mother added fat, juicy Chinese oysters to be stir-fried with the minced pork, chopped water chestnuts, and
bean sprouts. She lined the serving platter not only with lettuce leaves, but also
with crisp noodles. She then placed the cooked oyster and pork mixture on the
noodles surrounded by the lettuce; finally she sprinkled the dish with golden-
brown walnuts.

My mother created this dish when she was about forty-seven. Never considering herself a good cook or special in anything, she was an unassuming woman,
painfully shy. But in her village, she was the first college graduate and the village's
only female to marry according to her own choice. During the Second World
War, she wrote countless letters for neighbors and friends, since she was the only
woman in the area who could write. At least twice a week she read her favorite

legends to the villagers. Under the little oil lamp, men and women would laugh or silently weep at the stories conveyed by her lyrical voice.

When she departed, scores of unexpected people came. "Who was this woman, that so many mourn?" someone asked. She was neither nobility nor a celebrity, but a good departing soul whom they did not want to let go. She was fifty-four years of age.

## PREPARATION OF INGREDIENTS

1 head Boston lettuce: detach leaves, wash, dry
oil for deep-frying
1 ounce bean thread noodles
⅓ cup walnuts
1 teaspoon minced garlic
2 scallions: cut into pea-sized pieces, including green part
1½ cups (12 ounces) coarsely ground, lean pork
1 can (3⅔ ounce) smoked oysters in olive oil or cottonseed oil: drain, mince oysters coarsely
1 cup chopped water chestnuts in pea-sized pieces
1 cup coarsely chopped fresh bean sprouts or iceberg lettuce

## SAUCE MIXTURE (Mix in a bowl)

¼ teaspoon sugar
¼ teaspoon cayenne pepper
1 tablespoon thin soy sauce
2 tablespoons oyster-flavored sauce
1 teaspoon dry Sherry
1 teaspoon sesame oil

2 teaspoons cornstarch mixed with 1 tablespoon water

## DIRECTIONS FOR COOKING

1. Arrange Boston lettuce in a circle around the edge of a large serving platter.
2. Heat oil in wok to deep-fry temperature. Loosen bean thread noodles by pulling them apart. Test oil with a piece of noodle. If it pops up immediately, the oil is hot. Plunge noodles into oil. The noodles instantly become a white nest. Turn nest over and fry on the other side. (This takes less than 10 seconds.) Drain on paper towels.

3. Use the same oil to deep-fry the walnuts. Drain on paper towels. Put walnuts in plastic bag, crush them coarsely with a rolling pin. Set aside.

4. Slightly break the noodles into smaller pieces, and put in the center of the platter.

5. Remove all but 2 tablespoons of oil from wok. Heat oil, then slightly brown garlic and scallions. Add ground pork. Stir-fry until pork is no longer pink. Add oysters and stir-fry with pork for a minute. Add water chestnuts and iceberg lettuce or bean sprouts. Swirl in sauce mixture and stir well. Stir in cornstarch water and cook for a minute. Carefully place pork mixture over the noodles, then top with the walnuts. Serve hot.

To eat, put 2 to 3 spoonfuls of meat and oysters with noodles in the center of a piece of Boston lettuce. Fold lettuce into a package.

# CHILDBIRTH GINGER
## (PIG'S FEET, EGGS, AND GINGER IN SWEET VINEGAR)
Makes 8 to 14 bowls

In Kwangtung Province, after a woman give birth to a child, it was the duty of a mother-in-law to prepare a big pot of this ginger for her daughter in-law to regain her strength. The vinegar drew out the bone marrow of the pig's feet. The eggs, representing birth, turned dark brown while soaking in the vinegar. The ginger became sweet and mild. The sauce was the essence that the new mother had to drink. It was sweet, vinegary, gingery, and savory. No woman would refuse it.

The supply of the ginger, pig's feet, and eggs had to last for a month. And many extra pots had to be prepared in order to share with the relatives, neighbors, and friends. Distant neighbors, who sensed the aroma of the sweet vinegar, could bring bowls containing red envelopes with a little money for good luck; then their bowls would be filled with great pleasure.

The daughter-in-law was proud to be served this ginger dish, for it showed that her mother-in-law cared. It gave the new mother face and pride that she could show her relatives and friends that she was in a good family and was being well treated.

Unfortunately, in some families, if a girl was born instead of a boy, the disappointment was so great that no ginger was served, or only a small amount might be prepared. My grandmother still sighed, at the age of seventy-eight, because her ginger was accompanied by no eggs and no pig's feet. For she had given birth to a girl—my mother.

## PREPARATION OF INGREDIENTS

2 pounds fresh ginger: peel, break into small chunks, crack and flatten slightly with flat side of cleaver

2 pig's feet with hocks (about 2½ pounds): ask butcher to split them in half lengthwise and chop crosswise into 1-inch pieces; blanch in a big pot of boiling water for a minute, drain, discard water

2½ cups Chinese sweet vinegar

¼ cup white vinegar

1 cup water

½ teaspoon salt

8 hard-boiled eggs: remove shells

## DIRECTIONS FOR COOKING

1. Bring a big pot of water to a rapid boil. Add ginger and boil over medium heat for 20 minutes to reduce hotness of ginger. Drain in colander. Discard water.

2. Choose a 6-quart stainless steel pot or clay pot (be sure it can be used on stove), and add blanched pig's feet, ginger, sweet vinegar, white vinegar, water, and salt. Cover and cook over medium-low heat for about 1½ hours, or until pig's feet are tender. Stir from time to time while cooking. There should be about 2 cups of liquid left in pot at end of cooking time. Immerse eggs in sauce. Cover and allow the pot to stand for at least a day. Reheat on stove over low heat before serving hot.

NOTE: This dish is never served as a meal, but is eaten between meals. Serve the new mother two small bowls a day for a month—whether she gave birth to a girl or a boy.

# Beef and Lamb

*The Chinese character for "beauty" is composed of the characters for "big" and "lamb." It denotes that the ancient Chinese considered that what was most beautiful, most pleasing, and most desirable was a lamb, big and fat.*

*We are sometimes accused of synaesthesia, and that we think and see with our stomachs. I must admit that there is some truth to this, at least in my family. For the Leungs, it is almost impossible to enjoy the glorious orange hue of the morning sun and not associate it with a beautiful and delicious egg yolk. To us, it is only natural to think and talk about food and eating. Can we deny that food and drink remain among the few true joys in life. Who can forget one's stomach for long? So, to many Chinese and to my family, happiness is eating; and beauty is, indeed, a big, fat lamb.*

# BEEF AND LAMB

Two-thirds of the beef and lamb dishes in this book are from the west and north of China. Many of these dishes have strong Moslem, Mongolian, or Manchurian backgrounds. One easily forgets that China consists of many races, divided into five large groups: the Han people, the Manchus, the Mongols, the Moslems, and the Tibetans and other minority groups. Ninety-five percent of the Chinese are Han people. But the Mongols and the Manchus once ruled China in Beijing; and the Moslems have a substantial population spread through the north and the west of China. Many of these peoples do not eat pork, but rather beef and lamb. The Han people have adopted Moslem cooking and changed it into their own. The Beijing Fire Pot, Beef in Vinegar Sauce, Beijing Style, the Empress Dowager's Lamb, and many others are heavily flavored by Mongolian, Moslem, and Manchurian cooking.

For most Chinese, beef and lamb are eaten much less often than pork or poultry. It is not that the Chinese do not like beef and lamb, but rather because these commodities are low in quality and quantity. Chinese yellow cows and water buffaloes are lean and tough. And lamb is rare. Unlike America, there is not enough land in China for feed crops and for animals meant for slaughter. Many Chinese love American beef. When my uncle and aunt made their first visit to America from Hong Kong, they were eager to taste the famous American T-bone steak. My dining table was like a Texas spread. Aunt and Uncle soaked up and ate the bloody juice. Pictures were snapped of the diners for them to take home to show and tell about the famous American steaks and roasts.

For stir-frying, flank steak and leg of lamb are best. Never use more meat than the recipe calls for; it will alter the recipe and diminish the taste.

For red cooking (slow cooking), any kind of roast will do.

# AROMATIC SPICED BEEF ROAST
Makes 8 to 10 servings

## PREPARATION OF INGREDIENTS

4 pounds beef roast (eye round, top round, or cross-cut rib)
2 tablespoons oil
1 chunk (big as a walnut) fresh ginger: crush
3 cloves garlic: crush and peel
2 dried whole chili peppers

## SAUCE MIXTURE (Mix in a bowl)

2 tablespoons brown sugar
⅓ cup black soy sauce
⅓ cup dry Sherry

3 cups water
2 teaspoons five-fragrance powder
3 whole star anise
1 cinnamon stick, about 3 inches long

## DIRECTIONS FOR COOKING

1. Bring a big pot of water to a boil. Put in beef and let it boil for 2 minutes. Remove beef and pat dry with towel. Discard water.
2. Heat a wok or a Dutch oven and put in oil. When it is hot, slightly brown ginger, garlic, and chili peppers. Add sauce mixture, then beef. Turn beef all over to coat with sauce. Add 3 cups water, five-fragrance powder, star anise, and cinnamon stick. Cover and simmer over low heat for about 3 hours, or until beef is tender. Check beef from time to time while it is cooking; add more water if it is needed. There should be about 2 cups of sauce left in pot.
3. Discard ginger, chili peppers, garlic, cinnamon stick, and anise. Slice beef and put on platter. Pour sauce over beef slices and serve hot or serve cold without the sauce.

# ORANGE-FLAVORED BEEF
Makes 4 servings

PREPARATION OF INGREDIENTS

oil for deep-frying

BEEF MIXTURE (mix and marinate in a bowl)

1 pound flank steak: cut against grain into pieces ⅛-inch thick and 2 inches long
1 tablespoon cornstarch
2 teaspoons brown sugar
2 teaspoons black soy sauce
1½ teaspoons Sichuan sweet bean sauce or ground bean sauce
2 teaspoons dry Sherry

peel from 2 oranges: peel by hand and break into about 8 pieces
1 teaspoon minced fresh ginger
2 teaspoons minced garlic
3 scallions: cut into 1½-inch lengths, including some green part
2 teaspoons dry Sherry

SAUCE MIXTURE (Mix in a bowl)

2 teaspoons brown sugar
½ teaspoon cornstarch
1 teaspoon black soy sauce
2 teaspoons Chinese red vinegar
1 teaspoon water

¼ teaspoon orange extract

DIRECTIONS FOR COOKING

1. Heat oil in wok over high heat until almost smoking. Add beef mixture; stir to separate pieces. Blanch briskly until beef loses its red color. Remove with a drainer and put in a bowl.
2. Remove all but 3 tablespoons of oil from wok. Heat oil, then add orange peel and cook until golden brown. Add ginger, garlic, and scallions, and stir-fry them quickly. Be sure not to burn the garlic. Return beef to wok. Splash in Sherry.

*Beef and Lamb* • 141

Mix well. Stir in sauce mixture. Stir-fry until sauce is thickened. Add orange extract. Mix well. Put on plate and serve hot.

# BEIJING BEEF WITH SCALLIONS IN GARLIC SAUCE
Makes 4 servings

## PREPARATION OF INGREDIENTS

oil for deep frying

BEEF MIXTURE (Mix and marinate steak in a bowl for about 30 minutes)

1 pound flank steak: cut against grain into slices ⅛-inch thick and 1½ inches long
½ teaspoon sugar
1 tablespoon cornstarch
2 teaspoons ground bean sauce
2 teaspoons black soy sauce

8 ounces scallions: cut into 1½-inch lengths, including some green part
1 tablespoon minced garlic

SAUCE MIXTURE (Mix in a bowl)

½ teaspoon sugar
2 teaspoons ground bean sauce
1 tablespoon black soy sauce
3 tablespoons dry Sherry
2 teaspoons Chinese red vinegar

1 teaspoon sesame oil

## DIRECTIONS FOR COOKING

1. Heat oil in wok to deep-fry temperature. Add beef mixture. Quickly stir to separate pieces. Remove, with a drainer as soon as, beef loses its redness; be sure not to overcook. Press beef to drain. Set aside.

2. Remove all but 3 tablespoons of oil from wok. Heat oil over medium heat, then add scallions and stir-fry for about 30 seconds. Remove with a drainer to a bowl.

3. Keep wok hot over medium-high heat. Add garlic and cook briskly until golden. Stir and swirl in sauce mixture. Cook and stir until sauce begins to bubble. Return beef and scallions to wok. Swirl in sesame oil. Mix well. Put on serving platter. Serve hot.

# SPICED BEEF SHREDS, HUNAN STYLE
Makes 4 servings

## PREPARATION OF INGREDIENTS

oil for deep-frying

BEEF MIXTURE (Mix and marinate in a bowl)

1 pound flank steak: slice paper-thin against grain, shred slices into
     matchstick strips
1 egg white
¼ teaspoon salt
¼ teaspoon sugar
1 tablespoon cornstarch

1 teaspoon minced fresh ginger
2 teaspoons minced garlic
3 scallions: cut into pea-sized pieces, including some green part

SAUCE MIXTURE (Mix in a bowl)

1½ teaspoons sugar
¼ teaspoon cayenne pepper
1 tablespoon ground bean sauce
1 tablespoon rice wine or dry Sherry
1 tablespoon black soy sauce
2 teaspoons Chinese red vinegar or cider vinegar

6 water chestnuts: chop coarsely
2 tablespoons cloud ears: soak in hot water until soft, discard tough parts,
    tear each in half
½ cup water or canned, clear chicken broth
2 teaspoons cornstarch mixed with 1 tablespoon water
1 teaspoon sesame oil

DIRECTIONS FOR COOKING

1. Heat oil in wok to deep-fry temperature. Add beef mixture and stir to separate pieces. Blanch briskly until beef just loses its redness. Remove beef with a drainer to a bowl.

2. Remove all but 2 tablespoons oil from wok. Heat oil, then add ginger, garlic, scallions and stir-fry for several seconds. Stir in sauce mixture and cook until it bubbles gently. Add water chestnuts and cloud ears. Mix well. Pour in broth. When it begins to boil, stir in cornstarch water. Return beef to wok. Stir until sauce thickens. Add sesame oil. Mix and put on serving platter. Serve hot.

# SICHUAN SPICED BEEF SHREDS
# ON FRIED BEAN THREAD NOODLES

Makes about 4 servings

PREPARATION OF INGREDIENTS

oil for stir-frying
1 ounce bean thread noodles

BEEF MIXTURE (Mix in a bowl)

12 ounces flank steak: slice paper-thin against grain, shred slices into
    match stick strips
¼ teaspoon salt
2 teaspoons cornstarch
about ⅓ egg white
1 teaspoon dry Sherry

1 teaspoon finely minced fresh ginger
1 teaspoon minced garlic

2 scallions: cut into 1½-inch strips, including some green part
1½ cups bamboo shoots: cut into match stick strips
½ green or red bell pepper: cut into ¼-inch strips
2 dried chili peppers: tear into small pieces, do not discard seeds

SAUCE MIXTURE (Mix in a bowl)

½ teaspoon cayenne pepper
½ teaspoon sugar
2 teaspoons dry Sherry
1 tablespoon Chinese red vinegar or cider vinegar
1 tablespoon black soy sauce

1 teaspoon sesame seed oil
teaspoon flower peppercorn powder (optional; see page 312)

## DIRECTIONS FOR COOKING

1. Heat oil in wok to deep-fry temperature. Meanwhile, loosen noodles by pulling them apart. Test oil by dropping in a piece of noodle; if it pops up and turns white, the oil is right. Deep-fry noodles on both sides. (This takes less than 10 seconds.) Drain on paper towels; put a serving platter.
2. Keep oil hot. Add beef mixture and stir to separate pieces. Blanch briskly until beef just loses its redness. Remove with a drainer to a bowl.
3. Remove all but 2 tablespoons oil from wok. Heat oil, then add ginger, garlic, scallions, bamboo shoots, bell pepper, and chili peppers. Stir-fry for about 15 seconds. Stir in sauce mixture; cook and stir for several seconds. Return beef to wok. Mix well. Add sesame seed oil and flower peppercorn powder. Transfer entire contents of wok onto fried noodles. Serve hot.

# SPICY BEEF TRIPE
Makes about 4 cups

## PREPARATION OF INGREDIENTS

10 cups water
8 bay leaves
2 pounds honeycomb tripe: rinse thoroughly in running cold water
2 tablespoons oil
2 teaspoons fresh minced ginger

## SAUCE MIXTURE (mix in a bowl)

4 star anise
1 tablespoon sugar
3 tablespoons black soy sauce
2 tablespoons Sichuan chili bean sauce
1 teaspoon ground bean sauce
½ cup rice wine or dry Sherry
¼ cup canned beef or chicken broth

a small dish of Chinese chili sauce or Tabasco sauce (optional)

## DIRECTIONS FOR COOKING

1. Put water and bay leaves in a large pot, bring to a boil, and add tripe. When water again comes to a rapid boil, put lid on and turn off heat. Allow tripe to stay covered in hot water for 2 hours. (Do not peek or disturb the tripe during this time; the heat in the water will cook it to the right doneness.) Discard water and bay leaves. Cut tripe into pieces 1½ inches long and ½ inch wide. Put in colander and shake it to drain off excess water. Pat dry; keep in refrigerator until use.

2. Heat oil in a Chinese clay pot or a 3-quart pot over low heat for several seconds. When oil is hot, drop in ginger; stir and cook until it is golden. Pour in sauce mixture, stir, and cook for a few minutes. Add tripe and mix with the sauce. Cover and simmer for about 45 minutes. Remove from heat. Let tripe soak in sauce for a few hours or overnight. Just before serving, heat tripe in sauce over low heat until it is hot. Serve hot with or without chili sauce or Tabasco.

# BEEF WITH PEPPERS

Makes 4 to 6 servings

## PREPARATION OF INGREDIENTS

oil for deep frying

BEEF MIXTURE (Mix and marinate steak in a bowl)

1 pound flank steak: cut against grain into slices—⅛ inch thick, 2 inches long
1 tablespoon cornstarch
2 teaspoons brown sugar
1 pinch ground pepper
2 teaspoons sesame oil
1 tablespoon black soy sauce

½ pound green or red bell peppers: discard seeds and ribs, cut lengthwise into
   ½-inch strips (to add more color, use both green and red peppers)
1 teaspoon minced fresh ginger
1 teaspoon minced garlic
2 scallions: cut into 1½-inch lengths, including some green part

SAUCE MIXTURE (Mix in a bowl)

1 teaspoon cornstarch
2 teaspoons brown sugar
2 tablespoons black soy sauce
2 tablespoons dry Sherry
1 tablespoon water

DIRECTIONS FOR COOKING

1. Heat oil in wok over high heat until it is hot but not smoking. Add beef mixture. Stir quickly to separate pieces, and blanch briskly until meat loses its redness. Remove beef from wok with a drainer or a slotted spoon and put in a bowl.
2. Remove all but 3 tablespoons oil from wok. Heat oil, then add peppers and stir-fry for about a minute. Remove peppers with a drainer or a slotted spoon to a bowl.
3. Keep wok hot over high heat. Add ginger, garlic, and scallions and lightly brown them. Return beef and peppers to wok and stir-fry for about 20 seconds to reheat. Stir in sauce mixture and cook until sauce is thickened. Put on a serving platter. Serve hot.

# BEEF WITH BABY CORN AND CHINESE MUSHROOMS IN BLACK BEAN SAUCE
Makes 4 to 6 servings

PREPARATION OF INGREDIENTS

oil for dep-frying

BEEF MIXTURE (Mix in a bowl. Marinate steak no longer than 30 minutes)

1 pound flank steak: cut against grain into pieces ⅛ inch thick and 2 inches long
1 teaspoon sugar
1 tablespoon cornstarch
1 tablespoon thin soy sauce
1 tablespoon black soy sauce

1 teaspoon dry Sherry

20-ounce can baby corn: rinse in cold water, drain

SEASONINGS (Mix in a small bowl)

1 teaspoon finely minced fresh ginger
2 teaspoons minced garlic
½ teaspoon salt
½ teaspoon sugar
2 tablespoons salted black beans: rinse in hot water, drain and mash into paste
1 scallion: cut into pea-sized pieces, including some green part

6 Chinese dried mushrooms: soak in hot water until spongy, discard stems,
    leave caps whole
1 cup canned chicken broth mixed with 1 tablespoon cornstarch

DIRECTIONS FOR COOKING

1. Heat oil in wok to deep-fry temperature. Add beef mixture, and stir to separate
pieces. Blanch briskly until beef loses its redness. Remove with a drainer to a
bowl.
2. Keep oil hot over medium heat. Add baby corn, and blanch for a few seconds.
Remove with a drainer to a bowl.
3. Remove all but 2 tablespoons oil from wok. Heat oil over high heat, then add
the seasonings and mushrooms. Stir-fry until ginger and garlic turn golden. Stir
in broth and cornstarch mixture. Cook and stir until sauce is thickened. Return
beef and baby corn to wok. Stir-fry for about 10 seconds. Put on serving platter.
Serve hot.

# BEEF IN OYSTER SAUCE

Makes 4 to 8 servings

## PREPARATION OF INGREDIENTS

oil for deep-frying

BEEF MIXTURE (Mix and marinate steak in a bowl)

1 pound flank steak: cut against grain into pieces ⅛-inch thick and 2 inches long
¼ teaspoon sugar
1 tablespoon black soy sauce
1 tablespoon cornstarch

2 teaspoons finely minced fresh ginger
2 teaspoons minced garlic
4 scallions: cut into 1½-inch lengths, including some green part

SAUCE MIXTURE (Mix in a bowl)

½ teaspoon sugar
4 tablespoons oyster-flavored sauce
2 tablespoons rice wine or dry Sherry

¼ pound snow peas: break off ends, blanch in water

## DIRECTIONS FOR COOKING

1. Heat oil in wok to deep-fry temperature. Add beef mixture, and stir to separate pieces. Blanch briskly until meat just loses its redness. Remove with drainer or slotted spoon to bowl.
2. Remove all but 2 tablespoons oil from wok. Heat oil over high heat, then add ginger, garlic, and scallions and brown them slightly. Stir in sauce mixture; cook and stir until it begins to bubble. Return blanched snow peas and beef. Stir-fry for several seconds. Put on a serving plate. Serve hot.

# BEEF AND SCALLOPS IN OYSTER SAUCE

Makes 6 servings

PREPARATION OF INGREDIENTS

oil for deep-frying

BEEF MIXTURE (Mix in a bowl. Keep refrigerated before use)

1 pound flank steak: cut against grain into thin, 2-inch long pieces
1 tablespoon cornstarch
¼ teaspoon sugar
¼ teaspoon ground black pepper
1 tablespoon black soy sauce
2 teaspoons sesame oil

SCALLOP MIXTURE ( Mix in a bowl. Keep refrigerated before use)

½ pound sea scallops mixed with 2 teaspoons cornstarch

4 scallions: cut into 1½-inch lengths, including some green part
2 teaspoons minced, fresh ginger
2 teaspoons minced garlic
6 baby corn: rinse, cut each in half lengthwise or 12 fresh snow peas
6 water chestnuts: rinse, cut each in half
⅓ cup red bell peppers in thin strips

SAUCE MIXTURE (Mix in a bowl)

½ teaspoon sugar
4 tablespoons oyster-flavored sauce
3 tablespoons rice wine or dry Sherry
2 tablespoons water
1 tablespoon black soy sauce

DIRECTIONS FOR COOKING

1. Heat oil in wok until it is very hot, but not smoking. Add beef mixture and gently separate pieces. Cook beef for abut 1 minute. Remove to a plate.
2. Add scallops to hot oil and cook 15 seconds. Remove with drainer to a plate.

3 Remove all but 2 tablespoons oil from wok (save oil for cooking other seafood dishes). Heat oil until it is hot. Add scallions and ginger a few seconds before garlic. When garlic turns golden, add water chestnuts, baby corn or snow peas and bell peppers . Stir-fry for about 10 seconds or until they are heated through. Add sauce mixture and stir until it bubbles. Return beef and scallops (with juices) to wok. Stir-fry for about 15 seconds to reheat. Transfer to a platter. Serve hot.

# STEW BEEF WITH WHITE TURNIP, CANTONESE STYLE
Makes 8 to 12 servings

T his dish is one of the favorites among the Chinese. It is usually cooked at home or in Chinese restaurants that serve soul food—Chinese-style. This recipe will solve my brother Albert's entertainment problem, at least for a while. He wants to serve Chinese food without cooking it, or cooking it as little as possible. He likes something that tastes excellent, requires practically no work, can be cooked in advance and all in one pot.

I am sure that his guests will have this dish, in one big pot, served twenty times—Albert style.

## PREPARATION OF INGREDIENTS

3 tablespoons oil

2 chunks (each as big as a pecan) fresh ginger root: crack with flat side of cleaver
3 pounds stew beef or beef belly (the Chinese prefer the latter): leave stew beef in chunks; ask butcher to cut belly into 1-inch chunks

## SAUCE MIXTURE (Mix in a bowl)

½ teaspoon sugar
2 tablespoons rice wine or dry Sherry
¼ cup black soy sauce
1 cup water

2 to 3 cups water
1½ pounds Chinese white giant turnip: peel, cut into chunks slightly bigger than beef chunks

1. Heat a wok or Dutch oven over medium heat. When it is hot, add oil and spread it around to cover bottom of wok or pot. Add ginger and beef. Brown beef slightly and evenly. Pour in sauce mixture. Cover and cook over medium-low heat, adding water from time to time, for 1 hour.
2. Add turnips. Cover and continue to cook, adding water if needed, until beef and turnips are tender. It takes about another hour. There should be about 1 cup of sauce left in the pot at the end of cooking. Discard ginger. Serve hot.
NOTE: This dish can be cooked one or two days in advance. Reheat on stove over medium heat.

# THE EMPRESS DOWAGER'S LAMB
Makes 2 to 4 servings

It is said that this dish was created by one of the empress dowager, Ci Xi's chefs during the Qing Dynasty. The new dish was presented to the old dowager, and she was pleased by its sweetness and delicacy. She reordered it soon after, but did not know what to call it. "It tastes like honey," she said. Thus for the last 200 years this dish has been called Ta Si Mi, which means "It tastes like honey."

PREPARATION OF INGREDIENTS

5 tablespoons sesame oil

LAMB MIXTURE (Mix in a bowl and marinate lamb 30 minutes)

12 ounces leg of lamb: slice into thin pieces
2 tablespoons Sichuan sweet bean sauce or ground bean paste
1 teaspoon cornstarch

4 teaspoons sugar

SAUCE MIXTURE (Mix in a bowl)

½ teaspoon cornstarch
4 teaspoons Chinese red vinegar
1 tablespoon black soy sauce
1 tablespoon rice wine or dry Sherry
1 teaspoon minced fresh ginger

DIRECTIONS FOR COOKING

1. Heat wok over high heat. Swirl in 4 tablespoons of the sesame oil. When oil is hot (not smoking), add lamb mixture and stir-fry for about 2 minutes. Remove lamb with drainer or slotted spoon and put in a bowl.
2. Clean wok and dry it thoroughly. Reheat wok over high heat. Swirl in remaining sesame seed oil. Add sugar and stir-fry briskly. Pour in sauce mixture, and stir-fry for about 10 seconds. Return lamb to wok and stir-fry for another several seconds. Put on plate and serve hot.

# SLICED LEG OF LAMB, HUNAN STYLE
Makes 4 to 6 servings

PREPARATION OF INGREDIENTS

oil for deep-frying

LAMB MIXTURE (Mix in a bowl)

12 ounces leg of lamb: slice paper-thin
¼ teaspoon sugar
2 teaspoons cornstarch
2 teaspoons black soy sauce
1 teaspoon sesame oil

2 dried chili peppers: tear in half, do not discard seeds
1 teaspoon finely minced fresh ginger
1 teaspoon minced garlic
4 ounces scallions (about 1 bunch): cut into 1½-inch lengths,
    including some green part

SAUCE MIXTURE (Mix in a bowl)

½ teaspoon sugar
2 tablespoons ground bean sauce
2 tablespoons rice wine or dry Sherry
¼ to ½ teaspoon Chili Oil (see page 311) or cayenne pepper
1 tablespoon black soy sauce

DIRECTIONS FOR COOKING

1. Heat oil in wok. When oil is hot, add lamb mixture. Stir briskly until it is just done. Drain and put in a bowl.
2. Remove all but 3 tablespoons oil from wok. Heat oil, and drop in chili peppers, ginger, garlic, and scallions. Stir-fry until scallions just become soft. Remove from wok and put aside.
3. Keep wok hot over high heat. Swirl in sauce mixture. Stir and cook until sauce bubbles gently. Return lamb and scallions to wok. Mix well and stir to reheat. Serve hot.


# FRIED SWEETBREADS IN SWEET WINE SAUCE
Makes 4 to 6 servings

PREPARATION OF INGREDIENTS

4 cups water
2 tablespoons dry sherry
2 slices fresh ginger, each as big and thick as a quarter
1 pound sweetbreads: rinse in cold water
2 tablespoons cornstarch
oil for deep-frying
1 tablespoon minced garlic
2 scallions: cut into pea-sized pieces, including some green part

SAUCE MIXTURE (Mix in a bowl)

½ teaspoon sugar
3 tablespoons Sweet Wine Sauce (page 336) or orange liqueur
1 tablespoon tomato ketchup

1 teaspoon Chinese red vinegar
5 teaspoons black soy sauce
3 tablespoons rice wine or dry Sherry
½ teaspoon sugar

1 teaspoon cornstarch mixed with 4 teaspoons water

DIRECTIONS FOR COOKING

1. Pour water into a 3-quart pot, add Sherry and ginger, and bring to a boil. Immerse sweetbreads in water. Cover and cook over low heat for 5 minutes. Drain sweetbreads. Discard ginger and water.
2. Remove membrane and vein from sweetbreads as much as possible. Cut sweetbreads into ½-inch pieces.
3. Dredge sweetbreads in cornstarch.
4. Heat oil to deep-fry temperature. Deep-fry half the sweetbreads at a time until they just turn light gold. Remove with a drainer to a bowl.
5. Remove all but 2 tablespoons oil from wok. Heat oil, and drop in garlic and scallions. When garlic turns golden, swirl in sauce mixture. Stir and cook sauce until it begins to bubble. Stir in cornstarch water. When sauce thickens, return sweetbreads to wok. Stir-fry for about 15 seconds. Put on a serving platter. Serve hot.

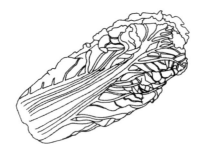

# Seafood

# SEAFOOD

Fish are plentiful in many parts of China. From the rivers, ponds, and lakes, we had freshwater shrimp, yellow perch, meaty crabs, and the king of Chinese fish, the plump and juicy carp. From the ocean we took the flounder, the red snapper, and the unbelievably expensive mouse garoupa, as well as many others. Fish packed in ice or frozen were unheard of in China. They were sold while they were swimming in buckets filled with water. You just pointed to the one you desired, and the fish seller would tie a long piece of straw around the fish's belly. Dangling from your finger, the shiny, lively creature would wriggle all the way home with you.

Fish were also sold in parts, especially the big ones. Fish heads, bellies, and tails could be bought separately. The Chinese have a great passion for fish heads, and red-cooked fish heads was a well-loved dish.

For many Chinese, one of the great pleasures of life was to have a banquet in a seafood restaurant. Most of these restaurants were located near a fish market by the water. Some of them were floating restaurants. Usually they did not carry a great amount of seafood. It was expected that the customers would pick up their own in the nearby fish stalls: there shrimp of all sizes swam in the water tanks; crabs rolled their eyes in baskets; lobsters timidly moved their feelers and stretched their claws; mounds of oysters in their shells were piled on the ground. Fish of all kinds swam with luxurious grace while the buyers and the sellers bargained their fate. The restaurants would cook whatever the customers brought and prepare it the way they wanted.

At such a banquet many kinds of fish and shellfish were included. Usually oysters were deep-fried in batter. Medium-sized fresh-water shrimp were steamed or blanched in the shells, dipped in sauce, then eaten with one's fingers. Lobsters were stir-fried with black bean sauce. Crabs were deep-fried, then stir-fried in ginger, garlic, and soy sauce. Some fish were steamed whole, while others were filleted and stir-fried. The fish head and backbones, augmented by fresh bean curd, made a big bowl of delicious soup. But always the very expensive fish were steamed whole with few seasonings added, so that the true flavor of the fish would be retained.

The banquet could go on and on, for as long as the diners' pockets could provide. Usually it concluded with a dish of noodles or fried rice. Then, full and happy, everybody stretched and sighed, "That was good."

Growing up near the sea, we were taught early how to choose a fresh fish, and were given these few practical rules, which you can easily follow: When a fish is fresh, the eyes are clear, the scales are shiny, the body is firm, and the gills are bright red. A bad fish has sunken dull eyes; its scales are loose and have no shine; the body is limp and smells bad too.

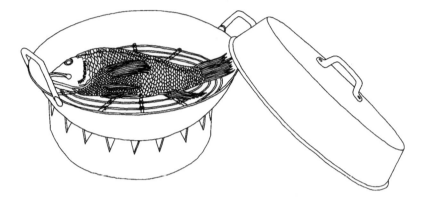

# TO CLEAN AND WASH SHRIMP

Shrimp, after they are cooked, should be crisp, firm, and resilient—not dull, hard, or tough. Rinsing fresh shrimp in the following method will help to achieve this result.

Shell and devein the shrimp. Put them in a bowl and wash them by gently massaging under cold running water for about half a minute. Then put shrimp in a colander and rinse them under fast-running cold water for about 3 minutes. (The cold water freshens and expands the shrimp, and the force of the running water stiffens them so that when they are cooked they become crisp and almost crunchy.)

Drain and dry shrimp thoroughly with paper towels. Cut or leave them whole according to the recipe. Keep refrigerated before use.

# TO BUTTERFLY SHRIMP OR PRAWNS

Peel shell off shrimp or prawn, except for the last section and the tail. Remove the back vein, then cut the shrimp or prawn from the underside (the stomach) almost through to the back (do not cut through!). Rinse the shrimp or prawn with cold water, and pat dry with paper towels. Arrange them split side up on a plate. Keep refrigerated before use.

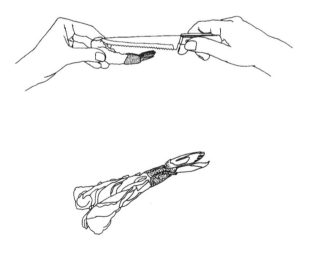

# STEAMED FISH WITH MUSHROOMS IN GINGER AND GARLIC SAUCE

Makes 4 to 6 servings

## PREPARATION OF INGREDIENTS

1 fresh fish: 1½ pounds (pike, red snapper, grouper, sea bass, or striped bass):
   ask your fishman to scale, clean, and leave the fish whole; slash several cuts,
   about ½-inch deep, on both sides of fish
1 tablespoon dry Sherry: use it to rub fish inside and out just before steaming
4 tablespoons oil
2 teaspoons minced garlic
4 slices fresh ginger, each as big and thick as a quarter: shred into
   very thin strips
6 Chinese dried mushrooms: soak in hot water until spongy, discard stems,
   cut into thin strips

## SAUCE MIXTURE (Mix in a bowl)

½ teaspoon sugar
2 tablespoons dry Sherry
2 tablespoons black soy sauce
2 tablespoons thin soy sauce

1 tablespoon sesame oil
2 scallions: cut into 1½-inch lengths, including some green part

## DIRECTIONS FOR COOKING

1. Heat a few cups of water in wok over high heat. When water comes to a rapid boil, put in a steamer or rack. Be sure that the rack or steamer is at least an inch above the boiling water
2. Place fish in steamer or rack. Cover and steam over high heat for about 12 minutes. Insert a fork into the thickest part of the fish. If the fork goes in easily, then the fish is done. Turn off heat. Cover and keep fish hot.
3. Two minutes before the fish is done, heat a small saucepan over medium heat. Add 4 tablespoons oil. When oil is hot, slightly brown garlic, ginger, and mushrooms.
4. Stir in sauce mixture. Cook over low heat until sauce begins to foam. Add sesame seed oil. Turn heat to very low to keep sauce hot.

5. Quickly remove fish from wok to a serving platter and decorate with scallions. Pour hot sauce evenly over fish. Serve hot at once.

NOTE: It is very important to eat the fish immediately.

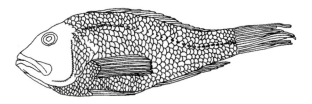

# STEAMED FLOUNDER WITH LILY BUDS
Makes 4 to 6 servings

## PREPARATION OF INGREDIENTS

1 fresh flounder, 1½ pounds: scale, clean, and leave whole
15 dried lily buds: soak in hot water until soft, pinch off hard ends,
    tear buds in half lengthwise
1 tablespoon cloud ears: soak in hot water until soft, pinch off tough parts
6 Chinese dried mushrooms: soak in hot water until spongy, discard stems
3 pieces fresh ginger, each as big and thick as a quarter: shred into thin strips
¼ cup shredded fresh fat pork or bacon, in strips 1½ inches long
4 tablespoons oil
2 scallions: cut into pea-sized pieces, including some green part

## SAUCE MIXTURE (Mix in a bowl)

¼ teaspoon sugar
2 tablespoons thin soy sauce
1½ tablespoons black soy sauce
1 tablespoon dry Sherry

1 tablespoon sesame oil

## DIRECTIONS FOR COOKING

1. Place fish on a heatproof plate. Arrange lily buds, cloud ears, mushrooms, ginger, and fat pork or bacon on fish.
2. Cover and steam fish over boiling water for about 12 minutes. (See Steamed Fish with Mushrooms in Ginger and Garlic Sauce, page 162.)
3. Meanwhile, heat a small saucepan. Add 4 tablespoons oil. When oil is hot, add scallions, sauce mixture, and sesame oil. Turn heat to low and cook until the sauce just comes to a boil. Pour hot sauce over fish. Serve hot at once.

# PAN-FRIED RED SNAPPER OR FLOUNDER WITH GINGER, GARLIC, AND TANGERINE SAUCE
Makes 4 servings

## PREPARATION OF INGREDIENTS

1 fresh red snapper or flounder, 1½ pounds: scale, clean, leave whole

MARINADE (Rub Sherry, ginger, and salt inside and outside fish. Refrigerate for 30 minutes)

¼ teaspoon salt
2 teaspoons dry Sherry
1 tablespoon finely minced fresh ginger

2 tablespoons flour
4 tablespoons oil
2 scallions: chop into pea-sized pieces, including some green part
2 teaspoons finely minced, fresh ginger
1 tablespoon minced garlic
1 piece dried tangerine peel (optional): soak in hot water 15 minutes or
    until soft, mince (to make about 1 teaspoon)

SAUCE MIXTURE (Mix in a bowl)

½ teaspoon sugar
2 tablespoons thin soy sauce
1 tablespoon black soy sauce

3 tablespoons dry Sherry
2 tablespoons water

DIRECTIONS FOR COOKING

1. Sprinkle and coat seasoned fish with flour.
2. Heat wok over high heat. Swirl in 4 tablespoons oil. When oil is hot, put fish in wok. Pan-fry over medium-low heat until both sides are golden brown (about 12 minutes each side). Remove fish and put into a warm oven to keep hot.
3. Reheat oil left in wok. Slightly brown scallions, ginger, garlic, and tangerine peel. Stir in sauce mixture and heat to boil. Return fish to wok. Spoon sauce over fish. Put on an oval platter. Serve hot at once.

# BROILED FISH OR SHAD ROES IN GINGER AND GARLIC SAUCE
Make 4 servings

In China, the Chinese always cook fish on the stove, because ovens are rare. The modern oven in the West is a blessing for cooking fish. It not only reduces the amount of oil in cooking, but also eliminates odor and splattering.

To celebrate the arrival of spring, use shad roes instead of fish. A heavenly dish.

PREPARATION OF INGREDIENTS

1 fresh flounder or red snapper, about 2 pounds: scale, clean and leave whole and pat dry or 2 pairs of shad roes: clean and pat dry

¼ cup dry Sherry
ground pepper
¼ cup all-purpose flour
4 tablespoons oil
10 scallions: cut into 1½-inch lengths, including some green part
3 tablespoons minced fresh ginger
3 tablespoons minced garlic

SAUCE MIXTURE (Mix in a bowl)

1 teaspoon sugar
⅓ cup thin soy sauce
⅓ cup dry Sherry
⅔ cup water

1 teaspoon sesame oil
½ red bell pepper: cut into thin pieces

DIRECTIONS FOR COOKING

1. Rub fish or shad roes inside and out with Sherry, then sprinkle with ground pepper and dust with flour.
2. Spray a large cast iron skillet or a broiler pan with non-stick oil spray. Add 2 tablespoons oil and spread evenly. Place flounder or shad roes in skillet or pan. Drip the remaining 2 tablespoons oil on top of the fish or shad roes.
3. Broil flounder for 15 minutes or shad roes for 7 minutes. Turn flounder or shad roes over. Add ginger, scallions, ginger, garlic, and sauce mixture. Broil flounder for another 15 minutes, shad roes for another 5 minutes.
4. Place flounder or shad roes on a serving platter. Add sesame oil and red bell pepper to the sauce in the skillet, stir to cook for about 10 seconds, and pour over flounder or shad roes. Serve hot at once.

# WHOLE FISH IN SWEET AND SOUR SAUCE
Makes about 6 servings

## PREPARATION OF INGREDIENTS

1 fresh sea bass, 1½ to 2 pounds: scale, clean, and leave fish whole, rinse in cold
  water, pat dry, cut deeply from stomach to back, but not splitting fish in half,
  score both sides about ½ inch deep into diamond design

MARINADE (Mix in a bowl)

1 teaspoon finely minced fresh ginger
1 scallion: mince, including some green part
½ teaspoon salt
⅛ teaspoon ground pepper
1 teaspoon dry Sherry

2 to 3 tablespoons cornstarch to dust fish

BATTER (Combine egg, water, oil, and soy sauce. add cornstarch, flour, and
baking powder. Mix with spoon until smooth)

1 beaten egg
3 tablespoons cornstarch
6 tablespoons all-purpose flour
2 teaspoons baking powder
3 tablespoons cold water
2 tablespoons oil
1 teaspoon thin soy sauce

oil for deep-frying

2 tablespoons oil
¼ cup frozen green peas, defrosted
½ red or green bell pepper: cut into thin slices
4 water chestnuts: cut into quarter-sized pieces
2 scallions: cut into pea-sized pieces, including some green parts

## SWEET AND SOUR SAUCE (Mix in a bowl)

7 tablespoons brown sugar
2 cloves garlic: mince
½ teaspoon salt
2 ounces shan zha bing or 3 tablespoons tomato ketchup
1 tablespoon black soy sauce
1 tablespoon thin soy sauce
⅓ cup cider vinegar
1 cup clear, canned chicken broth

2 tablespoons cornstarch mixed with 2 tablespoons water

## DIRECTIONS FOR COOKING

1. Rub fish inside and out with marinade, then dust with cornstarch. Dip fish in batter and thoroughly coat inside and outside.
2. Heat 5 to 6 cups oil in wok over medium heat to deep-fry temperature. Immerse fish in oil and deep-fry each side about 8 minutes or until crisp and golden brown.
3. Meanwhile, in a medium-sized pot, heat 2 tablespoons oil. Add peas, pepper, water chestnuts, and scallions. Pour in sweet and sour sauce. Cook over medium heat until it almost comes to a boil. Stir in cornstarch water. Stir and cook until sauce is thickened. Cover and keep warm over very low heat.
4. When fish is done, drain and put on a serving platter with stomach side down. Pour sauce over fish. Serve hot at once.

NOTE: The fish should be eaten immediately while it is hot and crisp. Be sure to gather your family or guests around the table to wait for the fish. Never let the fish wait for you!

# HUNAN CHANGSHA CRISP
# AND SPICY WHOLE SEA BASS

Makes about 4 servings

Hunan Province is the birthplace of Mao Tse-dong, and Changsha is the capital of Hunan, where he received his education, and from which he began the revolution. Hunan is like her neighbor, Sichuan, where the summer is hot and humid; her people like peppery food.

PREPARATION OF INGREDIENTS

1 whole sea bass, 1½ to 2 pounds: scale, clean, and leave whole, score both sides
   about ½ inch deep into diamond design, split fish along belly almost to
   bone, pat dry with towels

MARINADE (Mix in a small bowl)

1 teaspoon finely minced fresh ginger
1 teaspoon finely minced scallion
½ teaspoon salt
¼ teaspoon ground pepper
1 tablespoon dry Sherry

about 2 tablespoons cornstarch to dust fish
2 tablespoons oil
2 ounces ground pork
2 scallions: cut into pea-sized pieces, including some green part
¼ cup coarsely chopped red or green bell pepper

SAUCE MIXTURE (Mix in a bowl)

½ to 1 teaspoon cayenne pepper
2 teaspoons minced fresh ginger
2 teaspoons minced garlic
¼ teaspoon salt
5 tablespoons sugar
2 tablespoons tomato ketchup
2 tablespoons black soy sauce
2 tablespoons dry Sherry

2 tablespoons white vinegar
1 cup water

1 tablespoon cornstarch mixed with I tablespoon water
oil for deep-frying

BATTER (Beat egg, water, oil, and soy sauce together. Add flour, cornstarch, and
baking powder. Mix with a spoon until smooth)

1 egg
6 tablespoons all-purpose flour
3 tablespoons cornstarch
2 teaspoons baking powder
3 tablespoons cold water
2 tablespoons oil
1 teaspoon thin soy sauce

## DIRECTIONS FOR COOKING

1. Rub fish inside and outside with marinade.
2. Dust fish with cornstarch inside and out. Put it on a tray, stomach down.
3. Heat 2 tablespoons oil in a medium-sized saucepan. Add ground pork, and stir
to separate pieces. Cook until meat is no longer pink. Drop in scallions and bell
pepper. Pour in sauce mixture and cook over low heat until it bubbles gently. Stir
in the cornstarch water. Cook, stirring constantly, until sauce is thickened. Turn
off heat. Cover to keep hot.
4. Heat 5 to 6 cups oil in wok to deep-fry temperature. Meanwhile, pour batter
over and inside fish. Carefully put fish, stomach side down, in the very hot oil.
Deep-fry over medium heat for 8 minutes; then turn fish over and deep-fry for
another 10 minutes. Remove fish gently with the help of 2 spatulas and place it
on a big serving platter with its stomach down.
5. Pour sauce over fish. Serve hot at once.

NOTE: The fish should be eaten immediately while it is hot and crisp. Be sure to
gather your family or guests around the table to wait for the fish.

# FISH FILLETS IN SPICY VINEGAR SAUCE, BEIJING-STYLE
Makes 4 servings

## PREPARATION OF INGREDIENTS

1 pound fillets (flounder, red snapper, sole, or bass): cut into pieces 1 by 2 inches

MARINADE (Mix and marinate fish in a bowl. Refrigerate before use)

1 teaspoon finely minced fresh ginger
½ teaspoon salt
⅛ teaspoon white pepper
¼ teaspoon sugar
2 teaspoons dry Sherry
1 beaten egg

about ½ cup cornstarch for dredging fish
oil for deep-frying
4 dried chili peppers (or 2 if you do not like it so hot): tear into small pieces,
    do not discard seeds
1 teaspoon minced fresh ginger
1 teaspoon minced garlic
2 scallions: cut into 1½-inch lengths, including some green part
3 Chinese dried mushrooms: soak in hot water until spongy, discard stems,
    shred caps
4 ounces ground pork

SAUCE MIXTURE (Mix in a bowl)

4 teaspoons sugar
1 tablespoon white vinegar
3 tablespoons black soy sauce
2 tablespoons rice wine or dry Sherry
1 cup canned clear chicken broth

2 tablespoons cornstarch mixed with 3 tablespoons water
2 teaspoons sesame oil

## DIRECTIONS FOR COOKING

1. Dredge marinated fish slices in cornstarch.
2. Heat oil in wok to deep-fry temperature. Fry fish slices until they are light gold. Drain on paper towels. Put in warm oven to keep hot.
3. Remove all but 3 tablespoons oil from wok. Heat oil, then slightly brown chili peppers, ginger, garlic, and scallions. Add mushrooms and pork. Stir-fry until pork loses its pink color. Stir in sauce mixture and cook until it almost comes to a boil. Stir in cornstarch water and cook until sauce is thickened. Return fish slices to wok. Swirl in sesame oil. Put on a serving platter. Serve hot.


# FISH SLICES IN GARLIC AND BLACK BEAN SAUCE
Makes 4 servings

## PREPARATION OF INGREDIENTS

1 pound fillets (sole, red snapper, bass, or flounder): cut into 1-by-2-inch pieces

MARINADE (Mix and marinate fish in a bowl)

1 teaspoon finely minced fresh ginger
½ teaspoon salt
⅛ teaspoon white pepper
¼ teaspoon sugar
2 teaspoons dry Sherry
1 beaten egg

about ½ cup cornstarch
oil for deep-frying

SEASONINGS (Put in a bowl)

1 tablespoon salted black beans: rinse in hot water, drain, mash into paste
1 teaspoon finely minced garlic
2 scallions: cut into pea-sized pieces, including some green part
1 piece dried tangerine peel (optional): soak in hot water to soften,
    chop into rice-sized pieces to make 1 teaspoon

1 teaspoon finely minced fresh ginger

SAUCE MIXTURE (Mix in a bowl)

½ teaspoon sugar
¼ teaspoon salt
6 tablespoons water
2 tablespoons thin soy sauce
2 tablespoons dry Sherry

1 teaspoon cornstarch mixed with 1 teaspoon water

DIRECTIONS FOR COOKING

1. Roll marinated fish in cornstarch. Coat fish slices twice until they are not sticky.
2. Heat oil in wok to deep-fry temperature. Fry half the fish slices at a time to golden brown. Drain on paper towels.
3. Remove all but 3 tablespoons oil from wok. Heat oil until it is hot, slightly brown the seasonings. Pour in sauce mixture and cook to boil. Stir in cornstarch water and cook until sauce is thickened. Put fish slices into wok. Mix gently with sauce. Put on a serving platter. Serve hot.

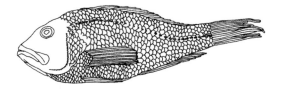

# BROILED TUNA WITH TOFU
# IN SOY-MUSTARD-DILL SAUCE

Makes 6-8 servings

## PREPARATION OF INGREDIENTS

1 pound tuna: cut into 1-inch cubes

### SAUCE MIXTURE (Mix in a bowl)

1 tablespoon Colman's mustard powder
1½ teaspoons sugar
¼ teaspoon cayenne pepper
2 tablespoons minced fresh dill
2 tablespoons minced garlic
2 teaspoons minced fresh ginger
⅓ cup scallions: cut into pea-sized pieces
3 tablespoons thin soy sauce
1 tablespoon black soy sauce
3 tablespoons Chinese red vinegar or cider vinegar
2 tablespoons sesame oil
¼ cup rice wine or dry Sherry

1 pound fresh, firm tofu: rinse in cold water, cut into ⅓-inch thick slices,
    drain, pat dry
½ cup canned clear chicken broth
½ cup red bell peppers: cut into thin strips
1 tablespoon cornstarch mixed with 3 tablespoons water

## DIRECTIONS FOR COOKING

1. combine tuna with half of the sauce mixture. Cover and marinate for at least
2 hours in refrigerator.
2. Drain tuna (save the marinade) and place on a broiler pan. Broil tuna turning
once until it is just cooked (about 4 minutes per side) . Set aside.
3. Add the remaining sauce mixture, red pepper, marinade, tofu and chicken
broth in wok. Cook over medium-low heat for 10 minutes. Stir in cornstarch-
water, stir and cook until sauce is clear and thickened. Return tuna to wok.
Cook to reheat. Serve hot.

# BROILED SALMON STEAKS WITH PORTOBELLO MUSHROOMS IN GINGER AND SCALLION SAUCE

Makes 6 servings

## PREPARATION OF INGREDIENTS

### MARINADE

¼ teaspoon sugar
½ teaspoon ground pepper
2 teaspoons minced fresh ginger
¼ cup rice wine or dry Sherry
¼ cup thin soy sauce

6 pieces of salmon steaks (about 3 pounds)
2 tablespoons oil
4 ounces portobello mushrooms: wash, pat dry, discard stems and cut caps into
    ¼-inch slices

### SEASONINGS

12 scallions: cut into 1-inch pieces
2 tablespoon minced garlic
2 tablespoons minced fresh ginger
½ cup chopped parsley

### SAUCE MIXTURE (Mix in a bowl)

¼ teaspoon ground pepper
½ teaspoon sugar
1 teaspoon Colman's mustard powder
1 teaspoon sesame oil
6 tablespoons thin soy sauce
⅓ cup rice wine or dry Sherry
½ cup water

## DIRECTIONS FOR COOKING

1. In a pan, marinate salmon for about 2 hours, turning occasionally. Keep refrigerated.

2. About an hour before cooking, drain marinade into a large bowl, add mushrooms and toss to mix well

3. Spray a baking pan with non-stick oil spray, add 2 tablespoons oil and roll pan to spread oil evenly. Arrange salmon on baking pan and broil for 10 minutes. Remove from heat.

4. Turn salmon over. place mushrooms with marinade between salmon pieces and top with ginger, garlic, scallions, parsley and sauce mixture.

5. Return salmon to broiler and broil for 10 minutes on the uncooked side or until your preferred doneness. Serve hot with rice or pasta.

# STARLIGHT SHRIMP
Makes 1 pound

There are places called "the poor people's nightclubs" throughout the Orient. One is in Kowloon around an old temple, the Queen of Heaven, not far from the harbor. There, a few classmates and I used to while away many evenings when we should have been studying in our college dorm.

It was not a disco or a cabaret, but caravans of food stalls and vendors jamming the back lanes and parking lots at night. In streams of brilliant lights oceans of fun seekers and crowd lingerers slowly flowed.

The sweet aroma of shellfish scented the air. Surging steam from the noodle stalls shot the dark still sky. Roasted ducks with golden skin and spiced innards excited appetites. This was "the poor people's nightclub" in which a poor man ate like a king—a place where gourmets enjoyed the best snake soup and plates of seafood without the dollars draining away.

It was also a place to listen to the amateur singers and musicians trying their art. If the sound pleased the crowd, someone would throw in a few coins; if not some would spit and mutter away.

The height of the evening was about ten, when hungry stomachs and restless spirits were eager to roam the night. We ate from stall to stall, at the small tables with tiny stools, or right off of bamboo skewers as we strolled the streets. With many others we strained our ears as fortune tellers told their humble clients' fate, or watched palmists examining worn and weathered hands. Sometimes we looked for bargains, bought a few things, or just followed the crowd.

If our purses were full, we treated ourselves at the shellfish stalls. Unaware of the stars above and the sweetness of our youth, we savored plates of shrimp, snails, and clams and leisurely watched the crowd pass by.

Many times since then I have returned to this nightclub of the poor. The richness of the night still remained. The same sweet aroma, voices, and salty air greeted the crowd. People still moved unhurriedly as before, except now and then tourists were herded like ducklings hastening by.

## PREPARATION OF INGREDIENTS

1 pound fresh medium-sized shrimp with shells: keep in ice water in
   refrigerator until use

## MARINADE

1 tablespoon sea salt
1 teaspoon sugar
1 teaspoon paprika
1 teaspoon five-fragrance powder
1 tablespoon fresh ginger juice (use garlic press) or minced ginger
1 tablespoon dry Sherry

6 tablespoons oil
¼ cup snipped parsley

## DIRECTIONS FOR COOKING

1. Holding shrimp with one hand, with the other hand take a sewing needle and go under the vein crosswise at third section (near the tail), lift the vein, and pull it out gently with the needle. Devein the others in the same manner. Rinse shrimp in very cold water, drain, and pat dry.
2. Combine deveined shrimp and marinade in a bowl, and keep it in refrigerator for an hour before use.
3. Heat wok over high heat. When it is hot, add oil and spread to heat until it begins to smoke. Quickly add shrimp, including its marinade. Stir-fry for about 3 minutes. Drop in the parsley and continue to stir-fry for another 2 minutes or until shrimp turns bright orange and is just cooked. Transfer to a serving platter. Serve hot. Eat with your fingers. Suck and taste the seasoning on the shell before peeling and eating the shrimp.

# DEEP-FRIED SHRIMP BALLS

Makes 4 servings

## PREPARATION OF INGREDIENTS

oil for deep-frying
1 small bowl of cold oil

### SHRIMP MIXTURE (Mix in a bowl)

1 pound fresh shrimp: shell, devein, rinse in running cold water, drain and dry,
    mince into paste
3 tablespoons minced pork fat or bacon fat
¼ teaspoon fresh ginger juice (use garlic press)
⅓ cup minced water chestnuts
1 pinch white pepper
½ teaspoon salt
1 teaspoon cornstarch
1 egg white, beat until slightly foamy
1 teaspoon sesame oil

Five-Fragrance Salt Dip (see page 312) or Plum Sauce Dip (see page 314)

## DIRECTIONS FOR COOKING

1. Preheat oven to low (only a warm oven is needed).
2. Heat oil in wok to deep-fry temperature. Have the small bowl of cold oil and
a soup spoon within reach.
3. Using your left hand, grasp a handful of the shrimp mixture and squeeze it
between the base of your thumb and your index finger. When it forms a walnut-
sized ball, scoop it with the spoon and put it into the heated oil. Dip the spoon
into the bowl of cold oil before scooping another shrimp ball. The cold oil keeps
the shrimp paste from sticking to the spoon. Repeat this until there are enough
shrimp balls in the hot oil. Fry until they are golden. Drain and put them in the
preheated oven until the others are done. Serve hot with dip.

# STUFFED PRAWNS
Makes 4 servings

## PREPARATION OF INGREDIENTS

8 big fresh prawns: shell, devein, and butterfly as illustrated on page 161
1 egg yolk

STUFFING (Mix in a bowl)

4 ounces ground pork
4 ounces fresh small shrimp: shell, devein, and rinse in cold water, pat dry,
    mince into paste
¼ cup minced water chestnuts
1 scallion: mince, including some green part
¼ teaspoon salt
¼ teaspoon sugar
1 big pinch ground pepper
1 teaspoon thin soy sauce
1 egg white: beat until slightly foamy

oil for deep-frying

BATTER (Mix in a bowl)

1 egg: beat until slightly foamy
2 tablespoons flour
¼ teaspoon five-fragrance powder
⅛ teaspoon salt
2 teaspoons cornstarch
½ teaspoon baking powder
1 tablespoon water

Soy-Vinegar Dip (see page 315) or Plum Sauce Dip (see page 314)

## DIRECTIONS FOR COOKING

1. Brush split side of prawns with egg yolk. Then spread stuffing generously on egg-yolked side of prawns.

2. Heat oil in wok to deep-fry temperature. Gently dip stuffed prawns into batter. Deep-fry until golden brown. Drain on paper towels. Serve hot with dip.

# PUFFED BUTTERFLY SHRIMP
Makes about 6 servings

## PREPARATION OF INGREDIENTS

1 pound (15 to 20) fresh shrimp: shell, devein, and butterfly as illustrated
    in this chapter

## GINGER JUICE MIXTURE (Mix in a small bowl)

¼ teaspoon fresh ginger juice (use garlic press)
1 teaspoon minced garlic
¼ teaspoon salt
1 teaspoon dry Sherry

1 cup all-purpose flour, unsifted
1 tablespoon baking powder
¼ teaspoon salt
5 tablespoons oil
⅔ cup cold water
2 tablespoons white sesame seeds
⅓ cup minced scallions, including some green part
oil for deep-frying

## DIRECTIONS FOR COOKING

1. Brush ginger juice mixture on split side of shrimp.
2. Mix flour, baking powder, and salt in a bowl. Add 5 tablespoons of oil gradually while stirring. Mix well. The dough should look like pie dough. Stir in water, a little at a time, until mixture becomes a thick batter. Add sesame seeds and scallions. Mix well. (To test whether consistency of the batter is right, hold a shrimp by the tail, dip it into the batter, then hold it over the bowl. The batter should drip down slowly from the shrimp.)
3. Heat oil, about 4 to 5 cups, to deep-fry temperature. Take each shrimp by the tail, dip it into the batter, then put directly into the hot oil. The shrimp should

puff up and swim to the surface immediately. If it stays on the bottom, the oil is not hot enough. (Deep-fry a few at a time; too many will cool down the oil temperature too much.) Turn the shrimp when the batter is set. Fry until light gold. Place on paper towels to drain. Serve hot or warm.

NOTE: You can put the shrimp in a warm oven. They will keep hot and crisp for half an hour or longer.

# SICHUAN SPICED SHRIMP
Makes 4 to 6 servings

PREPARATION OF INGREDIENTS

oil for deep-frying

SHRIMP MIXTURE (Mix and keep refrigerated for at least an hour before use)

1 pound fresh shrimp: shell, devein, cut into halves lengthwise, rinse in cold
    running water for a minute, drain, pat dry
¼ teaspoon salt
2 tablespoons flour
1 tablespoon cornstarch
1 egg, slightly beaten
¼ teaspoon baking soda
1 teaspoon thin soy sauce
1 teaspoon rice wine or dry Sherry

SEASONINGS (Put in a bowl)

1 teaspoon finely minced fresh ginger
2 teaspoons minced garlic
2 scallions: cut into pea-sized pieces, including some green part
2 to 3 dried chili peppers: tear into small pieces, do not discard seeds

SAUCE MIXTURE (Mix in a bowl)

1 tablespoon sugar
2 tablespoons black soy sauce
3 tablespoons tomato ketchup
1 tablespoonspoon dry Sherry
2 teaspoons white vinegar
1 tablespoon water

1 teaspoon sesame oil

## DIRECTIONS FOR COOKING

1. Heat oil in wok over medium heat to deep-fry temperature. Add shrimp mixture, half at a time, and stir briskly until shrimp turn whitish-pink (less than 10 seconds). Remove with a drainer to a bowl.
2. Remove all but 2 tablespoons oil from wok. Heat oil, then slightly brown seasonings. Stir in sauce mixture. Stir and cook until it begins to bubble. Return shrimp to wok. Stir-fry for several seconds. Swirl in sesame oil. Put on a serving platter. Serve hot.

# SHRIMP CANTONESE

Makes 4 to 6 servings

## PREPARATION OF INGREDIENTS

6 tablespoons oil

SHRIMP MIXTURE (Mix in a bowl. Refrigerate for at least an hour)

1 pound fresh shrimp: shell, devein, wash under running cold water, drain, dry
¼ teaspoon salt
⅛ teaspoon ground pepper
½ teaspoon baking soda
½ teaspoon dry Sherry
1 egg white
½ teaspoon sesame oil

SEASONINGS (Put in a bowl)

2 scallions: cut into pea-sized pieces, including some green part
1 teaspoon finely minced fresh ginger
2 teaspoons minced garlic
1 tablespoon salted black beans: rinse in hot, running water, drain,
    mash into paste

4 ounces ground pork
½ green or red bell pepper: cut into 1-inch squares

SAUCE MIXTURE (Mix in a bowl)

¼ teaspoon sugar
2 teaspoons cornstarch
1 tablespoon black soy sauce
2 teaspoons thin soy sauce
½ teaspoon sesame oil
½ cup clear, canned chicken broth
2 tablespoons rice wine or dry Sherry

2 eggs: beat until slightly foamy

DIRECTIONS FOR COOKING

1. Heat wok over high heat. Swirl in 4 tablespoons of the oil. When hot, add shrimp mixture. Stir-fry until shrimp just turn white-pink (less than 20 seconds). Remove with drainer or slotted spoon to a bowl. Clean and dry wok.
2. Heat wok over high heat until it is hot. Swirl in the remaining 2 tablespoons oil. When oil is hot, add seasonings. Stir-fry over high heat until garlic turns golden. Add pork. When pork loses its pink color, add bell pepper. Mix well. Stir in sauce mixture. Stir constantly. When sauce begins to bubble, return shrimp to wok. Mix well.
3. Pour eggs evenly over shrimp. Do not stir. Cover and cook over medium heat for 30 seconds or until eggs are slightly set around the edge. Stir to mix until eggs are just cooked. Put on a serving platter. Serve hot.


# SHRIMP IN PLUM SAUCE
Makes 4 to 6 servings

PREPARATION OF INGREDIENTS

6 tablespoons oil

SHRIMP MIXTURE (Mix in a bowl. Refrigerate for 1 to 2 hours)

1 pound fresh shrimp: Shell, devein, rinse in cold water, pat dry
1 teaspoon dry Sherry
⅛ teaspoon white pepper
about ½ egg white
¼ teaspoon sugar
½ teaspoon baking soda

2 teaspoons minced garlic
2 scallions: cut into pea-sized pieces, including some green part
4 ounces ground pork
¼ cup coarsely chopped water chestnuts

SAUCE MIXTURE (Mix in a bowl)

4 tablespoons plum sauce
1 tablespoon dry Sherry
1 tablespoon black soy sauce

DIRECTIONS FOR COOKING

1. Heat wok over high heat until it just begins to smoke. Swirl in oil. Add shrimp
mixture, and cook until shrimp turn whitish-pink (less than a minute). Drain
and put on a plate.
2. Remove all but 2 tablespoons oil from wok. Heat oil, add garlic, scallions, and
ground pork. Stir-fry until pork loses its pink color. Add water chestnuts. Stir in
sauce mixture. Cook and stir for about 15 seconds. Return shrimp to wok. Stir-
fry for 10 seconds. Put on a platter. Serve hot.

# SHRIMP WITH CASHEW NUTS
Makes about 6 servings

PREPARATION OF INGREDIENTS

5 tablespoons oil
⅓ cup uncooked cashew nuts
¼ cup Chinese dried mushrooms: soak in hot water until spongy, discard stems,
     cut caps into squares
⅓ cup quartered water chestnuts

SHRIMP MIXTURE (Mix in a bowl and refrigerate for at least 30 minutes)

1 pound fresh shrimp: shell, devein, rinse, drain, pat dry
⅛ teaspoon salt
½ teaspoon dry Sherry
about ½ egg white

SAUCE MIXTURE (Mix in a bowl)

¼ teaspoon sugar
1 tablespoon thin soy sauce

1 teaspoon black soy sauce
1 teaspoon dry Sherry

1 scallion: chop into pea-sized pieces, including some green part
1 teaspoon sesame oil

## DIRECTIONS FOR COOKING

1. Heat oil in wok to deep-fry temperature. Add cashew nuts, and turn heat to low. Deep-fry cashews slowly until they are golden brown. Drain on paper towels.
2. Reheat oil in wok over medium heat. Brown mushrooms slightly. Add water chestnuts, then shrimp mixture. Stir-fry until shrimp turn whitish-pink (about 1 minute). Stir in sauce mixture, and drop in scallion. Stir-fry for about 15 seconds. Add sesame oil. Throw in cashew nuts. Mix and serve hot.

# LOBSTER CANTONESE

Makes about 6 servings

## PREPARATION OF INGREDIENTS

3 pounds live lobster (three 1-pound lobsters)
2 tablespoons cornstarch
oil for deep-frying

## SEASONINGS (Put in a bowl)

3 tablespoons salted black beans: rinse in hot water, drain, mash into paste
¼ cup chopped scallions, including some green part
1 teaspoon finely minced fresh ginger
1 tablespoon minced garlic
4 ounces ground pork

## SAUCE MIXTURE (Mix in a bowl)

1 teaspoon sugar
¼ teaspoon salt

1 tablespoon cornstarch
1 tablespoon black soy sauce
2 tablespoons thin soy sauce
4 tablespoons Chinese rice wine or dry Sherry
1 cup clear canned chicken broth

¼ cup red or green bell peppers, in ½-inch squares
2 eggs: beat until slightly foamy
1 tablespoon sesame oil

DIRECTIONS FOR COOKING

1. Put lobster in boiling water for 2 minutes in order to kill it. Chop off each lobster's tail, and section it into desired pieces. Cut off claws, crack them. Cut off and discard feet. Split heads into halves, and cut halves crosswise. Discard gill and mouth area. Put lobster pieces in a colander to drain.
2. Mix lobster pieces and 2 tablespoons cornstarch in a bowl.
3. Heat oil in wok to deep-fry temperature. Add lobster pieces and deep-fry for about 10 minutes or until they are just done. Remove with a drainer or slotted spoon to a bowl.
4. Skim off residue from oil. Remove all but 2 tablespoons oil from wok. Heat remaining oil in wok over high heat, then add seasonings. Stir-fry until garlic turns golden. Add pork, break it into small pieces, and stir-fry until no longer pink. Stir in sauce mixture. Add peppers and stir and cook until sauce bubbles gently. Add lobster pieces. Turn heat to medium. Swirl eggs evenly over lobster. Cover and cook over low heat for about 30 seconds. When eggs are slightly set around the edge, stir to mix well. Stir and cook until eggs are done. Add sesame oil. Put on a serving platter. Serve hot.

NOTE: There is a lot of sauce in this dish. You might like to prepare more rice than usual.

# OYSTER FRITTERS WITH SOY-VINEGAR DIP

Makes 4-6 servings

The sign "Eat oysters, love longer" is seen here and there in fish stores in this country. I assume that some Westerners have the same idea as the Chinese—oysters enhance sexuality, especially in women. "It nourishes the Yin (female)," my grandmother used to say. Sea slugs were supposed to have the same effect.

In old China, the emperor had 3,000 women at his disposal in the palace, and his male subjects could have as many wives as their purses could afford; therefore sexual potency has always been a common concern among the Chinese. For thousands of years, the search for remedies to promote potency was perpetual. Ginseng was found, the rare Manchurian plant whose root resembles a man's figure. This manlike root, believed to restore health and to strengthen any body weakness, was revered as the root of life and happiness. But ginseng was too scarce and too expensive for most people. Therefore, they turned to more ordinary substances and created their own folk prescriptions. Dog meat (not the pet, but a special kind of Chinese dog) cooked with wine; mutton cooked with herbs; snake meat cooked with pork; mushrooms, ginger; and a special kind of chicken with dark meat called Zhu Si Ji were believed to heat one's body and reinvigorate the spirit of Yang.

My two grandfathers had ten wives between them; sometimes they held snake banquets at which dozens of snake dishes were prepared in many ways. It was said that the diners were stimulated for many days afterward.

Customarily, eating snake meat and dog meat occurred in the fall and winter, when one's body was cool and the spirit calm. In Hong Kong, dog eating was illegal, yet there were plenty of places away from the city where one could easily find a dog dinner. Once during my college years, I planned to join a dog-eating evening adventure, but dropped out when I imagined myself in jail, the headlines blaring: "College Girl Arrested for Eating Dog." I was told afterward by my fellow adventurers that all of them ate standing up, ready to run if the police came!

## PREPARATION OF INGREDIENTS

1 pound fresh oysters without shells
2 tablespoons salt

BATTER (Mix well in a bowl)

4 beaten eggs
⅔ cup flour
1 teaspoon baking powder
1 teaspoon salt
¼ teaspoon white pepper
2 tablespoons oil
½ cup chopped scallions, in pea-sized pieces, including some green part

4 to 5 tablespoons oil
double recipe Soy-Vinegar Dip (see page 315)
chili sauce (optional)

DIRECTIONS FOR COOKING

1. Add salt to oysters and massage them gently for about half a minute. Rinse in cold water and drain. Bring a small pot of water to a boil. Add oysters and blanch for 10 seconds. Drain in colander. Pat dry.
2. Add oysters to batter and mix well.
3. Heat a skillet. Add 2 tablespoons of oil. When oil is hot, spoon about 1 tablespoon batter with an oyster into skillet to make 1 fritter. You may pan-fry 4 to 5 fritters at a time. Turn heat to medium-low. Fry fritters until both sides are golden brown, then place in a warm oven. Serve hot with dip.

# LAKE DONG TING SCALLOPS

Makes 2 to 4 servings

Lake Dong Ting, the largest lake of China, is in the northern part of Hunan. The tranquil water of the lake, surrounded by green valleys, gentle hills, and stretches of densely forested mountains, portrays the beauty of the region.

This method of cooking scallops was taught by Lee, an old Hunanese friend. The scallops are enhanced by the delicious sauce, which is slightly sweet and spiced with chili peppers and garlic.

## PREPARATION OF INGREDIENTS

1 cup oil for deep-frying
1 pound fresh sea scallops: rinse and pat dry, then mix with 1 tablespoon
    cornstarch. Refrigerate before use.

## SEASONINGS (Put on a plate)

1 piece dried tangerine peel (optional): soak in hot water for about 15 minutes
    or until soft, mince (to make about 1 teaspoon)
2 to 3 dried chili peppers: tear into small pieces, do not discard seeds
1 teaspoon finely minced, fresh ginger
1 tablespoon minced garlic
3 scallions: cut into pea-sized pieces, including some green part
¼ cup green or red bell pepper (optional), in ½-inch squares

## SAUCE MIXTURE (Mix in a bowl)

1 tablespoon sugar
3 tablespoons tomato ketchup
2 tablespoons black soy sauce
1 teaspoon white vinegar
1 tablespoon rice wine or dry Sherry
1 tablespoon water

## DIRECTIONS FOR COOKING

1. Heat oil in wok to deep-fry temperature. Add scallops. Stir to separate them, and blanch in oil for about 30 seconds or until they are just done. Remove with a drainer to a bowl.

2. Remove all but 2 tablespoons oil from wok. Heat oil over medium heat, then

drop in seasonings. When garlic and ginger turn golden, swirl in sauce mixture. Return scallops to wok. Mix well. Cook and stir gently until sauce begins to bubble. Put on a serving platter. Serve hot at once.

# CARP IN BROWN SAUCE
4 to 6 servings

## PREPARATION OF INGREDIENTS

1 fresh carp, 1½ pounds (whole or section); slash several cuts, about ½ inch deep, on both sides of the fish, rinse, pat dry thoroughly
1 tablespoon cornstarch
oil for deep frying
2 tablespoons oil
1 tablespoon minced fresh ginger
1 tablespoon minced garlic
2 scallions, cut into 1½-inch lengths, including some of the green part

## SAUCE MIXTURE (Mix in bowl)

4 tablespoons ground bean sauce
2 tablespoons black soy sauce
4 teaspoons sugar
4 tablespoons Chinese rice wine or dry Sherry
1 tablespoon Chinese red vinegar

about ⅔ cup canned, clear chicken broth

## DIRECTIONS FOR COOKING

1. Dust carp inside and out with cornstarch.
2. Heat oil in wok over high heat. Gently slide in fish. Deep-fry each side for 8 minutes. The fish should be nicely browned, but not yet thoroughly cooked. Remove fish carefully with the help of 2 spatulas. Put on plate. Remove all the oil from the wok. (Save oil for frying fish in the future; keep refrigerated.)
3. Heat wok over high heat. Add oil. When oil is hot, drop in ginger, garlic, and scallions. When garlic turns light gold, add sauce mixture. Cook and stir until sauce becomes thick and pasty.

4. Return fish to wok. Pour in half the chicken broth. Cover and simmer for about 8 minutes. Turn fish over and add remaining broth if sauce seems to be drying out. Cover and simmer for another 8 minutes. Remove entire contents to a serving platter. Discard scallions. Serve immediately..

# SOFT-SHELL CRABS IN BLACK BEAN SAUCE
Makes 4 servings

When you buy soft-shell crabs, be sure that they are still alive. Usually they look quite dead, weak and limp. Touch their legs, eyes, or mouth. Even if they respond only slightly and slowly, they are still alive. Refrigerate them as soon as you get home.

Cleaning them is quite simple. Clip off the eyes and mouth. Lift the top shell and remove the soft feather-like gills and discard them. Turn the crab bottom up. Tear off and discard the cartilage (the shape of the female's is half oval, the male's is a narrow triangle).

PREPARATION OF INGREDIENTS

⅓ cup oil for pan-frying
4 soft-shell crabs: clean, roll in 2 tablespoons rice wine or dry Sherry, sprinkle
    with salt and pepper, coat generously with flour

SEASONINGS (Put in a bowl)

1 tablespoon salted black beans: rinse thoroughly in hot, running water,
    drain, mash into paste
1 teaspoon minced fresh ginger
2 teaspoons minced garlic
¼ cup scallions, in pea-sized pieces, including some green

4 ounces ground pork
½ cup chopped bell peppers

SAUCE MIXTURE (Mix in a bowl)

½ teaspoon sugar
1 tablespoon cornstarch

2 tablespoons black soy sauce
1 tablespoon thin soy sauce
1 tablespoon sesame oil
½ cup rice wine or dry Sherry
½ cup water

1 egg: beat until slightly fluffy

DIRECTIONS FOR COOKING

1. Heat oil in a frying pan; cover and pan-fry crabs over moderate heat for 12 minutes (6 minutes each side). Transfer to serving plate.
2. Remove all but 2 tablespoons of oil from pan. Reheat oil, add seasonings and stir to cook until ginger turns golden. Add pork and cook until it is no longer pink. Put in bell pepper and combine. Swirl in sauce mixture, cook and stir until it begins to bubble. Stir in egg, and stir to cook until egg is done and the sauce is thickened. Pour over the crabs. Serve hot.

# Vegetables
and Tofu

# VEGETABLES AND TOFU

M any Westerners cook their vegetables as if they were cooking potatoes. The peas, the beans, the broccoli, even the luscious asparagus are cooked so much that they all taste the same, like cooked potatoes—dull, mushy, and lifeless.

Cooking vegetables briefly in oil or water brings out a most beautiful green color that is even brighter and shinier than it was in the field. Short cooking preserves natural sweetness, crispness, and vitamins.

Vegetables are plentiful here, even the Chinese variety. Vegetables that were only available in urban Chinatowns are now sold in suburban Chinese grocery stores, where now you can find Chinese vegetables such as Chinese water spinach, long beans, silk melons, Chinese chives, giant white turnips, Shanghai bok choy, taros, pea shoots, and a newcomer called Taiwan green bean sprouts, with a delicious, nutty flavor. They look fresh and healthy and taste as good as in their mother soil.

But I have found that many people in this land do not know how to buy vegetables, and cannot tell the good from the bad. Perhaps this is why so many still use frozen vegetables. The suggestions in the following chapter might help on your next shopping trip. You will find an extensive list of Chinese vegetables and their use in Chinese cooking in the chapter CHINESE COOKING INGREDIENTS WITH INFORMATION ON BUYING AND STORING (see page 319)

# HOW TO MAKE SCALLION BRUSHES

Take a 2-inch-long piece from the white of the scallion. Slip a green ring from the stalk around it. Slice ends to form a brush. Put in ice water to curl brushes.

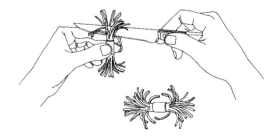

# SICHUAN SPICY CUCUMBERS
Serves 8 or more as an appetizer

## PREPARATION OF INGREDIENTS

4 firm cucumbers (about 3 pounds), wash, cut each in half lengthwise,
   scoop out and discard seeds and soft part, cut into strips 1 by 3 inches
2 tablespoons salt
1 tablespoon sugar
1 cup red bell peppers in thin strips
2 tablespoons thinly shredded fresh ginger
2 tablespoons oil
2 tablespoons sesame oil
4 dried chili peppers: break each in half (use seed, too)
1 teaspoon flower peppercorns

## SAUCE MIXTURE (Mix in a bowl)

¼ cup Chenkong (sometimes romanized as Chen-Chiang) vinegar
¼ cup sugar
1 tablespoon black soy sauce

DIRECTIONS FOR COOKING

1. Combine cucumbers with salt and sugar; allow to stand at room temperature for 15 minutes. Rinse cucumbers thoroughly in a large bowl under running cold water; drain in a colander; pat dry. In a large bowl, combine cucumbers with bell peppers and ginger shreds.
2. Head 2 kinds of oils in a small pot over low heat. Gently fry chili peppers and flower peppercorns to golden brown, then cool slightly. Add sauce mixture, and pour over cucumber mixture. Stir and toss to mix well. Refrigerate for a few hours or more. Serve as an appetizer or as a side dish.

NOTE: Keep the remaining vegetables in a covered jar with sauce: they will keep for 3 or 4 days.


# SWEET AND SOUR VEGETABLES, SOUTHERN STYLE
Makes 8 to 10 servings as an appetizer

PREPARATION OF INGREDIENTS

SAUCE MIXTURE (Mix in a large pot)

1 teaspoon cayenne pepper
2 teaspoons sea salt
2½ cups sugar
¼ cup shredded fresh ginger
2½ cups water

1 head of cauliflower or yellow cabbage: wash, cut into bite-sized pieces
1 cup red bell peppers, sliced

3 tablespoons white sesame seeds
2 tablespoons Sichuan peppercorn (optional)

DIRECTIONS FOR COOKING

1. Heat sauce mixture over moderate heat, stirring constantly, until sugar dissolves. Cool at room temperature. In a large bowl, add sauce mixture, cauliflower or yellow cabbage and bell peppers; toss to mix.

2. In a small pot, roast sesame seeds over moderate heat, stirring constantly until they turn golden. Remove from pot to cool.

3. In the same pot, roast Sichuan peppercorn until it turns black and begins to smoke. Remove from pot to cool.

4 Add roasted sesame seeds and peppercorn to vegetable; stir to mix well. Cover and refrigerate, steep for at least 8 hours before serving.

# ASPARAGUS OR PEA SHOOTS IN CRAB MEAT SAUCE
Makes 6 servings

## PREPARATION OF INGREDIENTS

1 pot water
4 tablespoons oil
1½ pounds asparagus: break off tough ends  or 1 pound pea shoots (see page 329): trim and discard large leaves and tough stems, wash and drain

## SAUCE MIXTURE (Mix in a bowl)

1 cup clear, canned chicken broth
1 tablespoon cornstarch
¼ teaspoon salt
¼ teaspoon sugar
1 teaspoon rice wine or dry Sherry
6 ounces fresh or frozen crab meat: thaw and drain on paper towels
2 egg whites, ⅛ teaspoon salt: beat together until foamy

## DIRECTIONS FOR COOKING

1. Bring water to rolling boil, put in 1 tablespoon oil, and add the asparagus or pea shoots. Cook asparagus over medium heat for 2 minutes or until done to taste, but leave the pea shoots in water for only five seconds. Drain and transfer to a serving platter. Cover asparagus or pea shoots while you are preparing the sauce.

2. Heat wok over high heat until hot. Add remaining oil. Stir in sauce mixture and turn the heat to medium. Cook and stir sauce constantly until it is clear. Add the crab meat and then the egg whites. Stir gently over low heat until sauce is thickened. Spoon over asparagus or pea shoots. Serve hot.

# STIR-FRIED SHRIMP AND SILK MELONS WITH CASHEW NUTS

Makes 4 to 6 servings

## PREPARATION OF INGREDIENTS

4 tablespoons oil
½ cup shredded scallions
2 teaspoons minced, fresh ginger
1 tablespoon minced garlic
½ cup loosely packed, chopped fresh parsley

## SHRIMP MIXTURE (Mix in a bowl)

1 pound large shrimp: shell, devein, wash under running cold water, drain,
    pat dry
1 egg white: beat until slightly foamy
¼ teaspoon ground white pepper
2 teaspoons dry Sherry
1 tablespoon thin soy sauce
1 teaspoon sesame oil

1½ pounds silk melon: peel and discard green skin, cut into ½-inch slices
⅓ cup dried cloud ears: soak in hot water, rinse thoroughly, pinch off and
    discard tough parts, drain

## SAUCE MIXTURE (Mix in a bowl)

2 tablespoons oyster-flavored sauce
2 tablespoons thin soy sauce
1 tablespoon dry Sherry
½ cup canned clear chicken broth

1 teaspoon cornstarch, mixed with 3 tablespoons water
1 teaspoon sesame oil
½ cup fried or roasted cashew nuts

## DIRECTIONS FOR COOKING

1. Heat wok over high heat. Swirl in 4 tablespoons oil. When oil is hot, add scallions, ginger, garlic and parsley. Stir-fry until garlic turns golden. Add shrimp mixture and stir-fry until shrimp just turns whitish. Remove with a strainer and put in a bowl.

2. Keep wok hot; add silk melons and cloud ears; stir and mix well. Swirl in sauce mixture and cook over medium heat for about 2 minutes or until melons are tender. Stir in cornstarch-water; stir and cook until sauce is clear. Return shrimp mixture to wok. Mix well and add sesame oil. Put on a serving platter and top with cashew nuts. Serve hot.

# BEAN SPROUTS WITH CHICKEN SHREDS AND ALMONDS

Makes 4 to 6 servings

## PREPARATION OF INGREDIENTS

4 tablespoons oil
⅓ cup uncooked sliced almonds
¼ cup shredded scallions
4 Chinese dried mushrooms: soak in hot water until spongy, discard stem, shred caps

## CHICKEN MIXTURE (Mix in a bowl)

1½ boned, skinless chicken breasts: shred into matchstick strips
about ⅓ egg white
¼ teaspoon salt
1 pinch white pepper
1 pinch sugar
1 teaspoon cornstarch

8 ounces fresh white bean sprouts: wash in cold water, drain
¼ cup shredded red or green bell pepper

**SAUCE MIXTURE (Mix in a bowl)**

¼ teaspoon sugar
¼ teaspoon salt
1 teaspoon cornstarch
4 teaspoons thin soy sauce
1 teaspoon black soy sauce
2 teaspoons dry Sherry
1 teaspoon sesame oil
2 tablespoons water

**DIRECTIONS FOR COOKING**

1. Heat 4 tablespoons oil in wok. Deep-fry almonds until they are a light gold color. Drain on paper towel.
2. Reheat oil in wok over high heat. Slightly brown scallions and mushrooms. Add chicken mixture and stir-fry until it is just cooked. Add bean sprouts and pepper. Stir-fry briefly to heat them. Swirl in sauce mixture and stir to cook until sauce is thickened. Put on a serving platter. Top with almonds. Serve hot.

# JADE GREEN BROCCOLI IN GINGER AND WINE SAUCE
Makes 4 to 6 to servings

C hinese broccoli looks a little bit different from its American cousin. It is slimmer, taller, and has more leaves with fewer flowers. But its taste is not much different. Don't shy away from the amount of sugar and wine in this recipe, for broccoli loves the company of sugar and wine.

In this dish the broccoli is very green and crunchy, and there is plenty of sauce for the rice.

**PREPARATION OF INGREDIENTS**

3 tablespoons oil
2 teaspoons minced, fresh ginger
2 teaspoons minced garlic
1 pound fresh broccoli: cut into finger-sized pieces, blanch in water,
    drain in colander (see Cooking Techniques, page 17)

SAUCE MIXTURE (Mix in a bowl)

2 tablespoons brown sugar
2 tablespoons thin soy sauce
1 tablespoon black soy sauce
1 teaspoon sesame oil
¼ cup rice wine or dry Sherry

1 teaspoon cornstarch mixed with 2 tablespoons water

## DIRECTIONS FOR COOKING

Heat wok over high heat and add oil. When oil is hot, brown ginger and garlic to golden. Add blanched broccoli. Stir in sauce mixture and mix well. Cover and cook for about 20 seconds. Stir in cornstarch water and cook until sauce is thickened. Put on a serving platter. Serve hot.

# SIMPLE PLEASURE
## (GREEN VEGETABLE WITH GARLIC IN OYSTER SAUCE)
Makes 6 servings

Green vegetables taste best when they are cooked simply. Blanching them in water for a few seconds not only retains their vitamins and crispness, but also turns their color to emerald green. Vegetables such as Shanghai bok choy, pea shoots, Taiwan green bean sprouts, Chinese broccoli, asparagus, or snow peas are all suitable for this simple, but delicious dish.

## PREPARATION OF INGREDIENTS

12 cups of water
4 tablespoons oil
1 pound trimmed vegetable as suggested: wash and drain
2 teaspoons minced garlic

SAUCE MIXTURE (Mix in a bowl)

2 tablespoons sesame oil
3 tablespoons oyster-flavored sauce
1 tablespoon black soy sauce

## DIRECTIONS FOR COOKING

1. In a large pot, heat water and 2 tablespoons oil to a rolling boil. Immerse vegetable in boiling water for 5 seconds, and quickly remove it with a drainer to a serving plate. Tilt plate to drain off water.
2. In a small pot, heat 2 tablespoons oil over moderate heat until it is hot. Add garlic and stir to cook until golden. Stir in sauce mixture and cook until it just bubbles evenly. Turn off heat. Pour sauce over vegetables and toss. Serve hot.

# BABY CORN AND BROCCOLI IN OYSTER SAUCE
Makes 4 to 6 servings

## PREPARATION OF INGREDIENTS

½ pound fresh broccoli: cut into finger-sized pieces
15-ounce can baby corn: drain
3 tablespoons oil for stir-frying
6 Chinese dried mushrooms: soak in hot water until spongy, discard stems, leave caps whole

## SAUCE MIXTURE (Mix in a bowl)

½ teaspoon sugar
3 tablespoons oyster-flavored sauce
1 tablespoon thin soy sauce
2 teaspoons dry Sherry
1 tablespoon water

1 teaspoon sesame oil

## DIRECTIONS FOR COOKING

1. Blanch broccoli and baby corn in water (see Cooking Techniques, page 17). Drain.
2. Heat wok over high heat. Swirl in oil. When oil is hot, add mushrooms, and brown lightly. Add broccoli and baby corn and cook for about 30 seconds. Stir in sauce mixture. Stir and cook for about 20 seconds. Swirl in sesame seed oil. Put on a serving platter. Serve hot.

# STUFFED PEPPERS WITH BLACK BEAN SAUCE
Makes 24

## PREPARATION OF INGREDIENTS

12 medium-sized frying peppers: wash, cut each in half lengthwise,
    discard seeds and ribs
about 2 tablespoons cornstarch

FILLING (mix in a bowl, stir vigorously with a spoon for a minute)

1 pound ground pork
⅓ cup minced water chestnuts
4 Chinese dried mushrooms: soak in hot water until spongy, discard stems,
    mince caps
½ cup minced scallions, including some green part
½ teaspoon sugar
½ teaspoon ground pepper
1 tablespoon cornstarch
2 teaspoons black soy sauce
1 tablespoon thin soy sauce
1 tablespoon dry Sherry

4 tablespoons oil for pan-frying
1 teaspoon minced fresh ginger
2 teaspoons minced garlic
2 tablespoons salted black beans: rinse in hot water, drain, mash to paste

BROTH MIXTURE (Put in a bowl)

1½ cups canned clear chicken broth
½ teaspoon sugar
2 tablespoons cornstarch
1 tablespoon thin soy sauce
2 tablespoons dry Sherry

## DIRECTIONS FOR COOKING

1. Dust insides of peppers with 2 tablespoons cornstarch
2. Stuff pepper with filling, pressing it down with a knife.

3. Heat a large skillet over medium heat. Swirl in 4 tablespoons oil. When oil is hot, arrange half the stuffed peppers, meat side down, in skillet. Pan-fry peppers until meat sides are golden brown but are not thoroughly cooked. Drain and let oil drip back to skillet. Transfer peppers to a heatproof plate, meat side up. Pan-fry the remaining stuffed peppers in the same manner. Keep the oil in skillet for later use.

4. Cover and steam stuffed peppers over high heat for 15 minutes. Turn off heat.

5. While the peppers are being steamed, heat oil that was left in skillet over medium heat. When oil is hot, drop in ginger, garlic, and black beans. Stir constantly. When garlic begins to turn golden, pour in broth mixture. Stir and cook until sauce thickens. (This sauce can be prepared in advance. Reheat in a small pot when it is needed.) Pour sauce over peppers. Serve hot as an appetizer or as a meal with rice.

# FIVE-FRAGRANCE EGGPLANT OR ZUCCHINI FRITTERS
Makes about 18

## PREPARATION OF INGREDIENTS

1 pound eggplant or zucchini: cut into thin rounds, then shred rounds into thin strips—do not use food processor
3 eggs, beaten
½ teaspoon salt
½ teaspoon sugar
1 teaspoon five-fragrance powder
2 tablespoons thin soy sauce
1 cup all-purpose flour
½ cup chopped scallions, including some green part
oil for pan-frying
Soy-Vinegar Dip (see page 315) and a small bowl of Chinese chili sauce or Tabasco sauce (optional)

1. In a mixing bowl, combine the above ingredients except the oil and dip. The mixture is thick; allow it to stand for about 30 minutes or until it becomes thinner. (This mixture can be prepared hours in advance.)
2. Heat a large skillet over medium-low heat. Add enough oil to cover bottom of skillet. When oil is hot, ladle about 2 tablespoonfuls of the mixture onto the skillet; pan-fry fritters, a few at a time, over medium-low heat until both sides are golden brown and edges are crisp. While cooking, press fritters occasionally with spatula to thin them; add more oil when it is needed. Transfer them to a wire rack, then place rack with fritters on a cookie sheet, and put in a 350-degree oven until the rest are cooked. (A 350-degree oven will keep the fritters hot and crisp for about 20 minutes; beyond that time they might become dry. A 300-degree or lower oven will keep them hot longer—but softer. Serve hot with dip.

# ROADSIDE FRIED TURNIP FRITTERS
Makes about 12

I first came upon these fritters when I was eight, in a small farming town whose name meant "river gate" near the Pearl River. It was a school field trip. Like little ducklings, we were herded through a busy food marketplace where everybody was either cooking, selling, yelling, or eating. The air was thick with the smell of steamed clams, snails, noodles, and the sweet aroma from the spiced innards of pork and beef.

Somehow I found myself all alone, with a mouthful and a handful of these fritters, standing and watching the vendors' hands as they quickly ladled the batter into the hot oil and scooped out other fritters.

Besides my hand getting five smacks from the ruler, I had to stay in school until dusk, finishing ten pages of "I should obey the teacher," before I could go home. The face of the anxious teacher has long gone; only the memory of those fritters has remained.

Twenty-five years later I found a woman cooking the same fritters on the roadside in Shatin, Hong Kong. I bought two dozen and chatted with her for two hours, learning about her grandchildren, her sons, and all about these fine fritters.

Here I give my thanks to this good woman and wish her well.

## PREPARATION OF INGREDIENTS

about 1 pound Chinese white giant turnip: strip off skin, then use potato peeler
    to shave turnip into thin strips (to make 2½ cups)
about 3 ounces raw sweet potato; peel and shave as with turnip (to make 1 cup)
1 cup canned clear chicken broth
1 cup flour
1 cup cornstarch
½ teaspoon salt
2 Chinese pork sausages: cut into thin slices
⅔ cup shredded scallions: strips 1½ inches long, including green part
oil for deep-frying

Soy-Vinegar Dip: in a small serving bowl, mix 4 tablespoons Chinese red rice
vinegar or rice vinegar with 4 tablespoons thin soy sauce, serve as dip.

## DIRECTIONS FOR COOKING

1. Combine all ingredients except oil and Soy-Vinegar Dip in a bowl in the
order listed. This batter can be prepared in advance and refrigerated.
2. Heat oil in wok over high heat to deep-fry temperature. Pour ¼ cup batter
into hot oil to make one fritter. Deep-fry both sides to light golden color. Two or
three fritters may be deep-fried at the same time, but too many fritters will lower
the oil's temperature and lengthen the frying time. Remove batter crumbs from
oil. The fritters should be crisp outside and soft inside. Drain on paper towels.
Put in 275-degree oven to keep warm while the fritters are frying. Serve hot
with dip.

# STIR-FRIED SNOW PEAS, WATER CHESTNUTS, AND BAMBOO SHOOTS

Makes 4 servings

PREPARATION OF INGREDIENTS

2 tablespoons oil for stir-frying
2 scallions: cut into 1-inch lengths, including some green part
4 Chinese dried mushrooms: soak in hot water until spongy, discard stems
½ pound snow peas: pinch off tips and ends
¼ cup sliced bamboo shoots
¼ cup water chestnuts: cut in half crosswise

SAUCE MIXTURE (Mix in a bowl)

¼ teaspoon sugar
¼ teaspoon salt
1 tablespoon thin soy sauce
1 tablespoon oyster-flavored sauce
1 tablespoon dry Sherry

1 teaspoon sesame oil

DIRECTIONS FOR COOKING

Heat wok over high heat. Swirl in oil for stir-frying. When oil is hot, drop in scallions, then mushrooms. Stir-fry for 10 seconds. Add snow peas, bamboo shoots, and water chestnuts. Stir-fry until snow peas turn bright green. Stir in sauce mixture and stir-fry for about 20 seconds. Swirl in sesame seed oil. Mix well. Put on a serving platter. Serve hot.

# STUFFED FIVE-FRAGRANCE EGGPLANT FRITTERS
Makes 4 to 6 servings

## PREPARATION OF INGREDIENTS

1 to 1½ pounds eggplant: cut crosswise into ½-inch-thick circles;
    slit edges of circles, but not all the way through, to make pocket for stuffing.

STUFFING (Mix and blend for about 1 minute or until stuffing becomes a sticky paste))

½ teaspoon sugar
½ teaspoon five-fragrance powder
1 big pinch pepper
½ pound ground pork
2 tablespoons Chinese dried shrimp (optional): soak in hot water to soften, mince
2 scallions: mince, including some green part
4 teaspoons thin soy sauce
1 teaspoon dry Sherry

2 eggs
½ teaspoon salt
⅔ cup cornstarch
oil for deep-frying
Soy-Vinegar Dip (see page 315)

## DIRECTIONS FOR COOKING

1. Fill each pocket of eggplant circles with 1½ tablespoons stuffing.
2. Beat eggs with salt. Dip stuffed eggplant circles into egg batter, then dredge it with cornstarch at least twice or until they are not sticky. Put aside.
3. Heat a skillet and pour in 4 tablespoons or enough to cover bottom of skillet. When oil is hot, pan-fry eggplant circles over medium-low heat for about 10 minutes or until both sides are golden brown. Drain and put in warm oven to keep hot while the others cook. Add more oil to skillet as necessary. Serve hot with dip.

# SICHUAN EGGPLANT IN CHILI GARLIC SAUCE
Makes 4 to 6 servings

## PREPARATION OF INGREDIENTS

2 pounds eggplant
3 tablespoons oil for frying
2 whole dried chili peppers
2 tablespoons minced garlic
2 scallions: chop into pea-sized pieces, including some green part

## SAUCE MIXTURE (Mix in a bowl)

2 teaspoons brown sugar
1 tablespoon Sichuan sweet bean sauce or ground bean sauce
1 tablespoon hoisin sauce
2 tablespoons black soy sauce
1 tablespoon dry Sherry
½ teaspoon cayenne pepper

1 teaspoon sesame oil

## DIRECTIONS FOR COOKING

1. Make 4 slashes around eggplant, about 1 inch deep. Steam eggplant over water until soft. Cool slightly. Tear eggplant into thin strips lengthwise. Discard part of the seeds.
2. Heat oil in wok over high heat. Fry chili peppers until dark brown, then discard. Add garlic and scallions and brown them slightly. Stir in sauce mixture and cook until it begins to bubble. Add eggplant strips. Stir-fry gently until eggplant is heated through. Add sesame oil. Serve hot.

# STEAMED STRING BEANS
# WITH GARLIC, NORTHERN STYLE
Makes 4 servings

I used to cook this dish the traditional way by deep-frying the string beans. But I have found that steaming them not only reduces a great amount of oil in this dish, but it gives it a fresher and purer taste. If you prefer a richer dish, deep-fry the string beans first, then stir-fry them as directed in this recipe. The success of this dish depends on fresh young string beans.

## PREPARATION OF INGREDIENTS

1 pound fresh string beans: wash, pat dry, break off tips and ends
2 tablespoons oil
4 ounces ground pork

SEASONINGS (Mix in a bowl)

1 tablespoon Sichuan pickle (optional): rinse, cut into rice-sized pieces
2 scallions: cut into pea-sized pieces, including some green part
2 tablespoons minced garlic
1 teaspoon salt
½ teaspoon sugar

1 tablespoon rice wine or dry Sherry

## DIRECTIONS FOR COOKING

1. Steam string beans for 15 minutes or until tender. Remove to a bowl.
2. Heat wok over high heat, add oil. When oil is hot, add pork and stir-fry until it is cooked. Add seasonings and cook until garlic turns golden. Splash in wine. Add cooked string beans immediately. Mix thoroughly. Put on a serving platter. Serve hot.

# STIR-FRIED CHINESE SPINACH OR
# WHITE LONG BEANS WITH BEAN CURD CHEESE
Makes 6 servings

The Chinese spinach is known as "tong cai," which means hollow vegetable. It has long, slender, hollow, green stems, and delicate, flat leaves. The stems and leaves are all edible; they are crispier and milder than the American spinach. Traditionally, it is cooked with strong seasonings, like that of garlic and bean curd cheese to bring out its delicate flavor.

The white long beans are 12 to 14 inches long and thick like crayons. They are actually pale green. The Chinese label them white, because they are paler in comparison with long green beans (see page 215 for recipe). They are prized for their tenderness and absorbency when cooked. Because of their mildness, it is best to cook them with pungent ingredients like the bean curd cheese. Choose those that are without black spots.

## PREPARATION OF INGREDIENTS

3 tablespoons oil
1 tablespoon minced garlic
1¼ pounds white long beans (to make 1 pound after being trimmed): discard
     ends, cut into 1½-inch pieces, rinse and drain
or 1½ pounds Chinese water spinach (to make 1 pound after being trimmed):
     cut off about 4 inches tough ends and discard; break spinach into 6-inch long
     pieces; wash thoroughly, drain

## SAUCE MIXTURE (Mix in a bowl)

1 tablespoon rice wine or dry Sherry
2 tablespoons white bean curd cheese
3 tablespoons water
½ teaspoon sugar
¼ teaspoon cayenne pepper (optional)

1 tablespoon sesame oil

## DIRECTIONS FOR COOKING

To cook water spinach: heat wok over high heat, until it is very hot. Swirl in 3 tablespoons oil, add garlic and brown to light golden. Add water spinach and stir-fry until it is almost wilted. Stir in sauce mixture; stir-fry until sauce bubbles vigorously. Toss with 1 tablespoon sesame oil. Serve with plain rice.

To cook white long beans: heat wok over high heat until it is very hot. Swirl in 3 tablespoon oil; add garlic and brown slightly. Add long beans and stir-fry for about 1 minute. Stir in sauce mixture and mix well. Cover and cook over medium-high heat for about 5 minutes or until long beans are tender. Stir in sesame oil. Serve with plain rice.

# SPICY SHRIMP WITH GREEN LONG BEANS AND PEANUTS
Makes 6 to 8 servings

6 tablespoons oil

EGG MIXTURE (Mix in a bowl)

4 eggs: beat with ¼ teaspoon salt until foamy
½ cup scallions in pea-sized pieces, including some green part

SHRIMP MIXTURE (Mix, refrigerate before use)

1 pound large shrimp in shells: shell, devein, wash under running cold water, drain, pat dry
⅛ teaspoon ground white pepper
¼ teaspoon salt
¼ teaspoon baking soda
1 teaspoon sesame oil
1 tablespoon rice wine or dry Sherry
1 egg white

SEASONINGS (Put on a plate)

1 teaspoon minced fresh ginger
2 teaspoons minced garlic
¼ teaspoon ground red pepper

8 Chinese dried mushrooms: discard stems, soak caps in hot water until spongy, cut caps into ⅓-inch squares, set aside

⅓ cup dried cloud ears: soak in hot water until soft, rinse thoroughly, drain, discard tough parts, set aside

8 ounces water chestnuts: quarter each, set aside

½ pound long green beans or string beans: wash, pinch off tips and ends, cut into ½-inch pieces

½ cup red bell pepper cut into ½-inch squares

SAUCE MIXTURE (Mix in a bowl)

4 tablespoons oyster-flavored sauce
2 tablespoons thin soy sauce
1 tablespoon black soy sauce
1 tablespoon rice wine or dry Sherry
½ cup canned clear chicken broth

½ cup roasted or fried peanuts

DIRECTIONS FOR COOKING

1. Heat wok over moderate heat. Swirl in 2 tablespoon oil and spread evenly. When oil is hot, add egg mixture and scramble them until they are firm but still moist. Remove from wok and cut into small chunks. Set aside.

2. Heat wok over high heat. Swirl in 3 tablespoons oil. When oil is hot, add shrimp mixture and stir briskly until shrimp turn whitish-pink (less than 10 seconds). Remove from wok and set aside.

3. Keep wok hot over high heat, add the remaining 1 tablespoon oil. When oil is hot, slightly brown the seasonings. Add mushrooms and cloud ears and stir to cook for about 30 seconds. Add long beans or string beans, bell pepper and sauce mixture; stir-fry until beans are cooked but still crisp. Return shrimp and egg chunks to wok. Combine and stir-fry for about 10 seconds. Transfer to a serving platter and top with peanuts. Serve hot.

# CHINESE CHIVES AND SAUSAGES WITH EGGS
Makes 4 to 6 servings

The Chinese chives are a grass-like, onion-flavored vegetable. They come in dark green or yellow. The yellow kind costs at least twice as much as the dark-green variety. They are not only delicious, but also have the effect of treating male sterility, according to traditional Chinese medicine.

## PREPARATION OF INGREDIENTS

4 tablespoons oil
3 Chinese sausages: cut each lengthwise, then dice
1 pound Chinese chives: wash; cut off about 2 inches of the whitish part
    and discard; cut chives into 1-inch lengths

## SAUCE MIXTURE (Mix in a bowl)

¼ teaspoon sugar
⅛ teaspoon ground pepper
1 tablespoon thin soy sauce
1 teaspoon sesame oil

6 large eggs: beat with ½ teaspoon salt until foamy

## DIRECTIONS FOR COOKING

1. Heat wok over high heat and swirl in oil. When oil is hot, add sausages and stir-fry for about 1 minute or until they are lightly browned. Add chives and stir-fry until they are tender. Add sauce mixture and stir to mix well.
2. Turn heat to medium. Swirl in egg mixture. Wait until parts of the egg are set, then scramble eggs with sausages and chives until eggs are done, but still moist. Serve hot.

# SCRAMBLED EGGS WITH CHINESE LEEKS
Makes 6 servings

The Chinese leek is a vegetable related to the onion family. It has a round, slender, dark-green stalk, with a small, white bulb at the top. It is crisp and mildly sweet. Choose those with tender, thin stalks, because the thicker stalks are tough.

## PREPARATION OF INGREDIENTS

4 tablespoons oil
1 pound Chinese leeks: cut and discard 2 inches of the base stems, wash and cut into 1-inch lengths

## SAUCE MIXTURE (Mix in a bowl)

½ teaspoon sugar
2 tablespoons thin soy sauce
1 tablespoon rice wine or dry Sherry

6 large eggs: beat with ½ teaspoon salt, until foamy
1 teaspoon sesame oil

## DIRECTIONS FOR COOKING

1. Heat wok over high heat, swirl in oil. When oil is hot, add leeks and stir-fry until tender. Add sauce mixture and mix well.
2. Turn heat to medium. Swirl in egg-mixture. Scramble eggs with leeks until eggs are done but still moist. Add sesame oil. Serve hot.

# LETTUCE IN OYSTER SAUCE

Makes 6 servings

I f you do not know that cooked lettuce tastes much better than raw lettuce, try this simple pleasure and heavenly dish. "Lettuce" in Chinese sounds like the word for "growing wealth"; therefore, it is often included in Chinese New Year dinner as a portent of prosperity.

## PREPARATION OF INGREDIENTS

3 tablespoons oil
1 large pot of water (about 12 cups)
1 head of iceberg lettuce: tear into large pieces

## SAUCE MIXTURE (Mix in a small pot)

2 tablespoons oil
2 tablespoons sesame oil
3 tablespoons oyster-flavored sauce
1 tablespoon black soy sauce

## DIRECTIONS FOR COOKING

1. Add 3 tablespoons oil to the water, and bring to a rolling boil. Add lettuce and immerse it. Immediately remove lettuce with a drainer to a serving platter. (The lettuce should not stay in the hot water for more than 3 seconds!) Drain off water.
2. Heat sauce mixture over medium heat. When sauce begins to bubble, remove from heat, and pour over lettuce. Serve hot.

# STIR-FRIED BITTER MELON WITH PORK SLICES
Makes about 6 servings

W hen we were children, we made faces and called this dish "the grownups' dish." The melon was bitter—it made our tongues quiver, even more so because our tastes were uncultivated. Then we were told that one day, after we had a few sorrows, some tears, and a little wisdom, the melon would seem mild.

Now that we have all aged and are somewhat seasoned by life, the bitterness of this melon has indeed become pleasant and mellow.

Yet, no Chinese would like to be called "a bitter melon," which means one is weepy and bitter. We would rather be called "a winter melon,"—big and clumsy—but that we don't mind.

## PREPARATION OF INGREDIENTS

6 cups water

½ teaspoon baking soda
1 pound fresh bitter melon: cut lengthwise, scoop out seeds and soft center,
     cut melon crosswise into thin slices
3 tablespoons oil
2 teaspoons minced garlic
2 scallions: cut into pea-sized pieces, including some green part ·

## PORK MIXTURE (Mix in a bowl)

8 ounces lean pork: cut into very thin slices (to make 1 cup)
1 tablespoon cornstarch
2 teaspoons black soy sauce
½ teaspoon sugar

## SAUCE MIXTURE (Mix in a bowl)

½ teaspoon sugar
4 tablespoons water
1 tablespoon black soy sauce
2 tablespoons rice wine or dry Sherry
1 teaspoon cornstarch

## DIRECTIONS FOR COOKING

1. Bring water to a boil. Add baking soda and melon. Simmer over medium-low heat for about 4 minutes (reduces the bitterness of the melon). Remove from pot and quickly rinse thoroughly in cold water. Drain in colander.
2. Heat wok over medium-high heat. Swirl in oil. When oil is hot, add garlic and scallions. Stir-fry until garlic turns golden. Put in pork mixture. Stir and cook until pork loses its pink color. Remove from wok with a drainer or a slotted spoon. Press to let oil drip back into wok. Put pork aside.
3. Keep wok hot over high heat. Swirl in sauce mixture. Cook and stir over medium-high heat until sauce bubbles gently. Add melon, then pork. Stir-fry for about 30 seconds to reheat. Put on a serving platter. Serve hot.


# POCKMARKED WOMAN'S SPICED TOFU
Makes 4 to 6 servings

I have not made up the name of this popular dish! It is said that the wife of a cook named Chan, who lived in Sichuan more than a century ago, created this tofu recipe. Mrs. Chan's face was pockmarked. So, the Chinese have always called this Pockmarked Woman's Spiced Tofu. This famous dish is hot, spicy, and extraordinarily smooth, and it makes one perspire. The emphasis is on the smoothness of the tofu. The key to success is to cook the tofu over low heat.

## PREPARATION OF INGREDIENTS

3 tablespoons oil
1 teaspoon finely minced fresh ginger
4 ounces ground pork

## SAUCE MIXTURE (Mix in a bowl)

½ teaspoon salt
½ teaspoon sugar
¼ teaspoon cayenne pepper
2 teaspoons ground bean sauce
1 tablespoon Sichuan chili bean sauce
1 tablespoon black soy sauce
1 tablespoon rice wine or dry Sherry

1 pound soft tofu: rinse in cold water, cut into ½-inch cubes
½ cup canned clear chicken broth
1 teaspoon cornstarch mixed with I teaspoon water
2 scallions: cut into pea-sized pieces, including some green part
¼ teaspoon flower peppercorn powder
1 teaspoon sesame oil

## DIRECTIONS FOR COOKING

1. Heat wok over high heat. Swirl in oil. When oil is hot, slightly brown ginger. Add pork and stir-fry until it is no longer red. Stir in sauce mixture. Cook and stir constantly for 10 seconds. Add tofu. Mix gently. Turn heat to low. Pour in broth, cover, and cook over low heat for 3 to 4 minutes. Stir in cornstarch water. Cook and stir constantly until sauce is thickened.
2. Add scallions, peppercorn powder, and sesame oil. Mix well. Put on a serving platter. Serve hot.

# HAKKA STUFFED TOFU
Makes about 6 servings

A small minority of people in the south of China are called Hakka, meaning "visiting family." They originated in the north and migrated to the south and southwest as early as the Q'in Dynasty, 221-207 BC They still speak a language which is closer to the Northern dialects than to those of the South. The women can be distinguished from the native women because they wear big broad hats with black ruffles hanging down around the rim, and they perform most of the manual labor in the fields. The men seem more inclined to domestic affairs. Hakka cooking is well-known for its tofu dishes. This stuffed tofu is one of the most popular and well-loved among the Chinese.

## PREPARATION OF INGREDIENTS

3 pieces firm tofu, each about 3 inches square: pat dry with paper towels, cut
    each square into 4 triangles, slice some tofu out of middle of one side each of
    triangle to make a pocket for stuffing.

STUFFING (Mix and blend in a bowl for about 1 minute)

¼ teaspoon sugar
¼ teaspoon salt
4 ounces ground pork
1 scallion: mince, including some green part
4 Chinese dried mushrooms: soak in hot water until spongy, discard stems, mince
1 tablespoon Chinese dried shrimp: soak in very hot water for about 20 minutes
    or until soft, peel off shells (if any), drain, mince
2 teaspoons thin soy sauce
1 teaspoon sesame oil

4 tablespoons oil
2 scallions: cut into 1½-inch strips, including some green part
4 Chinese dried mushrooms: soak in hot water until spongy, discard stems,
    cut caps into thin strips
4 ounces lean pork: cut into matchstick strips

SAUCE MIXTURE (Mix in a bowl)

¼ teaspoon sugar
½ teaspoon cornstarch
4 teaspoons thin soy sauce
2 teaspoons dry Sherry
½ cup canned clear chicken broth

Soy-Chili Dip (optional; see page 315)

DIRECTIONS FOR COOKING

1. Stuff tofu triangles with stuffing mixture.
2. Heat a skillet over medium heat. Swirl in 4 tablespoons oil. When oil is hot, arrange tofu triangles, meat side down, in skillet and pan-fry until meat sides are golden brown. Brown other sides. Remove from skillet.
3. Keep skillet hot. Slightly brown scallions, mushrooms, and pork strips. Pour in sauce mixture. Cook until sauce comes to a boil. Return tofu pieces to skillet and reheat them. Put on a serving platter and pour sauce over them. Serve hot with or without dip.

# STIR-FRIED TOFU WITH PORK SHREDS
Makes about 6 servings

## PREPARATION OF INGREDIENTS

6 tablespoons oil
1 pound firm tofu: slice ⅓-inch thick and size of pea pod
2 scallions: cut into 1½-inch lengths, including some green part
4 Chinese dried mushrooms: soak in hot water until spongy, discard stems,
    cut into thin strips
4 ounces lean pork: cut into matchstick pieces

## SAUCE MIXTURE (Mix in a bowl)

¼ teaspoon sugar
2 teaspoons black soy sauce
2 teaspoons thin soy sauce
2 teaspoons dry Sherry
½ cup canned clear chicken broth

1 teaspoon cornstarch mixed with 1 teaspoon water
¼ cup coarsely chopped fresh coriander (optional)

## DIRECTIONS FOR COOKING

1. Heat oil in wok to deep-fry temperature. Pan-fry tofu until both sides are golden. Remove from wok with a drainer to a bowl.
2. Remove all but 2 tablespoons oil from wok. Heat oil, add scallions, mushrooms and pork. Stir-fry over high heat until pork loses its pink color. Stir in sauce mixture. Stir and cook until sauce begins to bubble. Thicken sauce slightly with cornstarch water. Add coriander. Return tofu to wok. Stir-fry gently for about 15 seconds. Put on a serving platter. Serve hot.

# STIR-FRIED TOFU AND ASSORTED VEGETABLES IN OYSTER SAUCE

Makes about 8 servings

This nutritious, colorful dish can be served as a meatless meal.

## PREPARATION OF INGREDIENTS

3 tablespoons oil
1 teaspoon minced garlic
¼ cup diced scallions, including some green part
6 Chinese dried mushrooms: break off stems and discard, soak caps in hot water
    until spongy, squeeze off water, shred caps (save the mushroom–water)
10 pieces of baby corn (canned): cut each lengthwise
½ cup canned straw mushrooms: rinse in cold water, drain
4 ounces snow peas: pinch off tip ends
2 tablespoons dried cloud ears: soak in hot water until soft, drain
⅔ cup red bell peppers: cut into thin strips
2 pounds firm tofu: rinse in cold water, drain, cut into ⅓-inch slices

## SAUCE MIXTURE (Mix in a bowl)

½ teaspoon sugar
4 tablespoons oyster-flavored sauce
3 tablespoons black soy sauce
2 tablespoons rice wine or dry Sherry
½ cup mushroom water

2 teaspoons cornstarch mixed with ¼ cup mushroom–water.
1 tablespoon sesame oil

## DIRECTIONS FOR COOKING

Heat wok over high heat. Swirl in 3 tablespoons oil. When oil is hot, add garlic
and scallions. Cook until garlic browns slightly. Add shredded mushrooms, stir-
fry until they turn golden. Add baby corn, straw mushrooms, cloud ears, bell
pepper, snow peas, and tofu. Stir-fry them gently for about 30 seconds. Stir in
sauce mixture. Cover. Turn heat to medium-low and allow it to simmer for
about 7 minutes or until tofu is thoroughly heated. Stir in cornstarch-water; stir
gently, and cook until sauce is clear and thickened. Add sesame oil. Serve hot.

# STIR-FRIED TOFU AND MUSHROOMS WITH SPINACH IN OYSTER SAUCE
Makes 8 to 10 servings

This is a delicious and healthful dish for vegetarians and for those who like to eat less meat. Leftovers can be reheated in a microwave oven.

## PREPARATION OF INGREDIENTS

3 tablespoons oil
2 teaspoons minced fresh ginger
1 tablespoon minced garlic
4 scallions: cut into 1½ inch lengths, including some green part
8 Chinese dried mushrooms: break and discard stems, soak in hot water until spongy, cut caps into thin strips (save the mushroom-water)
4 ounces lean ground pork or beef (optional)
2 pounds firm tofu: rinse in cold water, cut into ⅓-inch thick slices, drain, pat dry

## SAUCE MIXTURE (Mix in a bowl)

½ teaspoon sugar
¼ teaspoon ground pepper
1 tablespoon rice wine or dry Sherry
3 tablespoons black soy sauce
¼ cup mushroom-water
¼ cup oyster-flavored sauce

2 teaspoons cornstarch mixed with ¼ cup mushroom-water

2 teaspoons sesame oil
2 bunches of fresh spinach (about 1 pound): break off roots and tough stems and discard, wash and drain

## DIRECTIONS FOR COOKING

1. Heat wok over high heat and swirl in 2 tablespoon oil. When oil is hot, add ginger and stir-fry for 10 seconds; drop in garlic and scallions and stir-fry until garlic is golden. Add mushrooms and stir-fry until golden brown. (If meat is used, add pork or beef; stir until meat is cooked.)

2. Add tofu and swirl in sauce mixture. Mix well. Turn heat to medium-low; cover and simmer until tofu is heated through and sauce is bubbling. Add corn-starch-water, stir and cook until sauce is clear and thickened. Add sesame oil. Turn off heat. Cover and keep hot.

3. Bring a pot of water to a rolling boil, add the remaining 1 tablespoon oil. Plunge in spinach. Allow spinach to stay in water for about 8 seconds. Pour into a colander immediately. Drain and put on a serving platter. Ladle tofu and mushrooms and sauce on spinach. Serve hot.

# MOO SHU TOFU WITH PORK OR CHICKEN

## PREPARATION OF INGREDIENTS

4 eggs
¼ teaspoon salt
5 tablespoons oil
1 teaspoon minced fresh ginger
2 teaspoons minced garlic
½ cup shredded scallions
8 Chinese mushrooms: break stems and discard, soak in hot water until spongy, cut caps into thin strips

## PORK OR CHICKEN MIXTURE (Mix in a bowl. Refrigerate before use)

8 ounces lean pork or boned, skinless chicken breast: cut into thin strips (to make a cup)
¼ teaspoon sugar
⅛ teaspoon ground pepper
2 teaspoons cornstarch
2 teaspoons black soy sauce
2 teaspoons dry Sherry
1 teaspoon sesame oil

8 ounces tofu noodles (also called bean curd strips)
8 ounces five-fragrance tofu: cut each cake into thin strips
1 cup shredded, canned bamboo shoots: rinse in cold water. Drain.
¼ cup cloud ears: soak in hot water until soft, rinse thoroughly, drain, pinch off hard parts, tear large pieces into halves. Set aside.

SAUCE MIXTURE (Mix in a bowl)

½ teaspoon salt
1 teaspoon sugar
3 tablespoons black soy sauce
2 tablespoons hoisin sauce
2 tablespoons dry Sherry
¼ cup water

1 teaspoon cornstarch mixed with 2 tablespoons water
2 teaspoons sesame oil

## DIRECTIONS FOR COOKING

1. Beat egg with salt until foamy. Heat wok until hot. Swirl in 2 tablespoons oil; add eggs and scramble. Do not overcook—eggs should be smooth and moist. Cut eggs into chunks, about the size of sugar cubes. Set aside.

2. Heat wok over high heat. When wok is hot, swirl in the remaining oil. Add ginger, garlic and scallions; stir-fry until garlic turns golden. Add mushrooms and stir-fry for about 20 seconds or until mushrooms become aromatic. Stir in pork or chicken mixture and stir-fry until pork or chicken is no longer pink. Add tofu noodles, five-fragrance tofu, bamboo shoots and cloud ears. Stir-fry until they are heated thoroughly. Stir in sauce mixture. Cook until sauce begins to bubble. Swirl in cornstarch water; stir until sauce is thickened. Add egg chunks and sesame oil. Toss to mix well. Serve hot with Mandarin Pancakes (see page 111) or with rice.

# STIR-FRIED FIVE-FRAGRANCE TOFU
# WITH CHICKEN SHREDS

Makes 6 to 8 servings

6 tablespoons oil
½ cup shredded scallions
1 teaspoon minced fresh ginger
2 teaspoons minced garlic
8 medium-sized Chinese dried mushrooms: break off and discard stems, soak
    caps in hot water until spongy, squeeze off excess water, cut into thin strips

CHICKEN MIXTURE (Mix in a bowl)

8 ounces boneless, skinless chicken breast: cut into thin strips (to make 1 cup)
¼ teaspoon sugar
¼ teaspoon ground pepper
2 teaspoons cornstarch
2 teaspoons black soy sauce
2 teaspoons dry Sherry
1 teaspoon sesame oil

8 ounces five-fragrance tofu: cut into thin strips
8 ounces tofu noodles (also called bean curd strips)
1 cup shredded bamboo shoots
1 cup shredded red bell peppers

SAUCE MIXTURE (Mix in a bowl)

¼ teaspoon five-fragrance powder
¼ teaspoon cayenne pepper
1 teaspoon sugar
1 tablespoon ground bean sauce
1 tablespoon Chinese red rice vinegar
1 tablespoon dry Sherry
2 tablespoons black soy sauce
½ cup canned, clear chicken broth

2 teaspoons cornstarch mixed with 3 tablespoons water
1 teaspoon sesame oil

*Vegetables and Tofu* • 229

1. Heat wok over high heat. Swirl in 2 tablespoons of the oil. When oil is hot, add scallions, ginger and garlic. Stir-fry until garlic turns golden; add mushrooms and stir-fry for about a minute or until they become aromatic. Transfer them to a plate.
2. Keep wok hot, swirl in the remaining 4 tablespoons of oil; add chicken mixture and stir-fry until chicken is no longer pink. Add five-fragrance tofu, tofu noodles, bamboo shoot strips, and shredded red peppers. Stir to mix well. Stir in sauce mixture and cook until sauce begins to bubble. Stir in the cornstarch-water, stirring until the sauce thickens and is clear. Stir in sesame oil. Put on a serving platter. Serve hot.

# SHRIMP AND TOFU IN SPICY SHA CHA SAUCE
Makes 6 to 8 servings

Sha cha sauce is a Chinese style of saté sauce, commonly labeled in English as Barbecue Sauce; made from chili peppers, oil, garlic, onions, dried shrimp, sesame and coconut. This spicy, fiery and aromatic sauce adds zest to insipid ingredients.

## PREPARATION OF INGREDIENTS

¼ cup oil
2 teaspoons minced fresh ginger
2 teaspoons minced garlic
4 scallions: cut into 1-inch pieces, including some green part

SHRIMP MIXTURE (Mix in a bowl. Refrigerate before use)

1 pound large shrimp: shell, devein, wash under running cold water, drain, pat dry
1 teaspoon cornstarch
½ teaspoon ground white pepper
¼ teaspoon baking soda
2 teaspoons dry Sherry
1 tablespoon sha cha sauce
1 egg white: beat until slightly foamy

## SAUCE MIXTURE (Mix in a bowl)

½ teaspoon cayenne pepper
2 teaspoons sugar
3 tablespoons black soy sauce
1 tablespoon dry Sherry
4 tablespoons sha cha sauce
½ cup water
2 pounds firm tofu: rinse in cold running water; cut into ⅓-inch thick slices, drain, pat dry

15-ounce can straw mushrooms: rinse and drain
1 cup snow peas: trim and blanch in water
½ cup red bell peppers, cut in thin strips
2 teaspoons cornstarch mixed with 2 tablespoons water
1 teaspoon sesame oil

## DIRECTIONS FOR COOKING

1. Heat wok over high heat. Swirl in oil. When it is hot, drop in ginger, garlic and scallions in that order. When garlic turns golden, add shrimp mixture and stir-fry until shrimp turns whitish. Remove shrimp with a drainer, let oil drain back into wok.
2. Keep wok hot; add sauce mixture and stir until it begins to bubble. Add tofu, straw mushrooms and mix well. Reduce heat to medium-low; cover and simmer until tofu is thoroughly heated (about 2 minutes). Add snow peas and bell peppers; stir and cook for about 10 seconds.
3. Turn heat to high. Return shrimp mixture to wok and gently mix with tofu. Stir in cornstarch water and cook until sauce is clear and thickened. Turn off heat; stir in sesame oil. Serve hot.

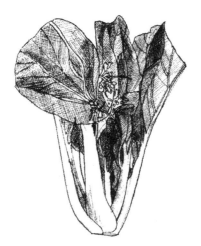

# Rice, Noodles, and Congee

# RICE

In southern China, rice is a must in our daily meals. Everything we eat without rice usually is considered a snack, not a real meal. I remember that when my uncle used to come home late from doing business, he always announced that he had not eaten for the whole day! A mutual understanding among the household was that he was far from starving, for he had eaten dumplings or noodles in the teahouses many times during the day. But he never considered that those were meals or that he had been eating at all. He was like many of the southern Chinese: a good healthy meal was plain rice, a bowl of soup, and a few dishes prepared at home.

There are many stories about rice. Here is one I remember. Thousands of years ago, before the Chinese had rice, their struggle for food was seen by the Goddess of Mercy, Kuan Yin. She reported this to the God of Heaven. Unfortunately, the All-Mighty was in a bad humor and refused to hear any bad news. But Kuan Yin could not bear to abandon the suffering. So she came down to earth seeking a way to help. Finding the fields full of rice plants, but without their ears filled, she squeezed her breasts and filled the ears of the rice plants with her milk. There were many ears of rice still to be filled. So she squeezed her breasts harder, so hard that blood mixed with milk flowed from her breasts and filled the rest of the rice plants. Therefore, in China we have not only white rice but also red rice.

Our ancestors were still starving, despite the Goddess's help and their hard work. They could feed themselves only one meal every 4 or 5 days. matter was brought to the attention of the God of Heaven. This time the All-Mighty was moved. He sent his heavenly Ox Star to tell our people that if they would work hard enough, they would be blessed with 1 meal every 3 days. The Ox Star was a good fellow, but not particularly bright, especially with numbers. On his way down to earth, he was confused—1 meal for every 3 days or 3 meals for every 1 day? He was not quite sure. The latter seemed right to him, and he told the people that they would eat three meals a day! The God of Heaven was furious because it was impossible for the people to provide three meals a day for themselves. Some help from the superpower was needed. Since it was the mistake of the Ox Star, he was sent to earth to help our people plow.

Leaving his heavenly home, the majestic-looking Ox Star became the water buffalo, and he has been working for our people ever since. His strength makes farming easier. A tireless and good-natured helper, he pulls the plow in the field as silently and patiently as the farmer. He never complains, never cries, for his mission is to help men.

China has always been a farming country. Most Chinese are farmers. Both of my grandfathers owned farms. As children, my younger brother and I tagged along with Ah Lin, my grandmother's maid, when she delivered lunch to the hired hands. We slogged through the muddy paddy fields; we trapped the tiny crabs, scared the frogs, and teased the water snakes with sticks. Our feared enemy was the water leech. We would shriek and cry when they fed on our legs. Ah Lin spat on the leeches to loosen their grip, and tore them away from our legs. Frightened by seeing our own blood, we bawled and cried some more, while the workers burst with laughter.

Before our tears were dried, the workers, bending down with their bare hands and feet, which fed the water leeches all day, resumed nursing the rice plants under the brutal sun.

As children, not wasting a single grain of rice was one of the very important lessons we learned. My grandmother used to threaten us: every grain of rice left in our bowls meant a pockmark on the face of our future mate. We giggled, but we shined our bowls; nobody dared to risk having a pockmarked mate!

Today, there are more varieties of rices that I can number. But the refined, long-grain, white variety remains the favorite in the Chinese kitchen; among them is a mildly fragrant new long grain from Thailand, known as jasmine rice. These white, long-grain rices are the basic, all-purpose rices in the Asian community. They are their staple, cooked without salt or seasonings.

The short- and medium-grain variety are considered to be lower grade, not suitable to grace the table. However, the plump, medium-grain, slightly glutinous sushi rice from Japan and Korea is gaining popularity among the Chinese for its robust and rich flavor.

The pearly white, glutinous rice, also called sweet rice, is used mainly in pastry and sweets or for stuffing. Recently, a brown, glutinous rice from Korea came to the Chinese markets. Its sticky and also delicately crunchy texture delights the palate as well as adding color and texture to certain dishes.

Brown rice and the new, exotic colored rices in red or black have not yet been accepted into the Chinese culinary mainstream, even though they are received with enthusiasm in the American kitchen. The colored rices are used mostly for making wine or as animal feeds.

Rice cooked with salt or butter is foreign to the Chinese. We like to eat it plain to enjoy its natural sweetness.

# PLAIN RICE
Makes about 6 cups of rice

## PREPARATION OF INGREDIENTS

2 cups long-grain rice: wash and rinse in cold water until water is not cloudy,
    drain
3 cups cold water

## DIRECTIONS FOR COOKING

1. Use a 3-quart pot with a tight lid. Put in the washed rice and add the water. Cook over medium heat without a cover. When it is boiling, you will see that the water is very foamy, almost obscuring the rice. Do not go away! Stand by and watch it closely. You will see the water evaporating to the point where many small holes (like craters) appear in the rice. The Chinese call them rice eyes.
2. Put lid on, turn heat to very low, and cook for 10 minutes. Then turn off heat, but do not remove the pot or uncover it. Let it stay covered for 15 minutes or more. (Do not peek during this 25 minutes! Otherwise the magic steam will escape; you will have half-cooked rice for not having faith!)
3. Remove the cover. Loosen the rice with a fork or chopsticks. Serve hot.


# RICE CRUST
## (FOR SIZZLING RICE SOUP)
Makes about 2 cups of crusts

You can also buy rice crust in Chinese grocery stores. It keeps for months without refrigeration.

## PREPARATION OF INGREDIENTS

4 cups long-grain rice: wash and rinse in cold water until water is not cloudy,
    drain
4 cups cold water

## DIRECTIONS FOR COOKING

1. Choose a heavy wide-bottomed pot with a tight lid; the best is a Dutch oven. Put in rice, add water, and cook over medium heat, watching closely until the appearance of "rice eyes," the small, crater-like holes that develop as water evaporates.

2. Put lid on, turn heat to medium, and cook for 10 minutes. Then turn heat to low and cook for 15 minutes. (Do not peek during these 25 minutes. You may hear a little cracking noise from the rice, or smell the aroma of the crust.) Turn heat off.

3. Loosen rice gently and remove it from pot, leaving the crust. Using a small spatula, work carefully under the crust, and try to remove it in big pieces. Leave them on a tray to dry overnight. Put crusts in plastic bag and keep refrigerated. Or they can be frozen indefinitely. Thaw before use.

# YANGCHOW FRIED RICE
Makes 6 to 8 servings

## PREPARATION OF INGREDIENTS

4 tablespoons oil for frying

EGG MIXTURE (Beat together until slightly foamy)

4 eggs
¼ teaspoon salt

⅓ cup chopped scallions, in pea-sized pieces, including some green part
8 Chinese dried mushrooms: soak in hot water until spongy, discard stems,
    cut caps into ¼-inch squares
6 ounces Smithfield ham or barbecued pork: cut into ½-inch cubes

SHRIMP MIXTURE (Mix in a bowl. Refrigerate before use)

4 ounces fresh shrimp: shell, devein, rinse in running cold water, pat dry,
    cut into peanut-sized pieces
½ teaspoon cornstarch
½ teaspoon dry Sherry

⅓ cup fresh or frozen green peas

SAUCE MIXTURE (Mix in a bowl)

¼ teaspoon salt
½ teaspoon sugar
⅛ teaspoon white pepper
2 tablespoons thin soy sauce
2 teaspoons black soy sauce

4 cups cooked rice
2 teaspoons sesame oil

DIRECTIONS FOR COOKING

1. Heat wok over high heat. Swirl in 2 tablespoons oil for. When oil is hot, pour half the egg mixture into wok and swirl it around, spreading it into a thin pancake. Turn pancake when it is set. Remove from pan before it is golden brown. Cook remaining egg mixture in the same manner. Cut pancakes into ⅓-inch squares. Set aside.
2. Heat wok over high heat. Add remaining 2 tablespoons oil. When oil is hot, add scallions, mushrooms, and ham or pork. Stir-fry for about 30 seconds. Add shrimp mixture. Stir-fry until shrimp turns whitish (less than 20 seconds). Add peas. Stir in sauce mixture. Mix well. Break up lumps in cooked rice, and add it along with egg squares. Stir-fry for 3 to 5 minutes or until rice is thoroughly hot. Swirl in sesame oil . Mix well. Put on a serving platter. Serve hot.

# LOTUS LEAF RICE
Serves 4 to 6 as a meal

The lotus is a sacred flower of the Orient. It resembles the water lily but does not belong to the same family: the lotus grows in muddy ponds but unlike the water lily, which floats on water, the lotus stands many feet above the water. Therefore, in China, the lotus symbolizes purity, for it grows in mud without being soiled.

Once it was granted me to visit 2 ponds of ethereal lotus in an old temple in Macao. The monks guarded them as if they were crown jewels, keeping them behind two locked iron gates and high spiked walls. There, in the man-made concrete ponds, high and majestic they stood, regal on their towering long stems. Some blossoms seemed as large as goddess heads, with luminous wide petals and tinted pink tips. Such an enthralling sight was like watching dawn on a mountain thousands of feet high. It is an awesome beauty.

In parts of the Orient, lotus ponds among rice fields are a common scene. Every part of the lotus is usable: the seeds and roots are eaten as fruit or as vegetable, the gently fragrant leaves are used to wrap and give flavor to food, and the flowers grace altar tables in homes and in temples.

In the summer, when the lotus was in glorious bloom, people would go to the teahouses and restaurants that had lotus ponds. When the weather was good, tables and seats were clustered abut the flower ponds. If the seeds and roots were young, they appeared on the menu. One would munch on the juicy marble-sized seeds and nibble slices of gently sweet crisp roots, while revering the splendid, sacred lotus.

The high point of the meal was the summer specialty, rice with assorted meats wrapped in fresh lotus leaves tied with straw. Bearing the streaming hot lotus package, the waiter also brought a pair of scissors. Then eyes and breath were seized by the scissors snipping a circle at the top of the leaves. When the circle was lifted, unveiling the fragrant treasures hidden within, spoons and chopsticks dived into the festive rice. Amid scented air, wriggling babies, unsettling children, soft and loud conversations, and bustling waiters, our hearts lightened, and troubles glided away with the summer clouds.

Before the summer ended, farmers would gather the lotus leaves and dry them under the sun, so that teahouses, restaurants and housewives could have rice in lotus leaves in other seasons. The delicately smoky dried leaves do not flavor the rice as much as fresh ones, but they never fail to bring the festive summer to a Chinese heart.

## PREPARATION OF INGREDIENTS

1 pound white, glutinous rice or sushi rice: soak in plenty of cold water for
    5 hours or until it is plump
4 tablespoons lard or oil

CHICKEN MIXTURE (Mix in a bowl. Refrigerate until use)

1 cup, boned skinned chicken in ½-inch cubes
½ egg white
¼ teaspoon salt
¼ teaspoon sugar
¼ teaspoon ground white pepper
1 teaspoon cornstarch
2 teaspoons sesame oil

10 Chinese dried mushrooms: soak in hot water until spongy, discard stems,
    cut caps into ½-inch squares
¾ cup lean pork cut in peanut-sized pieces

SHRIMP MIXTURE (Mix in a bowl. Keep refrigerated until use)

½ pound fresh shrimp: shell, devein, rinse in cold water, pat dry, cut in
    peanut-sized pieces
½ egg white, beaten
2 teaspoons cornstarch
½ teaspoon salt
1 teaspoon dry Sherry

SAUCE MIXTURE (Mix in a bowl)

½ teaspoon salt
¼ teaspoon sugar
1 tablespoon mushroom soy or black soy sauce
2 tablespoons oyster-flavored sauce
1 tablespoon sesame oil

2 large fresh or dried lotus leaves (or 24 dried bamboo leaves if lotus leaves are
    not available): soak dried lotus or bamboo leaves in warm water until soft;
    pat dry

## DIRECTIONS FOR COOKING

1. Steam soaked rice for 15 minutes or until done (see page 237).
2. Heat wok over high heat. Add 3 tablespoons lard or oil. When it is hot, add chicken mixture. Stir-fry about half a minute, until chicken is almost done. Remove from wok.
3. Turn heat to high. Add the remaining tablespoon of lard or oil to wok; drop in mushrooms; stir and cook for several seconds. Add pork; stir-fry until it is no longer pink. Add shrimp mixture; stir and cook until shrimp turns whitish and is almost cooked. Stir in sauce mixture. Return chicken to wok. Mix well, then turn off heat.
4. Remove half the meat and shrimp mixture from wok to a bowl and leave the other half in wok. Add cooked rice to wok and mix well with the meat and shrimp mixture.
5. Spread out one lotus leaf. Transfer the rice mixture to leaf, and top with the other half of meat and shrimp mixture. Put the other leaf on top. Wrap as you would wrap a round package. Tie it with straw or string. You may refrigerate the package until steaming. (If bamboo leaves are used, arrange leaves overlapping on a piece of heavy foil about 18 inches square. Transfer rice mixture to the center, then top with remaining meat and shrimp mixture. Place more leaves on top. Gather and fold the corners of the foil together to cover any opening.)
6. Steam the package over high heat for 30 minutes. Using scissors, cut the leaf from top at the table. Serve hot. (Do not eat the leaves, please!)

NOTE: You may divide the rice mixture into six equal portions. Wrap each portion in a lotus leaf, tie with string, and steam for about 15 minutes. Cut strings before serving. But let your family and guests have the pleasure, of opening them.

# CHINESE NOODLES

The Chinese eat not only rice, but also noodles, with as much passion as the Italians have for their pasta. Rice is not the national staple of all of China, but only the South, the primary staple in the North being noodles. In the North, rice is served only on occasion. Noodles of great variety cooked in numberless ways, along with bread, compose most of the daily meals. Often breakfast is a bowl of piping hot noodles, a virtual necessity for warmth, since Chinese houses are not equipped with central heat. In the South, noodles are the secondary staple, commonly favored as lunch, afternoon or late evening snacks. And throughout China, great long noodles are eaten at the end of a birthday dinner to symbolize longevity.

Noodles are especially popular in China because they make a good one-dish meal. A housewife can save time preparing a large noodle dish, combining vegetables with meat or seafood to feed her entire family without cooking a few dishes plus rice. Also, noodle dishes use less meat and are, therefore, less expensive. By adding more noodles, vegetables, and sauce, you can stretch a meal to feed as many as you wish.

# HOW TO COOK NOODLES

Fresh, thin noodles are cooked in seconds. Please believe it. The sizes of noodles and kinds vary, and no teacher can tell you exactly how many seconds of cooking they need to be perfectly done. So the word "about" is going to be used frequently. But, in general, it is preferable to undercook them rather than overcook them—in most recipes they are recooked with meat and other ingredients.

The noodles in these recipes are based on fresh noodles. And please do not substitute domestic, dried noodles or spaghetti lest the dish lose its authenticity.

Before cooking noodles, be sure you have a large colander or a large Chinese drainer. If not, you surely need one.

# PLAIN NOODLES
## (COLD OR HOT)

2 teaspoons salt
4 quarts water, in a large pot
8 ounces fresh noodles
½ cup cold water
2 tablespoons oil

## DIRECTIONS FOR COOKING

1. Place colander in sink under faucet.
2. Add salt to 4 quarts of water and bring to a rapid boil over medium heat. Add noodles. Stir to separate immediately. Allow noodles to stay in water for about 15 seconds. Pour in ½ cup cold water.
3. For cold noodles: Quickly pour noodles into colander and immediately run cold tap water over them thoroughly, tossing them with chopsticks or a fork to prevent further cooking. When noodles are no longer warm to touch, shake them in the colander for several seconds. Add oil. Toss to coat them evenly . The oil is to keep them from sticking to each other. Spread on a plate. These cold noodles are ready to be used in the required recipes.
4. For hot noodles: Quickly pour noodles into colander. Shake to drain off water. Add oil, tossing to coat noodles evenly. Since the noodles are still cooking by their own heat, it is better to use them as soon as possible or cook them just before you need them.

# SUMMER COLD SPICED NOODLES, SICHUAN STYLE
Serve 12 to 15 as an appetizer, 6 as a meal

This large platter of spicy noodles topped with succulent shrimp, lean pork strips, crispy celery, scallions, and other ingredients is an excellent summer dish or peppy appetizer for all seasons. Also, it can be prepared hours in advance.

## PREPARATION OF INGREDIENTS

1 pound fresh noodles: cook as in Plain Cold Noodles (see page 244)
2 slices fresh ginger root, the size of a quarter
4 cups water
2 tablespoons dry Sherry or rice wine
1 pound shrimp in shells

12 ounces lean pork or boned, skinned chicken breasts: steam for 15 minutes, cool, cut into thin strips
½ cups celery in thin strips 1¼-inches long
½ cup red bell pepper in thin strips
1 cup shredded scallions in 1½-inch lengths including some green part
¼ pound jellyfish skin (optional): rinse off salt, soak in plenty of cold water for at least 4 hours, immerse in a pot of boiling water, and rinse in cold water at once; cut into thin strips (can be kept in refrigerator a day or more)
2 ounces Sichuan mustard pickles (optional): rinse, mince, soak in a large bowl of cold water for about 15 minutes, squeeze off water

## SAUCE MIXTURE (Mix in a bowl)

1 tablespoon minced fresh ginger
1 tablespoon minced garlic
4 teaspoons sugar
½ teaspoon flower peppercorn powder
6 tablespoons back soy sauce
3 tablespoons Chinese vinegar or red rice vinegar
3 tablespoons sesame oil
½ teaspoon cayenne pepper or to taste

## DIRECTIONS FOR COOKING

1. Spread cooked, cold noodles on a large platter. Cover and put aside.
2. Add ginger to 4 cups water and bring to a rapid boil. Add wine, immediately drop in the shrimp, and count 35 seconds. Turn off heat. Quickly remove shrimp with a drainer and cool in refrigerator. Peel off shells and devein.
3. Arrange shrimp, shredded cooked pork or chicken, celery, pepper, scallions, and jellyfish skin shreds (they may be grouped or mixed together) on noodles; sprinkle Sichuan mustard pickles on top; add the sauce mixture just before serving. Serve cold or at room temperature.


# COLD SPICY NOODLES WITH PEANUT SAUCE
Makes 4 to 6 servings

## PREPARATION OF INGREDIENTS

½ pound fresh noodles: cook as in Plain Cold Noodles (see page 244 )
12 ounces fresh bean sprouts: blanch in water (see Cooking Techniques, page 17), drain in colander
3 scallions: cut into 1½ -inch lengths, including some green part, shred into thin strips

## SAUCE MIXTURE (Mix into a smooth sauce. Cover before use)

½ teaspoons cayenne pepper
1½ teaspoons sugar
3 tablespoons smooth peanut butter
3 tablespoons black soy sauce
1½ tablespoons Chinese red vinegar
1½ tablespoons sesame oil

## DIRECTIONS FOR COOKING

1. Toss cooked noodles and blanched bean sprouts together to mix well. Put on a serving platter and top with scallions.
2. Pour sauce mixture evenly over noodles. Toss before serving. Serve at room temperature.

# SESAME CHICKEN NOODLES, BEIJING FLAVOR

Serves 6 as a meal

T his colorful dish can be doubled or tripled and prepared in advance. It delights the palate and pleases the eyes. It makes an elegant meal for large gatherings,

## PREPARATION OF INGREDIENTS

8 to 10 ounces fresh noodles: cook as in Plain Cold Noodles (see page 244)
1 cup Chinese cabbage, cut crosswise in thin strips
6 bay leaves
4 quarts water
3 chicken breasts (about 3 pounds): cut each in half
¼ cup red bell pepper in pea-sized pieces
¼ cup snipped parsley
¼ cup sesame seeds: stir and roast in an ungreased small pot over low hear until
    golden brown, cool before use
1 tablespoon sesame oil
3 tablespoons corn oil

## SEASONINGS (Put in a bowl)

¼ teaspoon flower peppercorn powder
¼ teaspoon cayenne pepper
2 dried chili peppers: tear into small pieces (use seeds also)
2 teaspoons minced garlic
1 tablespoon minced fresh ginger
¼ cup scallions in pea-sized pieces, including some green part

## SAUCE MIXTURE (Mix in a blender or food processor or by hand)

2 tablespoons sugar
6 tablespoons black soy sauce
4 teaspoons Chinese red vinegar
2 teaspoons peanut butter

1. Spread cooked cold noodles on a large serving platter and sprinkle them with the cabbage. Cover with plastic wrap and set aside.
2. Put bay leaves and water in a large pot and bring to a rapid boil. Add chicken breasts. When water returns to a boil again, put lid on. Turn off heat; allow chicken breasts to poach in water for 20 minutes. Remove chicken breasts, drain, and cool in refrigerator.
3. Bone chicken breasts, and trim off excess skin (the Chinese love chicken skin, but if you dislike it, discard it). Cut chicken breasts crosswise into ½-inch strips and arrange them neatly on the cabbage and the noodles, then sprinkle them evenly with red bell pepper, parsley, and roasted sesame seeds.
4. Heat sesame oil and corn oil in a small pot over medium heat. When oil is hot, drop in the seasonings, and brown them slightly. Stir in sauce mixture, and cook, stirring, until it begins to foam. Remove from heat. Pour sauce over chicken evenly just before serving. (You may cook the seasoned sauce in advance and keep in a covered jar until use.) Serve at room temperature.

# TWO FACES YELLOW NOODLES, SHANGHAI STYLE
Serves 4 as a meal

Besides serving noodles soft or in soup, the Shanghainese pan-fry noodles the same way the Cantonese do: until the noodles are crisp outside but still soft inside. The Shanghainese call the noodles "Two Faces Yellow" because of their golden color on both sides. Like all noodle dishes, this one is good for a snack or lunch and also wonderful to serve as dinner.

## PREPARATION OF INGREDIENTS

1 cup oil for frying
½ pound fresh egg noodles: cook as in Plain Cold Noodles (see page 244)
2 teaspoons minced, fresh ginger
2 teaspoons minced garlic
½ cup scallions shredded in 1½-inch lengths, including some green part
⅓ cup Chinese dried mushroom: soak in hot water until spongy, discard stems, shred caps
2 cups shredded Chinese cabbage

SAUCE MIXTURE (Mix in a bowl)

¼ teaspoon salt
¼ teaspoon sugar
⅛ teaspoon ground white pepper
2 tablespoons black soy sauce
2 tablespoons dry Sherry
2 teaspoons sesame oil

1 cup canned clear chicken broth mixed with 4 teaspoons cornstarch

CHICKEN MIXTURE (put ingredients directly on chicken, mix, blanch chicken
mixture in water: (see Cooking Techniques, page 17)

1½ pounds boned. skinned chicken breasts: cut into matchstick strips
    (to make 1 cup)
⅛ teaspoon salt
2 teaspoons cornstarch
½ teaspoon black soy sauce
about ½ egg white

Soy-Sesame Dip (see page 315) and a small dish of Chinese chili sauce or
Tabasco sauce

DIRECTIONS FOR COOKING

1. Heat wok over high heat. Swirl in 1 cup oil. When oil is hot but not smoking,
spread noodles evenly on bottom of wok. Pan-fry noodles over medium heat
until golden brown on bottom. Turn noodles, and pan-fry until the other side is
also golden brown. Remove from wok to an ovenproof plate or tray. Place in a
300-degree oven to keep them hot and crisp.
2. Remove all but 3 tablespoons oil from wok. Heat oil over high heat, and add
ginger, garlic, scallions, and mushrooms. Stir-fry until garlic turns golden. Add
cabbage. Stir-fry for about 15 seconds. Stir and swirl in sauce mixture. When
sauce begins to bubble gently, stir in the broth with cornstarch. Stir and cook
constantly until sauce is slightly thickened. Add blanched chicken and cook
briskly to reheat.
3. Put noodles on a large serving platter and top with the chicken and cabbage
mixture. Serve hot with dip and chili sauce.

# SICHUAN SPICED BEEF STEW
# WITH VEGETABLE ON NOODLES
Serves 6 as a meal

The distant clapping of bamboo sticks and the jingling of bells woke the silence of the dawn. The sounds heralded the food vendors. Our breakfast was near.

Like most of the families in China, we often bought our breakfast on the streets. Besides offering great variety, the vendors had their specialties and secret recipes on which their livelihoods depended.

The Noodle Man clapped his bamboo sticks six times every time he paused to rest. The sound of bells signaled the Congee Woman, whose young son trotted beside her with a bell. The melancholy cry belonged to Bun Woman Wong: at night her husband hawked cakes and sweet almond soup.

Many a time, when we children feared a test, we pretended to be sick, but the approaching breakfast never failed to lift us out of our beds. As we gabbed about what we were going to eat, my grandmother's maid loosed her high call at the still silent street. "Buying!," a matinal command she thoroughly enjoyed. Swinging and springing in bouncy strides, the vendors raced to her call. Suspended from the ends of their thick shoulder poles were pots of steaming hot food on flaming stoves, plus sauces, ingredients, and even water for washing bowls.

We would choose from bowls of rice congee with chopped meats; noodles in tasty soup with slices of pork and beef; crispy fried crullers and meaty hot buns. From their portable kitchens they prepared our food, then quietly and proudly presented it to our table. While we savored every bite from our bowls, they patiently waited outside in the morning mist. Having rinsed and dried the bowls, we returned them, and the vendors moved on to other doors. Always they padded through streets and lanes, while we students in school studied how things ought to be.

Much has happened on the streets as the generations have progressed. Weddings and births have mended the sorrow of deaths. Old faces have vanished and new voices arise. But the sounds announcing the vendors continue to parade by. The call "Buying!," echoes in the streets much the same as it did in the past.

## PREPARATION OF INGREDIENTS

6 tablespoons oil
1 tablespoon minced fresh ginger
1 tablespoon minced garlic
½ cup chopped scallions, including some green

## BEEF MIXTURE (Mix in a bowl)

2 pounds stew beef chunks(use, beef with a little fat):cut chunks into ¼-inch-
    thick pieces
5 teaspoons Sichuan chili bean sauce
2½ tablespoons Sichuan sweet bean sauce or ground bean sauce

## SAUCE MIXTURE (Mix in a bowl)

2 teaspoons sugar
4 whole star anise
4 tablespoons black soy sauce
½ teaspoon flower peppercorn powder

3 cups water
8 to 10 ounces fresh noodles: cook as Hot Plain Noodles (see page 244)
½ pound fresh broccoli: blanch in water (see page 17)

## DIRECTIONS FOR COOKING

1. Heat oil in a 4–6quart pot. Add ginger, garlic, and half the scallions, and cook
for a few seconds. Add beef mixture, and cook until beef loses its redness. Stir in
the sauce mixture and mix well. Add 2 cups water; cover and simmer for 1 hour.
Add the remaining water and cook over low heat until beef is tender—about 1
hour. There should be 1½ cups sauce left in the pot when beef is done. Beef can
be cooked a day or two in advance; reheat on stove over low heat.
2. Put hot noodles and blanched vegetable on a large platter and top with beef
mixture and the remaining scallions. Serve hot.

# EGGPLANT WITH MEAT AND
# HOISIN SAUCE ON NOODLES

Serves

## PREPARATION OF INGREDIENTS

1 pound Chinese eggplant: slice each eggplant thinly crosswise ⅔ of the way
    through at an angle (you may use regular eggplants, quarter each length
    wise, then thinly slice the skins sides crosswise ⅔ of the way through
3 tablespoons oil
½ cup diced scallions, including some green part
1 teaspoon minced fresh ginger
2 teaspoons minced garlic
8 ounces lean pork or beef: ground coarsely in food processor
¼ cup cloud ears: soak in hot water until soft, rinse, drain, discard tough parts
⅓ cup coarsely chopped water chestnuts

## SAUCE MIXTURE ( Mix in a bowl)

½ teaspoon five-fragrance powder
¼ teaspoon cayenne pepper
2 tablespoons dry Sherry
2 tablespoons ground bean sauce
2 tablespoons black soy sauce
4 tablespoons hoisin sauce
1 cup canned clear chicken broth

2 teaspoons cornstarch, mixed with 2 tablespoons water
1 pound fresh noodles
1 tablespoon sesame oil
½ cup walnuts: deep-fry until golden brown, cool on paper towel, crush coarsely
    with a rolling pin

## DIRECTIONS FOR COOKING

1. Steam eggplants for 20 minutes or until they are soft and tender. Keep hot.
2. Heat wok over high heat. When wok is hot, swirl in 3 tablespoons oil. When
oil is hot, drop in scallions and stir-fry for about 10 seconds; add garlic and stir-
fry until it turns golden. Add ground pork or beef and stir-fry until it is cooked

thoroughly. Add cloud ears and water chestnut and mix well. Swirl in sauce mixture; stir and cook over medium heat until sauce begins to bubble. Stir in cornstarch water and stir to cook for about 10 seconds. Turn heat to very low. Cover and keep hot.

3. Cook noodles as directed in Hot Plain Noodles (see page 244). Transfer cooked, hot noodles to a serving platter and cover with the steamed eggplant. Ladle meat sauce over eggplant and noodles. Dribble sesame oil evenly on noodles. Top with walnuts. Serve hot.

# NOODLES IN MEAT SAUCE, BEIJING STYLE
Serves 4 as a meal

## PREPARATION OF INGREDIENTS

3 tablespoons oil
2 teaspoons minced garlic
½ cup chopped scallions, including some green part
1 pound pork or beef: grind coarsely in a meat grinder or food processor

## SAUCE MIXTURE (Mix in a bowl)

4 tablespoons Sichuan sweet bean sauce or ground bean sauce
1 teaspoon sugar
2 tablespoons rice wine or dry Sherry

½ cup canned clear chicken broth
1 tablespoon sesame oil
4 quarts water
2 teaspoon salt
10 to 12 ounces fresh noodles

## DIRECTIONS FOR COOKING

1. Heat wok over high heat. Swirl in oil. When oil is hot, drop in garlic and half the scallions. When garlic turns golden, add ground pork or beef. Stir-fry until pork or beef loses its pink. Stir in sauce mixture, stir and cook for about 2 minutes. Add the broth. Mix well. Simmer over low heat for about 7 minutes, stirring constantly. Add sesame oil and mix well. Cover to keep hot or reheat just before serving.

2. Bring 4 quarts of water to rapid boil. Add the salt and then the noodles. Stir immediately: they are done in less than 30 seconds, before the water returns to a boil. It is better to undercook than to overcook them.

3. Quickly pour noodles into a colander. Shake the colander to drain off the water. Add 1 tablespoon oil to toss and coat noodles evenly. Put on a serving platter and top with the meat sauce and the remaining scallions. Serve hot at once.

# VELVET CHICKEN LO MEIN
Makes 4 to 6 servings

In Cantonese, "lo" means "toss," mein means "noodles."

## PREPARATION OF INGREDIENTS

3 tablespoons oil
2 teaspoons finely minced fresh ginger
1 tablespoon minced garlic
6 Chinese dried mushrooms: soak in hot water until spongy, discard stems,
    shred caps

2 cups fresh Chinese cabbage, shredded

CHICKEN MIXTURE (Mix in a bowl. Blanch in water (see Cooking Techniques, page 17)

1½ boned, skinless chicken breasts: cut into match stick strips (to make 1 cup)
⅛ teaspoon salt
1 tablespoon cornstarch
½ teaspoon thin soy sauce
about ½ egg white

SAUCE MIXTURE (Mix in a bowl)

½ teaspoon sugar
¼ teaspoon salt
1 tablespoon thin soy sauce
1 tablespoon black soy sauce
2 tablespoons oyster-flavored sauce
2 teaspoons sesame oil
¼ cup water

½ pound fresh noodles: just before use, cook as in Plain Noodles (see page 244)
4 scallions: cut into 1½-inch lengths, including some green part
Soy-Chili Dip (optional; see page 315 )

DIRECTIONS FOR COOKING

Heat wok over high heat, then swirl in oil. When oil is hot, drop in ginger, garlic, and mushrooms. Stir-fry until garlic turns golden. Add the Chinese cabbage and cook until soft; add blanched chicken. Mix well. Swirl in sauce mixture. Stir-fry for about 30 seconds. Add noodles and scallions. Turn heat to medium. Stir and toss for about 2 minutes. Put on a serving platter. Serve hot with or without dip.


# BEEF WITH SAH HO RICE NOODLES OR FEN
Serves 3 to 4 as a meal

Sah Ho is a small area in Kwangchow, China, where these noodles originated. These fresh soft, white, wide noodles are made with rice powder daily by noodle shops in marketplaces and in Chinatown. They are also known as fun. Few Chinese families make their own because of the equipment involved. The noodles come in a large, round sheet and are already thoroughly cooked. Each sheet weighs about a pound, and usually comes uncut and folded for easy handling. Cut it into 12-inch-wide strips before using it. They are also known as fen.

These noodles are very white, smooth, and flimsy; unusual by Western standards, but absolutely delicious.

## PREPARATION OF INGREDIENTS

1 cup oil for blanching

BEEF MIXTURE (Combine and refrigerate until use)

12 ounces flank steak: cut against the grain into pieces ⅛-inch thick and
    2 inches long
1 teaspoon brown sugar
1 tablespoon cornstarch
1 tablespoon black soy sauce
2 teaspoons dry Sherry
2 teaspoons sesame oil

1 teaspoon minced fresh ginger
1 teaspoon minced garlic
¼ cup scallions in 1½-inch lengths, including some green part
⅓ cup green or red bell pepper strips

SAUCE MIXTURE

¼ teaspoon salt
¼ teaspoon sugar
2 tablespoons black soy sauce

1 pound sha ho rice noodles (fen), in ½-wide strips
2 cups fresh bean sprouts
Soy-Sesame Dip (see Page 315) and a small dish of Chinese chili sauce or
    Tabasco sauce

1. Heat wok over high heat. Swirl in oil. When oil is hot (but not smoking), add
beef mixture. Stir quickly to separate pieces, and blanch briskly, until meat just
loses its redness. Remove beef from wok with a Chinese drainer or a large slotted spoon, and put in a bowl.
2. Remove all but 3 tablespoons oil from wok. Heat oil over medium heat, and
add ginger, garlic, scallions, and pepper. Stir-fry for about 10 seconds. Swirl in
sauce mixture and stir quickly for a few seconds; return beef (with juice) to wok
and mix briskly. Add rice noodles; stir and toss gently until noodles are evenly
coated with sauce. Drop in the bean sprouts. Stir and toss constantly until noodles
are hot. Put on a platter. Serve hot with dip and sauce.

# SAH HO RICE NOODLES WITH
# PORK SHREDS AND BEAN SPROUTS
Serves 3 as a meal

## PREPARATION OF INGREDIENTS

5 tablespoons oil
6 scallions: cut into 1½-inch lengths, including some green part
6 Chinese dried mushrooms: soak in hot water until spongy, discard stems,
     shred caps
12 ounces lean pork: cut into matchstick strips
½ pound fresh bean sprouts: wash and drain

## SAUCE MIXTURE (mix in a bowl)

¾ teaspoon salt
¼ teaspoon sugar
4 teaspoons black soy sauce
1 teaspoon thin soy sauce
2 teaspoons dry Sherry

1 pound Sah Ho rice noodles (fen), in ½-inch-wide strips

## DIRECTIONS FOR COOKING

Heat wok over high heat. Swirl in oil. When oil is hot, drop in half the scallions
and add the mushrooms; stir-fry for about 30 seconds. Add pork strips and cook
until they are no longer pink. Add bean sprouts, then stir in sauce mixture. Stir
and cook for about 20 seconds. Add the rice noodles. Stir-fry gently over medium heat until the noodles are just heated through. Add remaining scallions. Put
on a serving platter. Serve hot.

# SILK THREADS FROM HEAVEN
## (STIR-FRIED SHREDDED PORK WITH VEGETABLES
## ON CRISP BEAN THREAD NOODLES)
Makes 6 to 8 servings

PREPARATION OF INGREDIENTS

oil for deep frying

2 ounces bean thread noodles
2 eggs with ⅛ teaspoon salt: beat well to mix yolk and white
1 teaspoon minced garlic
½ cup shredded scallions, including some green part

PORK MIXTURE (Put ingredients directly on pork and mix in a bowl)

1 pound lean pork: cut into matchstick strips (to make 2 cups)
⅛ teaspoon salt
½ teaspoon sugar
¼ teaspoon white pepper
2 teaspoons cornstarch
1 teaspoon sesame oil
2 teaspoons thin soy sauce

VEGETABLES (Put on a plate)

½ cup Chinese dried mushroom: soak in hot water until spongy, discard stems,
    shred caps
½ cup shredded, salted mustard greens: soak in 2 cups cold water for 10 minutes,
    squeeze off water
2 cups shredded celery in 1½-inch matchstick strips
1 cup shredded bamboo shoots, in 1½-inch matchstick strips
¼ cup shredded red bell pepper, in matchstick strips

## SAUCE MIXTURE (Mix in a bowl)

¼ teaspoon salt
2 teaspoons cornstarch
2 tablespoons black soy sauce
1 tablespoon dry Sherry
½ teaspoon sugar
1 tablespoon sesame oil
¼ cup canned clear chicken broth

## DIRECTIONS FOR COOKING

1. Heat oil in wok to deep-fry temperature (375 degrees). Pull and separate noodles into two portions. Then again pull to loosen each portion. Test oil by dropping in a piece of noodle; if it pops up instantly, the oil is right. Immerse noodles in oil, the noodles immediately turn into a white nest. Turn nest over and fry the other side. (This procedure takes only a few seconds.) Drain on paper towels. The noodles can be fried hours in advance; cool and put in a plastic bag.

2. Remove oil from wok except about 2 tablespoons. Turn heat to medium. When oil is hot, pour in eggs. Slowly swirl the eggs by turning the wok clockwise to form a large pancake. Turn pancake over when it is no longer runny. When it is set, transfer to a cutting board. Cut pancake in thin strips. Put aside.

3. Heat wok over high heat. Swirl in 4 tablespoons oil. When oil is hot, drop in garlic and half the scallions. As soon as garlic turns light gold, add pork mixture. Stir-fry until pork loses its pink. Add mushrooms, stir, and cook for about 15 seconds; put in the vegetables; mix and stir well. As soon as the celery begins to soften, swirl in sauce mixture. Stir constantly until sauce thickens. Turn off heat.

4. Put fried noodles on a large platter, and transfer contents of the wok onto noodles. Top it with egg shreds and the remaining scallions. Serve hot.

# STIR-FRIED RICE NOODLES, SING CHOU STYLE

Serves 4 as a meal

Sing Chou is the Chinese name for Singapore, where many of our kin emigrated for centuries. For generations, this has been one of the favorite noodle dishes among many Chinese. We love the flavor of the curry paste that spices and jazzes up the noodles, and its aroma delights us with a whiff of the tropical.

You can find this dish easily in teahouses in this country as well as in China.

## PREPARATION OF INGREDIENTS

6 tablespoons oil
2 eggs: beat to combine yolks and whites well
1 teaspoon minced garlic
6 scallions: cut into 1½-inch lengths, shred, including some green part
½ pound Cantonese Barbecued Pork (see page 126): cut into matchstick strips
8 Chinese dried mushrooms: soak in hot water until spongy, discard stems, shred caps

### SHRIMP MIXTURE (Mix in a bowl. Refrigerate before use)

½ pound fresh shrimp: shell, devein, rinse in cold water, pat dry, cut each in half lengthwise
¼ teaspoon baking soda
⅓ egg white
1 teaspoon dry Sherry

⅓ cup bell pepper (preferably red) in long, thin strips

### SAUCE MIXTURE (Mix in a bowl)

1 tablespoon yellow curry paste
1 teaspoon curry powder
¼ teaspoon cayenne pepper
½ teaspoon sugar
1 tablespoon black soy sauce
1 tablespoon thin soy sauce
1 tablespoon dry Sherry

½ pound dried rice sticks; soak in very warm but not burning tap water for 15 minutes, or until they just soften, but are still resistant (do not oversoak them); drain in colander; put in plastic bag to keep from drying
2 cups fresh bean sprouts: clean in cold water, drain
2 teaspoons sesame oil

## DIRECTIONS FOR COOKING

1. Heat wok hot over medium heat. Swirl in 2 tablespoons oil. When oil is hot, swirl in eggs and spread into a large pancake. Turn pancake when it is set. Remove from wok when it is no longer running. Cut pancake into thin strips. Set aside.

2. Heat wok over high heat. Swirl in 4 tablespoons oil. When oil is hot, drop in the garlic. When it turns golden, add half the scallions and stir-fry for a few seconds. Add barbecued pork, then mushrooms, and stir-fry for about 20 seconds. Put in shrimp mixture, stir, and cook until shrimp just turns whitish. Add bell pepper. Immediately swirl in sauce mixture, mixing well. Turn heat to medium. Add rice sticks, toss, mix, and cook until they are evenly coated with sauce. Drop in bean sprouts. Toss and stir until rice sticks are thoroughly heated. Swirl in sesame oil. Add remaining scallions; mix well. Transfer to a large serving platter. Serve hot.

# STIR-FRIED RICE STICKS WITH PORK AND SHRIMP
4 to 6 servings

## PREPARATION OF INGREDIENTS

5 tablespoons oil
3 eggs: beat until slightly foamy
1 teaspoon minced garlic
3 scallions: cut into 1½-inch lengths, shred, including some green part

PORK MIXTURE (Mix in a bowl. Refrigerate before use)

8 ounces lean pork: cut into matchstick strips (to make 1 cup)
1 teaspoon cornstarch

SHRIMP MIXTURE (Mix in a bowl. Refrigerate before use)

6 ounces fresh medium-sized shrimp: shell, devein, rinse in cold water, pat dry
about 1 teaspoon dry Sherry
⅓ egg white

1 cup fresh bean sprouts or 1 cup matchstick-sized celery strips

SAUCE MIXTURE (Mix in a bowl)

½ teaspoon sugar
½ teaspoon salt
2 tablespoons thin soy sauce
1 tablespoon black soy sauce
1 tablespoon oyster-flavored sauce

½ pound dried rice sticks: soak in hot water for 15 minutes or a little longer,
    drain, cut through rice sticks once or twice with scissors

DIRECTIONS FOR COOKING

1. Heat wok over high heat. Swirl in 1 tablespoon oil. When oil is hot, pour in
beaten eggs and spread into a thin pancake. Turn pancake when it is set. Do not
brown. Remove from wok and cut pancake into strips ¼-inch wide and 3 inches
long. Set aside.
2. Heat wok over high heat. Swirl in remaining 4 tablespoons oil. When oil is
hot, slightly brown garlic. Add scallions and pork mixture. Stir-fry until pork
loses its pink color. Add shrimp mixture and stir-fry until it just turns whitish.
Drop in bean sprouts or celery. Mix well. Stir in sauce mixture. Turn heat to
medium. Add rice sticks and shredded eggs. Mix well by constant tossing and
stirring. Stir-fry for about 2 minutes or until rice sticks are thoroughly hot. Put
on a serving platter. Serve hot.

# WONTON-NOODLE SOUP, SOUTHERN STYLE

Wonton-noodle soup is one of the most popular and cheapest snacks or meals among the Chinese. There Are hundreds of wonton-noodle houses and thousands of street stalls on back lanes and alleys in China.

Good wonton-noodle houses are always small and crowded. The furnishings are seldom more than a dozen bare tables with wooden chairs and stools on a tile floor, and a few hand-written menus pasted on the stark walls.

Nobody minds or expects more, for we know it is not a place to stretch one's legs, or hold hands with loving eyes. A frugal professor of mine lost all his dates over bowls of wonton-noodle soup. For his ladies lost half their hearts across the still-wet table, and the other half was wiped out by the loud-voiced waiter, who took and called out their orders before they could reach their seats. No love could spring and flow under the dozens of hungry eyes measuring the noodles in your bowl, and faces flashed: eat and out! I need your table to have my bowl!

Unlike the regular restaurants that cook in their kitchens in the back, the wonton-noodle houses do all the cooking visibly at one side of the entrance.

The delicious scent of freshly cooked noodles and wontons sweeps over you as you step in from the street. At one side stands the cook, enveloped in clouds of hazy steam, billowing from huge pots of boiling soup and stock. His hands move with lightning speed, flying among bowls of chopped scallions, oils, sauces, trays of uncooked wontons, fresh noodles, tender broccoli or yu choy (a delicious Chinese rape) and stacks of serving bowls.

Usually the menu has fewer than six items to choose from. Along with the specialty, wontons in soup, with or without noodles, small plates of tender vegetables in soy-oil or oyster sauce are the most favored side order to accompany the meal. If one prefers a more meaty snack, small dishes of spiced, stewed beef brisket and tasty tender pig's feet are also on the menu to complement the wontons and noodles.

It is not uncommon to wait for twenty minutes to sit down then share a table with blank-faced strangers. No head waiter helps you locate a seat. Experienced eyes sweep across the tables searching for a bowl that is nearly empty, then dash to stand guard by its holder, fearful that he or she may order another bowl.

Finally the bowl, surging with an irresistible aroma, is delivered to the table. The world becomes a void of sweet contentment, consisting only of the luscious wontons and noodles.

No one would dare to linger at the table when the last drop of soup is drained. As you are barely emerging from the sphere of sheer gratification, the waiter mops up right under your nose, calling out at the top of his lungs to the cashier guarding the door, "Come four dollars and one week," meaning four dollars plus seven dimes .The satisfied creature pays according to the call, retaining every cent of change, willing to leave the alluring scent—temporarily.

## PREPARATION OF INGREDIENTS

8 ounces fresh egg noodles
45 to 50 wonton skins: cover to keep from drying

FILLING (Mix in a bowl. Refrigerate before use)

½ pound ground pork
½ pound fresh shrimp: shell, devein, rinse in running cold water, pat dry,
    cut into peanut-sized pieces
¼ teaspoon salt
¼ teaspoon sugar
⅛ teaspoon ground pepper
2 teaspoons dry Sherry
2 teaspoons sesame oil
1 tablespoon thin soy oil
1 beaten egg
2 scallions: cut into pea-sized pieces, including some green part

1 large pot of water (about 7 pints)

BROTH MIXTURE (Mix in a 3-quart pot)

4 cups canned clear chicken broth
¼ teaspoon sugar
salt to taste
½ cup scallions: cut into pea-sized pieces, including some green part
1 tablespoon sesame oil
½ pound fresh broccoli, cut into finger-sized pieces, or 1 bunch of watercress

Soy-Sesame Dip (see page 315) and chili sauce

## DIRECTIONS FOR COOKING

1. Cook egg noodles as for Plain Cold Noodles (see page 244).Put noodles in a large serving bowl. Set aside.

2. Prepare a small bowl of water for sealing wontons. Take a wonton skin and keep the rest covered. Put about 1 heaping teaspoon of filling in the middle of a wonton skin. Moisten edges with water and fold skin in half; press edges together and seal tightly; bring the folded corners over each other and seal with water. Put wonton between linen towels. Prepare the others in the same manner.

3. Bring the large pot of water to a rapid boil, and at the same time, simmer the broth mixture over very low heat.

4. Drop wontons in boiling water and cook over moderate heat for about 5 minutes; remove wontons with a Chinese drainer or a large slotted spoon, and place them on top of the cooked noodles in the serving bowl. (Save water for cooking the vegetable.)

5. Pour broth over wontons and noodles, and add scallions and sesame oil.

6. Bring water back to a rapid boil. Immerse broccoli or watercress in water; remove it right away with a Chinese drainer and add it to the wonton-noodle soup.

7. Serve each person a bowl of wonton-noodle soup with vegetables, a small dish of dip, and sauce. Eat wontons and noodles with dip or sauce, adding it to the spoon, but try not to mix sauce or dip with soup; otherwise you have peppery soy sauce soup.

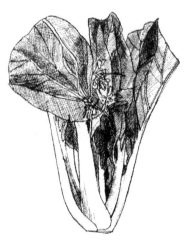

# STIR-FRIED TOFU NOODLES
# WITH CHICKEN AND MUSHROOMS
Makes 6 to 8 servings

## PREPARATION OF INGREDIENTS

¼ cup oil
1 teaspoon minced fresh ginger
2 teaspoons minced garlic
6 Chinese dried mushrooms: break stems and discard, soak in hot water until
   spongy, cut caps into thin strips

## CHICKEN MIXTURE (Mix in a bowl. Refrigerate before use)

8 ounces boneless and skinless chicken breast; cut into thin strips
¼ teaspoon sugar
⅛ teaspoon ground pepper
2 teaspoons Chinese rice wine or dry Sherry
1 tablespoon black soy sauce
1 tablespoon cornstarch

1 pound tofu noodles
1½ cups shredded bamboo shoots
1 cup red bell peppers, cut into strips

## SAUCE MIXTURE (Mix in a bowl)

2 tablespoons hoisin sauce
2 teaspoons Sichuan sweet bean sauce or ground bean sauce
1 tablespoon dry Sherry
2 tablespoons black soy sauce
¼ teaspoon ground red pepper
½ cup canned. clear chicken broth
½ cup water

2 teaspoons cornstarch mixed with 2 tablespoons water
2 teaspoons sesame oil

## DIRECTIONS FOR COOKING

1. Heat wok over high heat. Swirl in the oil. When oil is hot, add ginger and stir-fry for about 10 seconds. Drop in garlic and mushrooms. When garlic turns golden, add chicken mixture and stir-fry until it is no longer pink. Add tofu noodles, bamboo shoots, and sauce mixture. Stir and cook until sauce begins to bubble. Stir in cornstarch-water. Cook and stir until sauce is clear and thickened. Stir in sesame oil. Put on a serving platter. Serve hot

# BEEF CONGEE WITH CONDIMENTS
Makes 8 to 12 servings

In Chinese, congee is called "jook." It is served as breakfast, an informal meal, or a late evening snack. But it is never served on a formal occasion.

## PREPARATION OF INGREDIENTS

oil for deep-frying
½ cup uncooked skinless peanuts
1 ounce bean thread noodles or rice sticks
20 wonton skins: cut into ¼-inch-wide strips
10 cups water
1 cup rice: soak in water for 2 hours or more, drain before cooking

BEEF MIXTURE (Mix in a bowl. Refrigerate before use)

1 pound flank steak: cut against grain into pieces ⅛ inch thick and 2 inches long
1 teaspoon finely minced fresh ginger
2 teaspoons cornstarch
½ teaspoon sugar
1 tablespoon black soy sauce
1 tablespoon thin soy sauce
2 teaspoons sesame oil

SAUCE MIXTURE (Mix in a bowl)

1 tablespoon thin soy sauce
½ teaspoon sugar

⅓ cup chopped scallions, in pea-sized pieces, including some green part
⅓ cup chopped fresh coriander (leaves only)
1 small bowl thin soy sauce
1 small bowl sesame oil

## DIRECTIONS FOR COOKING

1. Heat oil in wok to deep-fry temperature. Deep-fry peanuts until golden brown. Drain, cool, and put in a small serving bowl.
2. Reheat oil to deep-fry temperature. Loosen noodles or rice sticks by pulling them apart. Test oil by dropping in a piece of noodle or rice stick; if it pops up and turns white, the oil is right. Deep-fry noodles; they will pop up and turn into a white nest instantly; quickly turn over the nest and fry the other side. (This takes less than 10 seconds.) Drain on paper towels. Put on a serving plate.
3. Loosen wonton strips by pulling them apart, then deep-fry half at a time until they are golden brown. Drain on paper towels. Put on a serving plate.
4. Bring 10 cups of water to a rapid boil. Add soaked rice. Uncover and cook over medium heat for about 2 hours or until rice becomes like a thin gruel. There should be 8 cups congee left in the pot at the end of cooking time.
5. Keep congee bubbling over medium heat. Add beef mixture and stir to separate pieces. Stir and cook until beef just loses its redness. It takes less than 30 seconds. Turn off heat. Stir in sauce mixture. Salt to taste.
6. Serve congee hot in individual bowls. Bring peanuts, fried noodles, fried wonton strips, scallions, coriander, soy sauce, and sesame oil to the table in small bowls. Let each person add these condiments to his or her congee. Sesame oil should be used sparingly. Taste the congee before adding thin soy sauce; it might not need it.

# SAMPAN CONGEE
Makes 8 to 12 servings

In the hot southern summer, when dusk deepened, the light of the Pearl River became more brilliant. Like millions of fireflies, the sampans' lights flickered on the water. The noise became so loud that one had to shout. Flocks of fun seekers assembled at the shore to take a boat ride in hopes of cooling off on the river while the moonbeams shone.

Like a school of fish, the sampans gathered where the fun seekers stood. Since there was never a fixed fare, bargaining preceded the ride. A good bargainer would start at a price insultingly low. The oarsman would yell back, cursing sometimes. The customer would look away, pretending not to hear. A good actor would turn slowly as if to walk away. The voice from the sampan would soften. The customer would slightly raise the price. The oarsman would be mad, spit, then plead: life had been hard; too much rain; no fun seekers; children to feed. The bargaining went on. When finally it was settled, one of them always felt cheated. But when the sampan was loaded, no grudge would be held. Then we all floated and rolled on the gentle river in peace.

The highlight of the evening was not the soft rock of the Pearl River, the moon and the summer stars, or even the ladies and gentlemen in the other boats that my mother would not allow us to stare at. It was the food hawkers' boats that we desired. They would stop and pass us, often, making our mouths water. At last the night snack signal would be given. The oarsman would spring from his silence, yelling and waving. In seconds, we would be almost swallowed by half a dozen boats. Some boats sold only congee, noodles, and wontons. Some carried only steamed clams, snails, and spiced innards. The sampan congee was always so good that we all would have some. Uncle would order his usual clams and snails. The innards would be plentiful for everyone. The children chose the noodles and wontons in soup. The oarsman graciously accepted a bowl.

Under the Milky Way in that small little boat, who cared to seize the moment of wholeness that was ours? It was so long, long ago. Now we are all scattered like those distant stars. Some have gone beyond them. But voices and laughter do remain.

## PREPARATION OF INGREDIENTS

oil for deep-frying
½ cup uncooked skinless peanuts
1 ounce bean thread noodles or rice sticks
20 wonton skins: cut into strips ¼-inch wide
10 cups water
¾ cup long grain or medium-grain rice: soak in water for 2 hours or more,
    drain before cooking
¾ teaspoon salt
1 tablespoon oil for rice

## FISH AND SQUID MIXTURE (Mix in a bowl. Keep refrigerated before use)

¼ teaspoon white pepper
¼ teaspoon sugar
1 teaspoon finely minced fresh ginger
1 pound fish fillets (sea bass or flounder): cut crosswise into thin slices
½ pound fresh cleaned squid (optional): rinse in cold water, drain, cut crosswise
    into ½-inch strips
1 tablespoon sesame oil
1 teaspoon Chinese red vinegar
2 teaspoons thin soy sauce

1 cup canned abalone cut into strips, ¼-inch thick and wide by 2 inches long
1 cup soaked jellyfish skin (optional) cut into strips, ¼-inch wide by
    2 inches long
1 tablespoon sesame oil
⅓ cup scallions: cut into pea-sized pieces, including some green part
⅓ cup fresh coriander (leaves only)
1 small dish white pepper
1 small bowl thin soy sauce
1 small bowl sesame oil

## DIRECTIONS FOR COOKING

1. Heat oil for deep-frying in wok. Deep-fry peanuts until golden brown. Drain and cool on paper towels. Put in a small serving bowl.
2. Reheat same oil to deep-fry temperature. Loosen noodles or rice sticks by pulling them apart. Test oil by dropping in a piece of noodle or rice stick; if it

pops up and turns white, the oil is right. Deep-fry noodles. They will pop up and turn into a white nest instantly; quickly turn over the nest and fry the other side (this takes less than 10 seconds). Drain on paper towels. Put on a serving plate. Crumble noodles slightly.

3. Loosen shredded wonton skins, and deep-fry half at a time, until golden brown. Drain on paper towels. Put on a serving plate.

4. Bring 10 cups of water to a rapid boil. Add rice, salt, and oil for rice. Uncover and cook over medium heat for about 2 hours or until rice becomes like thin gruel. There should be 8 cups congee left in the pot at the end of cooking time. Add boiling water to maintain the 8-cup level if necessary.

5. Keep congee bubbling over medium heat. Add fish and squid mixture. Stir to separate pieces. Cook for about 30 seconds, then turn off heat. Add abalone and jellyfish skin, and swirl in sesame oil. Mix well.

6. Bring cooked peanuts, fried wonton skins, fried noodles, scallions, coriander, white pepper, soy sauce, and sesame oil to the table in individual bowls. Let each person add condiments to congee.

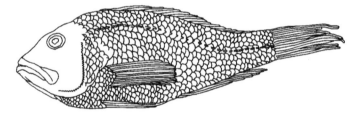

# Soups and Firepots

# SOUPS

The presence of a big bowl of soup on a Chinese dinner table was as indispensable as water and milk to a Western table. The soup was neither the first course nor the last. It was there to stay from the beginning of the meal until the end. "Finish your soup!"—as children we were urged constantly to drink soup at every dinner.

The Chinese drink soups not only for nourishment and pleasure but also for medicinal purposes. Soups are supposed to aid circulation, to help digestion, to induce liang (cool) air and clear excessive yeh (hot) air out of the system to balance of yin and yang forces in one's body. Many Chinese believe that the balance of yeh and liang in one's body is the key to good health. Lots of foods are considered either yeh or liang, and to keep a good balance of both, one eats food that equalizes the body's heat and coolness.

For example, watercress soup purifies the lungs; mustard green soup cools down the overheated faculties; shark's fin soup and bird's nest soup strengthen potency; mung bean with seaweed soup clears up pimples. The terribly bitter-tasting soup of the lotus seed hearts is supposed to be good for sour-tempered children. It certainly made us more docile, since we became exhausted from crying and screaming at being forced to drink such hair-raising stuff.

Chinese soups come in many varieties, from thin to thick, sweet to sour, and hot to mild. A sample of each appears in the following pages. Some are easy to prepare, others have to be slaved over. But they are all good for your health in some way. If it does not soothe your cranky child or calm your nerves, at least is cleansing and nourishing.

# PORK AND BOK CHOY SOUP
## (A ONE-DISH MEAL)
Serves 4 to 6

If I were allowed to serve my family only one dish for an entire month, I would choose this dish without hesitation. This dish is known for its healthful effects: cleansing, restoring and nourishing. Although it is simple to prepare, pure and unpretentious in ingredients, it is never lowly. Rather, it evokes all that is good in life—warmth, wellness, hospitality and the comfort of home. Most important of all, it is delicious and loved by family of all ages.

Recently, while I was waiting for my order at the counter of my Chinese butcher, a Chinese employer asked for 25 pounds of pork for this soup. Instantly, we swelled with a sense of well being and shared appreciation of the good life. The butcher nodded in approval and admiration for this caring and generous boss, who smiled in satisfaction and in anticipation. And I thought of my son and daughter, whose visits I never let end without plenty of this wonderful soup.

## PREPARATION OF INGREDIENTS

4 quarts water
2 pounds boneless, skinless pork shoulder: rinse and pat dry
1 chunk of ginger (golf-ball size): crush
6 Chinese dried, red dates or regular dried dates
3 pounds bok choy (do not use Shanghai bok choy): wash, drain, cut into
    4-inch pieces
½ teaspoon salt or to taste
soy-sesame dip: mix ½ cup black soy sauce with 2 tablespoons sesame oil

## DIRECTIONS FOR COOKING

1. Bring water to a rolling boil in an 8-quart pot. Add pork, ginger and dates. Cover and cook over medium heat for 1½ hours or until pork is very tender (It should almost come apart). Add bok choy, cover and cook for 15 minutes. Add salt to taste. Discard ginger.
2. Slice pork and put on a serving platter. Arrange bok choy around sliced pork. Serve hot with soy-sesame dip. Plain rice is excellent to accompany this dish.

NOTE: this dish can be doubled or tripled. Reheat leftovers on stove.

# EGG FLOWER SOUP
## (EGG DROP SOUP)
Makes about 8 servings

In order to have the beautiful cloud-like egg flowers floating in the soup, do not stir when you swirl in the eggs.

## PREPARATION OF INGREDIENTS

3 cups water
¼ teaspoon sugar
½ teaspoon salt or to taste
2 cups canned clear chicken broth
1 tablespoon cornstarch mixed with ¼ cup cold water
2 eggs: beat until slightly foamy
2 scallions: cut into pea-sized pieces, including some green part
2 teaspoons sesame oil

## DIRECTIONS FOR COOKING

1. In a 3-quart pot, add sugar, and salt to water and broth. Bring to a rapid boil. Stir in cornstarch-water. Stir and cook until soup is no longer cloudy. Slowly swirl in beaten eggs. Do not stir! Turn off heat at once. Allow eggs to form feathery mass.
2. Drop in scallions and sesame oil. Now you can stir gently. Pour into a serving bowl. Serve hot.

# CHICKEN AND WATERCRESS SOUP

Makes 6 to 8 servings

## PREPARATION OF INGREDIENTS

BROTH (Mix in a 3-quart pot)

3 cups water
2 cups canned clear chicken broth
¼ teaspoon sugar
½ teaspoon salt or to taste

4 ounces watercress: discard hard stalks, wash, rinse

CHICKEN MIXTURE (Mix in a bowl)

2 teaspoons cornstarch
1 boned, skinless chicken breast: cut into match stick strips
½ teaspoon thin soy sauce

1 teaspoon sesame oil

## DIRECTIONS FOR COOKING

1. Bring broth mixture to a boil. Add watercress. Cook over medium heat for a minute or until watercress just turns bright green.
2. Add chicken strips. Stir to separate pieces. Cook briskly until chicken just turns white (about 30 seconds). Turn off heat immediately. Swirl in sesame oil. Serve hot.

# HAPPY FAMILY DUMPLING SOP

Serves 4 to 6 as a meal

These marble-sized smooth, soft, glutinous dumplings signified more than just a snack or meal in our life. They were a symbol of family happiness. The smoothness and roundness of the dumplings represented a family, full and whole without rough edges; the stickiness symbolized the inseparability and unbreakableness of a family.

Prior to every Chinese New Year, we would assemble around the table, rolling plenty of these glutinous dumplings, taking care to say only things that were cheery and sweet. And the first thing that touched our lips on New Year's Day was these dumplings in sugared soup, so that we as a family would be sweet and whole in the year to come.

During the Chinese New Year holidays we did nothing but chat and eat. To reinforce our wishes we made more dumpling soup, now with meat and vegetables.

As we gathered and enjoyed the dumplings leisurely, my grandmother's eyes would beam on us, and I knew a wish had been fulfilled.

PREPARATION OF INGREDIENTS

2 tablespoons oil

EGG MIXTURE (Beat together until slightly foamy)
3 eggs
¼ teaspoon salt

1½ cups white glutinous rice powder
2 teaspoons sugar
about ½ cup cold water

BROTH (Mix in a 3-quart pot)

2 cups water
4 cups canned clear chicken broth
½ teaspoon sugar
½ teaspoon salt (or to taste)

1 cup Cantonese Barbecued Pork (see page 126) or Smithfield ham or cooked sandwich ham cut in small squares.

3 Chinese pork sausages: cut each lengthwise, then dice

10 Chinese dried mushrooms: soak in hot water until spongy, discard stems, cut caps into small squares

2 tablespoons Chinese dried shrimp (optional): soak in hot water until softened, cut into small pieces

3 cups Chinese cabbage in thin strips

2 scallions: cut into pea-sized pieces, including some green part

DIRECTIONS FOR COOKING

1. Heat wok hot over medium heat and swirl in the oil. When oil is hot, pour in egg mixture. Slowly swirl mixture by turning the wok clockwise to form a large pancake. Turn pancake over when it is no longer runny; when it is set, transfer to a cutting board; cut into thin strips; put aside.

2. Combine rice powder and sugar in a mixing bowl, add water gradually, and mix with hand to form a smooth dough. Divide dough into three portions. Roll them into ½-inch sausages; then pinch the "sausages" into cherry-sized pieces. Put a small piece in the center of your palms and roll it into a marble-sized dumpling. Repeat the others in the same manner; put dumplings between towels.

3. Add pork or ham, and sausages, mushrooms, and shrimp to broth and bring it to a rolling boil. Add cabbage and cook until tender. Add dumplings and cook over medium heat. As soon as all the dumplings float to the top, turn off heat. Add scallions and egg strips. Serve hot.

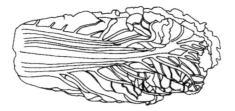

# CHICKEN FU YUNG SOUP
Makes 6 to 8 servings

## PREPARATION OF INGREDIENTS

3 cups water
1 teasoopn salt or to taste
½ teaspoon sugar
2 tablespoons cornstarch mixed with 2 tablespoons water

### CHICKEN AND CORN MIXTURE (Mix in a bowl)

½ boneless, skinless chicken breast: mince or grind into fine paste
1 egg white: beat slightly, but do not create bubbles
17-ounce can cream-style corn

2 egg whites: beat slightly, but not until foamy
½ teaspoon salt or to taste

## DIRECTIONS FOR COOKING

1. Bring water to a boil; add salt and sugar. Stir in cornstarch water. Stir and cook over medium heat until broth is clear and not cloudy.
2. Pour in chicken and corn mixture. Cook and stir until it bubbles gently. Slowly swirl in beaten egg whites. Do not stir! Allow a few seconds for egg whites to form a mass of white clouds in the soup. Turn off heat at once. Stir. Serve hot.


# EIGHT PRECIOUS JEWELS
# WHOLE WINTER MELON SOUP
Makes 8 to 12 servings

This soup is a summer event. The whole melon comes to the table, looking like a green pumpkin, soft from cooking and piping hot. It is filled with soup containing eight delicious ingredients: mushrooms, barbecued pork, shrimp, lotus seeds, chicken, straw mushrooms, abalone, pork. These are called jewels.

The soup should be clear, tasty, and not rich because winter melon is believed to cool and clear out summer heat. After the soup is finished, the soft and tender melon pulp is scooped out and eaten.

With this soup, I first experienced the power that comes with the ability to cook. I was twelve years old then. In China in those days, the role of a father was to be strict. Kindness and tenderness came only from the mother. My father accurately played his role, which he had learned from his father. We used to be in awe when he spoke, silently retreating from a room when he entered. He was such a handsome man, flamboyant, fun, always joking with his friends. But to his children, he was distant, aloof, and restricted by his role.

It was his birthday. I requested that the family cook permit me the honor of surprising my father with this winter melon soup. With help from the cook, I did the preparing and the cooking. Carving the melon, however, was my chore alone. It was not a piece of stunning art, but on it were cut all the good words that a Chinese cherishes—happiness, prosperity, good health, and longevity—and that a child could carve.

I can still see the shine of those many pairs of eyes when the cook announced and presented my majestic soup. My father's face quivered and his eyes grew moist. I did not get a pat on my shoulder, but rather several generous nods. For many days, though, I did not have to practice my fifteen minutes' straight walk for my pigeon toes.

Time has carried away many old memories. But neither my father nor I have forgotten this winter melon soup.

## PREPARATION OF INGREDIENTS

10-pound good-looking winter melon (that will fit into a big pot)

BROTH (Mix in a bowl)

5 cups canned clear chicken broth
½ teaspoon sugar
¾ teaspoon salt

15 dried skinless lotus seeds: boil in water until tender, drain
4 Chinese dried mushrooms: soak until spongy, discard stems,
    cut caps into ¼-inch squares
⅓ cup diced Cantonese barbecued pork or Cantonese roast duck

## CHICKEN AND PORK MIXTURE (Mix in a bowl)

1 boned, skinless chicken breast: cut into ¼-inch cubes
⅓ cup lean pork cubes: cut like chicken
1 teaspoon cornstarch
2 teaspoons dry Sherry
¼ teaspoon salt

## SHRIMP MIXTURE (Mix in a bowl)

6 ounces fresh shrimp: shell, devein, rinse in running cold water, drain, pat dry,
    cut into peanut-sized pieces
½ teaspoon cornstarch
½ teaspoon dry Sherry
1 big pinch white pepper

½ cup canned straw mushrooms: rinse in cold water, drain in colander
⅓ cup canned abalone: cut into ¼-inch cubes
chrysanthemum flowers or greens for garnishing

## DIRECTIONS FOR COOKING

1. Cut about a quarter of the melon off the top. Scoop out seeds and soft center. Cut edge into a zigzag pattern. Carve designs on the melon's skin if you wish.
2. Rinse inside of melon with a pot of boiling water. Discard water and dry melon with a towel.
3. Place a big piece of cheesecloth under melon. Put broth, lotus seeds, and dried mushrooms into melon. Loosely tie corners of the cheesecloth on top of melon. (This is to help lift it out of the pot after it is cooked.) Place melon in pot big enough to allow steam to circulate. Fill pot with water one-third of the way up the melon. (If melon begins to float, remove some water.) Cover and cook over medium heat for about 1 hour. Add barbecued pork or duck to broth in melon. Cover and cook for another 15 minutes.
4. Add chicken and pork mixture to piping hot broth in melon. Stir to separate pieces. They should be cooked almost instantly. Add shrimp mixture, straw mushrooms, and abalone. Turn off heat.
5. Grasp cheesecloth and lift melon out gently. Place it on a big round serving platter or in a big bowl. Remove cheesecloth carefully. Decorate around the melon with flowers or greens. Bring melon to the table. Serve hot.

NOTE: Eat melon pulp only after finishing the soup because the shell is needed to hold the soup.


# SIZZLING RICE SOUP WITH SHRIMP AND CHICKEN
Makes 4 to 6 servings

S erving this soup is a pleasure. It always creates excitement when the piping hot rice crusts sizzle noisily at the table, catching the guests by surprise. The main ingredient is the rice crusts. Formerly, you had to make them yourself, but now you can purchase them in Chinese grocery stores.

## PREPARATION OF INGREDIENTS

BROTH (Mix in a medium-sized pot)

2 cups water
2 cups canned clear chicken broth
½ teaspoon salt
¼ teaspoon sugar

1½ tablespoons cornstarch mixed with 3 tablespoons water

CHICKEN MIXTURE (Mix in a bowl. Keep refrigerated before use)

½ boned, skinless chicken breast: cut into very thin strips
⅓ egg white
1 teaspoon cornstarch
⅛ tablespoon salt

SHRIMP MIXTURE (Mix in a bowl. Keep refrigerated before use)

1 teaspoon cornstarch
⅛ teaspoon salt
6 ounces fresh shrimp: shell, devein, rinse in running cold water, drain, pat dry, cut lengthwise
½ teaspoon dry Sherry

⅓ cup canned baby corn: cut crosswise into thin round pieces
2 tablespoons green peas (frozen will do)
¼ cup canned straw mushrooms
1 scallion: cut into pea-sized pieces, including some green part
1 teaspoon sesame oil
4 cups oil for deep-frying rice crusts
1 cup rice crusts, about half-dollar size (see page 237)

## DIRECTIONS FOR COOKING

1. Bring broth mixture to a gentle boil over medium heat. Stir in cornstarch water. Cook, stirring constantly, until broth is clear.
2. Keep broth bubbling gently. Add chicken and shrimp mixtures. Quickly stir to separate pieces. Add corn, peas, and mushrooms. Immediately turn the heat to very, very low to wait for the rice crusts.
3. Put scallions and sesame seed oil in a big serving bowl which will hold the soup.
4. While the soup is cooking, heat oil for deep-frying in wok over high heat until very hot. Test by dropping in a small piece of rice crust; it should pop and float to the top immediately. Add rice crusts and deep-fry until they are golden color. Remove with a drainer or a slotted spoon to a small serving plate.
5. Quickly pour the hot soup into the serving bowl. Immediately bring soup and rice crusts to the table. Immerse rice crusts in soup at once. Be proud of the sizzling sound. Stir and serve hot.

# HOT AND SOUR SOUP
Makes 6 to 8 servings

This is an excellent soup for a cold winter day. It warms your body and clears your nose. It is an offering from Sichuan. Where else?

Who else would think of pouring vinegar and ladling pepper into the soup? The cook who invented this must be mad! However, we love it.

## PREPARATION OF INGREDIENTS

10 dried lily buds: soak in hot water for 15 minutes
2 tablespoons cloud ears: soak in plenty of hot water for 15 minutes
4 cups canned clear chicken broth
6 ounces lean pork (or boneless, skinless chicken breast):
 cut into matchstick strips
½ cup firm tofu: cut into thin strips
¼ cup bamboo shoots: cut into matchstick strips
6 Chinese dried mushrooms: soak in hot water until spongy, discard stems,
 cut caps into thin strips

## SAUCE MIXTURE (Mix in a bowl)

¼ teaspoon sugar
¾ teaspoon salt
1 tablespoon thin soy sauce

2 tablespoons cornstarch mixed with 3 tablespoons water
1 egg: beat until slightly foamy

## VINEGAR AND PEPPER MIXTURE (Put in a big serving bowl to hold the soup)

3 tablespoons Chinese red vinegar
½ teaspoon ground white pepper
2 teaspoons sesame oil

2 scallions: cut into pea-sized pieces, including some green part

## DIRECTIONS FOR COOKING

1. Pinch off tough parts of soaked lily buds and cloud ears. Tear cloud ears and lily buds into halves lengthwise. Put aside.
2. In a 3-quart pot, bring chicken broth to a boil. Add pork (or chicken), tofu, bamboo shoots, lily buds, cloud ears, and mushrooms, and cook for a few minutes. Stir in sauce mixture and cornstarch-water. Stir and cook until soup boils gently. Slowly swirl in the beaten egg. Turn off heat immediately. Do not stir! (This allows the egg to set slightly. it will resemble a mass of yellow clouds.) After the egg sets slightly, stir to mix. Pour soup into serving bowl containing vinegar and pepper mixture. Add scallions. Stir gently to bring up vinegar and pepper mixture from the bottom. Serve hot.

# HOT AND SOUR FISH SOUP
Makes about 8 servings

## PREPARATION OF INGREDIENTS

1 pound fish fillets (sole or flounder): marinate in 1 tablespoon dry Sherry
    not more than 20 minutes
⅓ cup cornstarch to coat fish
oil for deep-frying
5 cups canned clear chicken broth
4 Chinese dried mushrooms: soak in hot water until spongy, discard stems,
    shred caps
1 tablespoon cloud ears: soak in hot water until soft, tear into small pieces
½ cup firm tofu cut into small strips

## SAUCE MIXTURE (Mix in a bowl)

½ teaspoon sugar
¾ teaspoon salt
4 teaspoons thin soy sauce
1 teaspoon black soy sauce

4 tablespoons cornstarch mixed with ¼ cup water
1 egg: beat until slightly foamy

VINEGAR AND PEPPER MIXTURE (Put in a big serving bowl to hold the soup)

3 tablespoons Chinese red vinegar
½ to ¾ teaspoon ground, white pepper
1 tablespoon sesame oil

2 scallions: cut into pea-sized pieces, including some green part
I tablespoon coarsely chopped fresh coriander (optional)

DIRECTIONS FOR COOKING

1. Coat fish slightly in cornstarch. Put aside.
2. Heat oil in wok to deep-fry temperature. Deep-fry fillets until they are just golden brown. Gently remove from wok. Drain.
3. Heat broth in a 3-quart pot to a boil. Add mushrooms, cloud ears, and tofu. Stir in sauce mixture, then cornstarch-water. Stir and cook over medium heat until broth is clear and thickened. Add fish. Stir gently. As soon as broth bubbles again, slowly swirl in the egg. Turn off heat immediately. Do not stir! (This allows the egg to set slightly. It will resemble a mass of yellow clouds.) Allow egg to set for several seconds, then stir to mix.
4. Pour soup into serving bowl containing vinegar and pepper mixture. Add scallions and coriander. Stir gently to bring up vinegar and pepper from the bottom. Break fillets into big chunks. Serve hot at once.

# FU YUNG BIRD'S NEST SOUP
Makes 6 to 8 servings

They are the nests of sea swallows of Southern Asia. Instead of using grass and twigs, the swallows digest seaweed and sea plants and turn them into a gelatinous fluid which they spit out to build their nests.

The sea swallows build their nests on high cliffs along the coast. Monkeys were trained to fetch these precious nests in the olden days. The nests of top quality are free from feathers, shaped like small petals of the water lily, hard and wax-colored. Less expensive nests are darker in color, with some tiny feathers attached. The most popular kinds served in restaurants are pieces of broken nests or crumbs of ground-up nests that are made into balls or patties.

In spite of its desirability, the nest is almost odorless and tasteless. Its flavor depends solely on being cooked in good broth, borrowing flavors from the other ingredients. Like its celebrated sister, the shark's fin, the swallow's nest is the rich man's whim, the poor people's dream, and a formal banquet's necessity.

## PREPARATION OF INGREDIENTS

2 ounces dried bird's nest: soak in plenty of hot water for at least 3 to 4 hours
    (makes about 2 cups after soaking), drain before cooking
2 scallions: leave whole
4 slices fresh ginger, each as big and thick as a quarter
2 tablespoons dry Sherry
4 cups canned clear chicken broth
½ teaspoon sugar
1½ tablespoons cornstarch mixed with 2 tablespoons water

## CHICKEN MIXTURE (Mix in a bowl. Refrigerate before use)

1 whole boned, skinless chicken breast: cut into matchstick strips
    (to make about 1 cup)
1 egg white
2 teaspoons cornstarch

2 eggs: beat until just slightly foamy
salt to taste (1-1½ teaspoons)

## DIRECTIONS FOR COOKING

1. Pour enough water into a 3-quart pot to reach two-thirds up the sides. Add soaked bird's nest and boil over medium-low heat for 30 minutes. Drain in colander.

2. Heat dry wok over high heat, then throw in 1 whole scallion, 2 slices of ginger, and I tablespoon of Sherry. Quickly add 4 cups of water and the bird's nest. Cook over medium heat for 10 minutes. Drain in colander. Discard scallion and ginger. Repeat this entire process with remaining scallion, ginger, and Sherry. Then put bird's nest in a bowl. Cover until use.

3. Heat chicken broth and sugar in a 3-quart pot and bring to a boil. Add bird's nest and cornstarch water. Stir and cook until broth is clear and thickened. Add chicken mixture, stir to separate pieces, and cook briskly for several seconds. As soon as broth bubbles again, slowly swirl in beaten eggs. Turn heat off immediately. Do not stir in order to allow the eggs to form a mass of clouds. (It takes only several seconds). Salt to taste. Stir to mix well. Pour into a serving bowl. Serve hot.

# FIRE POTS

The cooking of northern China has been very much influenced by Mongolian cooking, for the Mongols conquered China and ruled in Beijing for eighty-eight years. It was they who planned and built a large part of Beijing. It was their ascendancy that Marco Polo so lavishly described. Most of the Mongols lived in tents and cooked and ate around the fire. Their cooking was distinguished by barbecued ducks and meat, sliced lamb and beef cooked in hot broth, then dipped in spiced sauces. The famous Peking duck and the Beijing fire pot still have much of the Mongolian flavor even though these dishes have long since been refined by the Chinese.

In the north, when winter fell and the wind from Inner Mongolia started to blow, fire pots were a familiar sight on the tables of families and restaurants. Chinese homes did not have central heating; therefore, gathering and eating around a blazing fire pot and dipping food into piping hot broth was not only fun but sometimes a necessity.

In the Beijing fire pot (which is also called "Mongolian Fire Pot or "Mongolian Rinsed Lamb"), the chief ingredient is the thinly sliced lamb, which is accompanied by Chinese cabbage, tofu, bean thread noodles, shao-bings (sesame seed rolls), and sauces. The fire pot looks like a giant bowl with a big chimney rising high in the middle. Charcoal burns in the base under the chimney, and the broth is held around the chimney. The intense heat keeps the broth bubbling (electric fire pots are available in Chinese food stores). Each person immerses one or two slices of lamb in the piping hot broth, which cooks the lamb in a matter of seconds (it is cooked as fast as if one just rinsed the lamb in broth). Then the lamb is dipped and eaten with sauces. In order not to lose the food that is put into the broth, little wire strainers with long handles are provided for everybody to immerse his own food.

The fire pot is not exclusively a Northern spread. It is also very popular in the South, where winter is not bitter but damp and chill. The Southerners prefer the chrysanthemum fire pot, in which everything delicious can go into the pot: shrimp, fried shrimp balls, oysters, sliced chicken, liver, lettuce, bean thread noodles, fish fillet, and so on.

If you do not have a fire pot, a chafing dish or an enamel pot placed on an electric stove or a hibachi will do. Many Chinese are not equipped with fire pots either; they use a clay pot on a portable charcoal stove.

Eating around a fire pot is always a joyful event, and it often lasts for hours. Somehow one seems unable to stop eating until the last drop of soup is gone. Then stomachs are full, bodies are warm, eyes begin to feel heavy, and no one seems to mind the north wind raging.

# BEIJING FIRE POT

Serves 8 to 12 persons

## PREPARATION OF INGREDIENTS

6 pounds boned leg of lamb (save the bone): slice paper-thin when half-frozen, arrange slices slightly overlapping on two serving plates, brush lightly with sesame oil, garnish plates with scallion brushes, cover and refrigerate before use

6 to 8 pieces firm tofu: slice into ⅓-inch-thick pieces, arrange on two serving plates, garnish plates with snow peas or scallion brushes, cover and refrigerate before use

8 ounces bean thread noodles: soak in plenty of hot water for about 10 minutes or until soft, drain in colander, cut with scissors 3 or 4 strokes to shorten a little, put in two serving bowls, cover

2 pounds Chinese cabbage: cut off stem, separate stalks, cut into bite-sized pieces, put in a serving bowl

⅓ pound snow peas (optional): break off ends, wash, dry, put on a plate, cover

1 head iceberg lettuce (optional): separate leaves, wash, dry, break into big pieces, put in a big serving bowl

12 Scallion Brushes (see page 198)

SAUCE (Mix in a bowl until smooth. Put in a serving bowl. Cover)

4 tablespoons brown sugar
¼ cup black soy sauce
⅓ cup sesame oil
½ cup rice wine or dry Sherry
⅔ cup smooth peanut butter mixed with ½ cup boiling water
2 tablespoons Chinese red vinegar
4 tablespoons Chinese red bean curd cheese: mash into paste
½ teaspoon cayenne pepper
5 to 6 quarts water: cook lamb bone in water for an hour or until 4 quarts of broth are left in pot; discard bone and skim off scum and fat. Salt to taste

## DIRECTIONS FOR COOKING

1. Give each person a small drainer, specially made for a fire pot, a small bowl for dip, a bigger bowl for food and soup, a plate under the soup bowl, and spoons.
2. Arrange all the ingredients on table, except water.

3. Bring water to a boil on stove. Salt to taste, cover and simmer.

4. Put charcoal (about 15 pieces) on a shallow pan and place it under the broiler (as close as possible). Turn oven to broil until part of each piece of charcoal becomes red. Transfer charcoal to the base of the fire pot.

5. Pour lamb broth into fire pot. Cover broth with lid. Carry the fire pot to the table before people gather around it. (The base of the fire pot will be very hot. Be sure you put a lot of heatproof material under it, otherwise the intense heat will burn your table.)

6. When the charcoal is burning happily and the broth is boiling, seat your family and guests.

7. If small strainers are provided, put one or two slices of lamb in a drainer and immerse it in the broth. Take it out in about 7 seconds. With chopsticks, dip lamb into the sauce and eat. (If small strainers are not available, hold on to the meat with chopsticks.) Dip vegetables, noodles, and tofu in broth and eat in the same manner. Add more charcoal when the heat gets low; add more water to the fire pot if it begins to cook down. Do not drink the broth at the beginning, but wait until the end of the meal. By then, the broth will be seasoned with the lamb and other ingredients.

# CHRYSANTHEMUM FIRE POT
Serves 8 to 12 persons

## PREPARATION OF INGREDIENTS

3 whole boned, skinless chicken breasts: slice paper-thin while half-frozen, arrange slices slightly overlapping on serving plate, brush with a little sesame oil, garnish with scallion brushes, cover, refrigerate before use

1 pound (23 to 25) fresh shrimp: peel off shell except tails, devein, butterfly (see Seafood Chapter), rinse in cold running water, pat dry, arrange slightly overlapping on a serving plate, brush with sesame oil, cover, refrigerate before use

2 pints oysters: blanch in water (see Cooking Techniques, page 17), drain, put in a serving bowl, refrigerate before use

½ pound fresh chicken livers: slice thinly, mix with ½ teaspoon finely minced fresh ginger root and ½ teaspoon sesame oil, put in a covered bowl, refrigerate before use

½ pound fresh fish fillet (sole, striped bass, or sea bass): slice paper-thin, arrange slightly overlapping on plate, cover, refrigerate before use

1 pound lean pork or flank steak: slice paper-thin while half-frozen, brush with a little sesame oil, arrange slices slightly overlapping on a plate, cover, refrigerate before use

8 ounces bean thread noodles: soak in plenty of hot water for about 10 minutes or until soft, drain in colander, cut with scissors 3 or 4 strokes to shorten a little, put in a serving bowl, cover

6 pieces firm tofu: slice into ⅓-inch-thick pieces, put on a serving plate, garnish with snow peas or scallion brushes, cover, refrigerate before use

⅓ pound snow peas: break off ends, wash, dry, put on a serving plate, cover

1 head iceberg lettuce: separate leaves, wash, dry, break into big pieces, put in a serving bowl

½ pound watercress (optional): discard tough stalks, wash, dry, put in a bowl

2 big chrysanthemum flowers from the florist: leave them whole

## SAUCE INGREDIENTS (Put each item in an individual bowl)

¼ cup brown sugar
½ cup thin soy sauce
½ cup black soy sauce
½ cup Chinese red vinegar
⅔ cup hoisin sauce

½ cup sesame oil

¼ cup chili oil

3 to 4 eggs: beat to mix yolks and whites

¼ cup rice wine or dry Sherry

⅔ cup chopped scallions: in pea-sized pieces, including some green part

5 to 6 quarts water: salt to taste

Plain Rice for 6 to 8 persons (see page 237)

## DIRECTIONS FOR COOKING

1. Give each person a small drainer, specially made for a fire pot, a small bowl for dip, a bigger bowl for food, rice, and soup, a plate under the soup bowl, and spoons.

2. Arrange all the ingredients on table, except rice.

3. Put water on stove and bring it to a boil. Cover and simmer to wait for the charcoal.

4. Put charcoal (about 15 pieces) on a shallow pan and place it under the broiler (as close as possible). Turn oven to broil until part of each piece becomes red. Transfer charcoal to base of fire pot.

5. Pour water into fire pot. Cover with lid. Carry fire pot to table before people gather around it. (The base of the fire pot will be very hot. Be sure you put a lot of heatproof material under it, otherwise the intense heat will burn your table.)

6. When the charcoal is burning merrily and the water is bubbling, seat your family and guests.

7. Begin the meal with this little opening ceremony: as host or hostess, uncover the lid of the fire pot. Pick up a chrysanthemum flower, detach a few petals, and drop them into the broth. Your family and guests can follow you in this procedure if they wish. The petals are edible.

8. Each guest makes his own sauce by mixing his choice of sauce ingredients in the small bowl.

9. If small strainers are provided, put one or two pieces of meat or seafood in a drainer and immerse it in water. Take it out after several seconds. With a pair of chopsticks, dip meat or seafood in the sauce and eat. (If small strainers are not available, hold on to the meat with chopsticks.) Dip vegetables, noodles, and tofu in water and eat in the same manner. Serve rice during the meal. Add more charcoal when the heat gets low; add more water to the fire pot if it begins to cook down. Drink broth at the end of the meal, not at the beginning, when it is still watery.

NOTE: Appetizers such as Jiaozi (see page 28), Spring Rolls (see page 44-52), and Crisp Scallion Cakes (see page 52), or dishes such as Deep-Fried Shrimp and Balls (see page 178) can also be served during the meal.

# Chinese Sweets

# CHINESE SWEETS

Except for banquets, the Chinese do not include dessert in their meals. Fresh fruit is served after the meal. Since milk and cream and other dairy products are not included in our diet, traditional Chinese sweets are generally heavy and quite plain; usually they are made with rice, rice powder, sugar, and sweet bean paste. But one of the very popular desserts is sweet soup, made with beans, seeds, or nuts ground up and liquefied. The pastries and tarts that are filled with cream and sold in Chinese pastry shops reflect the influence of the British colonials.

During banquets, because the endless courses may dull one's palate, light sweet dishes are served in between and at the end to refresh one's tastebuds.

Sweets that are frequently presented at banquets as desserts are almond float, eight-jewel rice pudding, and glazed apples. Almond float was served as one of the sweet dishes at the banquet given for Mr. and Mrs. Nixon in Beijing.

The Chinese do like sweets, but usually eat them between meals. Pie and cake are too heavy to conclude a Chinese meal. If you are uncertain as to what to serve for dessert, fresh fruit is always welcomed.

# CHINESE NEW YEAR-EIGHT JEWEL RICE PUDDING IN GRAND MARNIER SAUCE

Makes 8 to 10 servings

Every year, for over twenty years, I have served this pudding for Chinese New Year. No relative or friend is allowed to leave without the blessings of this pudding. It conveys best wishes for a happy new year and sweet and gluey relations that will not come apart. No one has ever left without this sumptuous pudding, ever since I infused the tasteless, traditional sauce with Grand Marnier.

## PREPARATION OF INGREDIENTS

### PUDDING

1 pound white, glutinous rice: soak in cold water overnight or until plump;
    steam for 20 minutes or until it is done
2 tablespoons lard or butter
½ cup sugar

1½ cups sweet red bean paste
⅓ cup assorted candied fruit (such as fruitcake mixture) for decorating

### SAUCE MIXTURE (Mix in a pot)

1 cup water
½ cup sugar
rind from one orange: cut into very tin strips
2 tablespoons cornstarch, mixed with ¼ cup water
Grand Marnier to taste

## DIRECTIONS FOR COOKING

1. Combine hot, glutinous rice with ½ cup sugar and 2 tablespoons lard or butter. Set aside.
2. Line a 9-inch, round-bottomed, 2-inch deep plate with plastic wrap. Evenly spoon half of the rice on plate and, evenly spread sweet red bean paste on top of rice. Spoon and spread remaining rice on bean paste.
3. Turn the plate with rice upside down on a slightly larger serving plate. Decorate pudding with candied fruits. (You may prepare pudding up to this point;

cover and refrigerate for at least 3 days.) Steam pudding (see page 17) until it is hot and soft (about 30 minutes).

4. Prepare sauce about 10 minutes before serving pudding. Heat sauce over medium-low heat; stir and cook until it almost comes to a boil, add cornstarch-water. Cook and stir until it is clear and thickened. Add Grand Marnier, and stir to mix well. Remove from heat.

5. Serve each portion of hot rice pudding with hot Grand Marnier sauce on top.


# GLAZED APPLES
Makes 4 to 6 servings

## PREPARATION OF INGREDIENTS

3 firm apples: peel, cut each into 6 wedges, discard cores
2 eggs: beat until slightly foamy
½ cup cornstarch
about 4 cups oil for frying

## SUGAR MIXTURE (Mix in a bowl)

3 tablespoons oil
1 cup sugar
¼ cup water

1 tablespoon black sesame seeds
1 big bowl cold water with ice cubes

## DIRECTIONS FOR COOKING

1. Dip sliced apples in eggs, then roll pieces in cornstarch to coat evenly. Put aside.

2. Generously brush a serving plate with oil.

3. Heat the 4 cups of oil in a medium-sized pot to deep-fry temperature. Deep-fry half the apples at a time until golden brown. Remove with a drainer. Drain on paper towels and keep hot in a 300-degree oven.

4. While you are frying apples, heat sugar mixture in a wok over medium heat until sugar becomes a syrup ready for glazing: it should spin a long thread when a drop falls from the tip of a chopstick, or it should form a hard ball when

dropped in cold water. Add sesame seeds.

5. Quickly roll fried apples in syrup to coat evenly, then put them on the greased plate.

6. Quickly bring glazed apples and the bowl of ice water to the table. Let your family or guests have the pleasure of dipping the apples in the ice water to harden the syrup before eating. The glaze should be crisp and hard like a layer of thin glass.


# ALMOND FLOAT
Makes 8 to 12 servings

## PREPARATION OF INGREDIENTS

2 envelopes unflavored gelatin
½ cup cold water
2 cups boiling water
½ cup sugar
1 teaspoon almond extract
1 cup milk
a few drops red food coloring (optional)
20-ounce can lychee fruit, mandarin oranges, or mixed fruit cocktail: chill

## DIRECTIONS FOR COOKING

1. Empty gelatin into a mixing bowl. Add cold water and stir well. Add boiling water, sugar, almond extract, and milk. Stir until sugar completely dissolves. Add food coloring if you wish.

2. Pour mixture into two pie plates. Chill in refrigerator for about 6 hours.

3. Using a knife, slice almond float into small cubes and put into a serving bowl. Top with chilled lychee, oranges, or fruit cocktail and the juice from the can. Serve in small bowls.

# FRIED SWEET SESAME BALLS
Makes 12 balls

This recipe for sesame-seed balls was taught to. me by my grandmother's maid, Noble Face, when my husband and I visited her in her village home in China in the spring of 1979.

Unlike the sesame-seed balls in bakeries in Chinatowns and Hong Kong, and the ones I learned to make from dim stim chefs in Hong Kong, these will stay soft and fresh for a few days instead of becoming hard and unpalatable in a matter of hours.

## PREPARATION OF INGREDIENTS

2 cups white, glutinous rice powder
6 tablespoons plus ½ cup water
½ cup sugar

FILLING (Mix in a bowl)

¼ cup sweetened, flaked coconut
¼ cup sugar
¼ cup white sesame seeds: roast in an ungreased pot over medium heat, stirring
   constantly, until golden brown; cool and crush with a rolling pin or grind
   coarsely in a spice or meat grinder

ALTERNATE FILLING

12 tablespoons sweet red bean paste: roll into 12 balls

about ½ cup white sesame seeds for coating: put on a plate
oil for deep-frying

## DIRECTIONS FOR COOKING

1. Mix ½ cup glutinous rice powder with 6 tablespoons of cold water into a thin batter in a mixing bowl.
2. In a pot, stir sugar in ½ cup water until it dissolves; bring it to a boil. Add batter and stir quickly for several seconds over low heat until batter is clear and thickened. Remove from heat.
3. Combine 1½ cups rice powder with the hot batter and stir. When the dough

is not too hot to touch, put it on a slightly powdered surface. Knead until soft and not sticky. If the dough seems dry, wet your hands with water and knead to soften dough. Divide dough into 12 equal sections and roll each into a round ball between your palms. Cover them with a damp cloth.

4. Take a dough ball and make a hollow in the center. Fill hollow with a heaping teaspoon of filling or a bean-paste ball. Close the opening by squeezing edges together with your thumb and your forefinger. Pinch edges to seal and smooth out pinch mark.

5. Wet your hands with water and roll balls in your hands to moisten them. Roll wet dough balls in sesame seeds to coat generously. Wash and dry hands. Roll balls again in hands to make sesame seeds stay firmly on dough.

6. Pour oil in wok to reach about 3 inches deep. Heat oil over medium-high heat. When oil is moderately hot, put sesame seed balls on a large Chinese drainer or a large slotted spoon and put in oil. Allow sesame seed balls to stay on the drainer until they begin to float. Remove drainer. With a spatula, press each ball firmly against the wok. (This pressing action enables the sesame seed balls to expand.) Turn heat to medium-low, so that sesame seed balls will not turn brown too quickly, but allow the dough to cook thoroughly. Roll balls in a circling motion with the bottom of the drainer. And again press balls with spatula. Roll and fry balls until they are golden brown. Drain on paper towels. Cool for a few minutes before serving.

# COCONUT ANISE RICE CAKE
Serves 6 to 8

This is Andrew, my godson's, favorite sweet, as well as his three brothers' and their grandmother. I believe that their blonde haired, blue-eyed and fair-skinned Vermont family has consumed more glutinous rice than most Chinese I know. Each visit I have to make each of them a plate to relieve the pain of sharing.

## PREPARATION OF INGREDIENTS

1 pound white, glutinous rice: soak in plenty of water for at least 4 hours
    or more, drain
½ cup sweetened, flaked coconut
1 to 2 tablespoons anise seed

⅔ cup sugar
3 tablespoons lard or butter

DIRECTIONS FOR COOKING

1. Cook soaked, glutinous rice as in Plain Rice (see page 237).
2. While the cooked rice is still hot, stir in coconut, anise seed, sugar, and lard or butter. Mix well.
3. Brush an 8- to 8½-inch baking dish with vegetable oil. Pour in rice mixture, press, and spread it evenly. When it is cool, cut into squares. Serve at room temperature as a snack.


# SUGARY OLD MEN
## (SUGAR EGG PUFFS)
Makes about 20

These sweet, airy puffs are favorites among the countless breakfast and snack items in China. In the morning, as we children walked to school, they were hawked on the streets. Round and golden, frosted with glittering white sugar, they often lured away the lunch money in our fists.

In China, the name of this sweet actually means "sugary old men"; however, no one I have asked could tell me the origin of this name. It might be that the white sugar on the puffs was seen as the white hair of an old man.

These sugary old men can be made hours in advance. Be sure to follow the instructions carefully, frying them in warm oil in the beginning. They are excellent for dessert or as a tea snack.

PREPARATION OF INGREDIENTS

1 cup plus 2 tablespoons water
2 tablespoons lard or butter
1 cup all-purpose flour
½ teaspoon baking ammonia (obtain in drugstore)
5 large eggs
oil for deep-frying
about 1 cup sugar

## DIRECTIONS FOR COOKING

1. In a medium-sized pot, place water and lard or butter and bring to a rolling boil. Turn off heat. Immediately stir in flour and baking ammonia. Add eggs, one at a time, stirring constantly until batter is thick but smooth. Set aside.

2. Heat oil over low heat. When oil is a little hotter than lukewarm, drop in about 2 tablespoons of batter for each puff. Deep-fry puffs slowly, a few at a time, turning from time to time, until puffs expand four times their original size. This process is usually slow. When puffs reach their maximum size, turn heat to a higher temperature, about medium or medium-high. Deep-fry egg puffs until they turn a rich golden color or a pale brown, and are firm and crisp outside. Drain on paper towels, and roll in sugar to coat evenly while they are still warm.

3. Cool oil to low temperature before putting in batter for another batch of egg puffs; repeat, cooking the remaining egg puffs in the same manner. Serve warm or at room temperature. They can cooked a few hours in advance, then covered with paper napkins.

Note: If egg puffs do not expand as much as they should, or are still battery inside, turn heat down to very low. Egg puffs expand in low temperature—not instantly, but slowly—so be patient. Also, be sure to raise the oil temperature after egg puffs finish expanding, so that they are firm and crisp outside.

# ALMOND COOKIES
Makes about 30

$\mathrm{T}$ he Chinese call these walnut cookies, and they are at least twice as large as the American-made almond cookies. A walnut is pressed on each cookie instead of an almond, but you may use either walnuts or almonds.

Walnut cookies are among the traditional wedding pastries which the groom's family gives by the hundreds to the bride-to-be. Her family gives them to relatives and friends as a way of announcing the coming wedding, and showing pride that their daughter is well-considered by her new family.

This tradition is still very strong among many Chinese. My family, especially my grandmother, felt very sorry when I told them that I was not going to ask for wedding pastry from my American groom-to-be. Grandmother, then seventy-two, had always been open-minded and considerate. But the notion of marrying off her eldest granddaughter without the wedding pastry was a shame that she could not bear. Even her maids received pastry, she said; how could she face the spirits of her ancestors?

Already in a daze from learning that he had to provide twenty tables of wedding banquet, my groom-to-be was too numb to run or to fight. We compromised. I received one-hundred dozen Chinese pastries and one-hundred dozen Western cream-filled pastries, which were much cheaper than the Chinese pastry.

My grandmother was pleased. So were my parents. My groom-to-be gained his first respect and acceptance, being complimented that he did look Chinese, if one did not notice his eyes and nose.

## PREPARATION OF INGREDIENTS
1½ cups sugar
1 teaspoon vanilla extract or almond extract
8 ounces lard or butter
4 cups sifted all-purpose flour
1 teaspoon baking soda
1 teaspoon baking powder
3 eggs: beat until slightly foamy
½ cup uncooked walnuts or almonds
1 egg (for brushing cookies): beat until slightly foamy

## DIRECTIONS FOR COOKING

1. In a mixing bowl, cream together sugar, vanilla or almond extract, and lard.

2. Combine flour and baking soda and powder, and mix with the creamed sugar and lard or butter. Pour in the 3 beaten eggs. Mix until dough forms into a smooth ball.

3. Roll dough into a 2-inch-diameter sausage (a smaller-diameter sausage can be used to make smaller cookies), then cut into ½-inch-thick rounds. Slightly flatten the edge of each round with your hand. Gently press a walnut or almond in the center of each cookie. Brush cookies with the beaten egg.

4. Arrange cookies on cookie sheet lined with aluminum foil. Do not preheat oven. Put cookies in cold oven, turn oven to 325 degrees, and bake for 20 to 25 minutes or until cookies are golden brown. Let oven cool completely before baking the remaining cookies. Repeat procedure. Cool before storing in cookie jar.

# Sauces and Dips

# SAUCES AND DIPS

## BEAN SAUCE DIP
Makes about ⅓ cup

4 tablespoons Sichuan sweet bean sauce or ground bean sauce
4 teaspoons sugar
4 teaspoons sesame oil

Heat all the ingredients in a small pot over low heat. Stir constantly until it is smooth and hot. Put in individual serving dishes. Serve warm.

## CHILI OIL
Makes about 1½ cups

Chili oil is available in Chinese grocery stores. But it is best to prepare your own. The following recipe will provide you with enough chili oil for years.

For this chili oil, use regular chili peppers, those the size of your little finger. They are hot but not unbearable if you swallow one. Most Chinese and Italian grocery stores sell them in packages.

2 cups corn oil
1½ cups dried red chili peppers: tear or chop into small pieces,
      do not discard seeds
5 teaspoons cayenne pepper

1. In a small pot, heat oil over medium-low heat. The oil should be hot, but not yet to deep-fry temperature. (Test by dropping a pepper in oil. If pepper sizzles gently, then oil is right. If pepper turns black quickly, oil is too hot; cool it down before adding the rest of peppers.) Add peppers and their seeds. Cover and cook gently over low heat, stirring from time to time, until all the peppers turn black. Turn off heat and let oil cool a little, about 15 minutes, before adding cayenne. (If oil is too hot, it will burn the cayenne.)
2. Add cayenne, stir, and mix well. Cover and let peppers, cayenne, and oil stand

at room temperature overnight.

3. Strain chili oil, which is orange-red in color, through cheesecloth into jar. Cover and keep in refrigerator—it will last for years! (The chili oil will become cloudy in the refrigerator, but it will clear up quickly at room temperature.)

## FIVE-FRAGRANCE SALT DIP
Makes about ⅓ cup

6 tablespoons salt
¼ teaspoon five-fragrance powder
½ teaspoon ground pepper

Heat a small dry pot. Put in salt and stir it constantly. When salt is very hot, add five-fragrance powder and ground pepper. Mix well and turn off heat. Cool; put in a covered jar. It will keep for months. Use sparingly. Put small amount into small dishes and serve as a dip. It is also very good to use as a table salt.

## FLOWER PEPPERCORN POWDER
Makes about ⅓ cup

6 tablespoons flower peppercorns or more

Heat a small dry pot over medium heat. Add flower peppercorns. Stir constantly until peppercorns turn deep brown and become aromatic. (They smoke slightly.) Remove from heat. Grind roasted peppercorns to a powder in a pepper mill. Put in a covered jar. It will keep for months.

## FLOWER PEPPERCORN AND SALT DIP
Makes about ⅓ cup

2 teaspoons flower peppercorn powder (see preceding recipe)
4 tablespoons salt
1 teaspoon ground pepper

Mix all the ingredients. Store in a covered jar; it will keep for months. Use sparingly. Put small amount into small dishes and serve as a dip.

# FRESH CHILI-SOY DIP
Makes 4 servings

¼ cup fresh hot chili peppers cut into small rings, do not discard seeds
6 tablespoons black soy sauce
2 tablespoons Chinese red vinegar
2 tablespoons peanut oil or corn oil

Put peppers, soy sauce, and vinegar in a serving bowl. Heat oil and pour over mixture. Mix together and serve.

# GINGER-SCALLION DIP
Makes 4 servings

3 tablespoons peanut oil or corn oil
2 tablespoons sesame oil
3 tablespoons finely minced ginger
1 cup finely shredded scallions
1 teaspoon salt

Heat peanut or corn oil. Add sesame oil, cool, then pour over ginger, scallions, and salt in a serving bowl. Mix together and serve.

# GINGER-VINEGAR DIP
Makes 4 servings

3 tablespoons finely shredded fresh ginger
6 tablespoons Chinese red vinegar or cider vinegar

Mix in a bowl and serve.

# HOISIN SAUCE DIP
Makes 4 servings

8 tablespoons hoisin sauce
1 tablespoon sesame oil

Heat hoisin sauce and sesame oil in a pot over low heat. Stir constantly until it is hot. Put in individual serving dishes. Serve warm.

# MUSTARD-OIL DIP
Makes about 4 servings

2 tablespoons Colman's mustard powder
1 teaspoon sesame oil

Mix mustard with enough water to make a thin paste. Then put in a serving bowl and top with sesame oil.

# PLUM SAUCE DIP
Makes about 2 cups

4 tablespoons sugar (optional)
4 tablespoons water
1-pound can plum sauce

Dissolve sugar in water over low heat. Mix sugar water with plum sauce. Put in a container and refrigerate. Serve at room temperature.

# SOY-CHILI DIP

Makes 4 servings

4 tablespoons black soy sauce
2 teaspoons chili oil

Mix in a serving bowl and serve.


# SOY-SESAME DIP

Makes 4 servings

4 tablespoons black soy sauce
1 tablespoon sesame oil

Put soy sauce in a small serving dish. Add oil and serve.


# OIL-OYSTER SAUCE DIP

Makes 4 servings

6 tablespoons oyster-flavored sauce
1 tablespoon peanut oil or corn oil
1 teaspoon sesame oil

Put oyster-flavored sauce in a serving bowl. Heat oils in a small pot, pour it over oyster-flavored sauce, and serve warm.


# SOY-VINEGAR DIP

Makes about 4 servings

4 tablespoons Chinese red vinegar or cider vinegar
4 tablespoons black soy sauce

Mix in a serving bowl and serve.

# Chinese Cooking Ingredients

# CHINESE COOKING INGREDIENTS WITH INFORMATION ON BUYING AND STORING

ABALONE
The canned variety mostly comes from Japan or Mexico. It is already cooked and ready to be served from the can. It is best to use in stir-fry dishes, congee, or as an appetizer. Cooking time should be short. Excessive heat will toughen it, and it becomes chewy. Liquid from the can is good for soup and congee.

STORING: Drain and rinse. Store in covered jar with enough fresh cold water to cover. Refrigerate. Change water every day. Will keep for about 2 weeks.

AGAR-AGAR (TAI CHOY)
A dried seaweed with no flavor. Sold in packages, mostly from Japan. Resembles a cross between rice sticks and bean thread noodles. Functions like unflavored gelatin in sweet dishes. Cook in water until dissolved, then chill. For use in salad dishes, soak in cold water and cut into 1½-inch lengths.

STORING: Needs no refrigeration. Keeps forever.

ANISE (STAR)
Chinese spice, looks like a ½-inch eight-pointed star, reddish-brown, hard and dried, smells like licorice. Used to flavor meat and poultry. Sold by weight (usually with the points apart).

STORING: Store in covered jar at room temperature; will keep forever.

ASPARAGUS
Choose stalks that are firm and green and moist-looking, with closed tips. Avoid those that have long white bases and droopy heads.

STORING: refrigerate in paper bag; use as soon as possible.

BABY CORN
(See recipe, Beef with Baby Corn and Chinese Mushrooms in Black Bean Sauce.,

page 148)
STORING: Keep in water, changed daily, refrigerated. Will keep for weeks.

## BAMBOO SHOOTS
Young shoots of tropical bamboo, ivory in color; sold in tub in Chinese grocery stores; must rinse thoroughly before use. Because all the so-called fresh bamboo shoots have been par-boiled before sending to the markets, the canned variety is as good as the fresh one. In many ways, they are more convenient, because they are available in slices, strips or in chunks; rinse thoroughly before use.

STORING: in refrigerator in a covered jar with enough water to cover them, change water every other day, will keep for two weeks.

## BEANS, LONG (GREEN)
They are 12-14 inches long and thin like pencils. Choose those that are deep green and firm, so that they will be crisp when cooked. Do not pick those that have black spots. They are sold in bundles in Chinese food stores.

STORING: in refrigerator, they will keep for about three days.

## BEANS, BLACK (SALTED)
Black beans preserved in ginger, garlic, salt, and spices; used as seasoning. Before cooking, they are strong, pungent, and salty in taste; rinse in hot water before use. After cooking, they give a delicious flavor to food. Sold in cans or bags.

STORING: Keep in covered jar; no refrigeration needed; will keep for months.

## BEANS, WHITE, (LONG) [See page 214]

## STRING BEANS
The young string beans are slender and moist. Pick one up and break off the tips from both ends. The break should be easy and have a crisp, snappy sound, revealing moisture. If the tips come off along with small strings, the beans are old.

STORING: keep refrigerated, use within 3 days.

## BEAN CURD (see TOFU)

## BEAN CURD CHEESE (RED AND WHITE)
The red variety is also labeled as red bean cheese, brick-red, 2 inches square and about 1 inch thick. Fermented with beans, red rice, salt water, and rice wine. Strong, pungent, and salty in taste. Mostly used in seasoning. The white bean curd cheese is fermented with the same ingredients except the red rice. Smoother

and less pungent than the red variety. Sold in cans or jars.

STORING: Place in clear glass jar and refrigerate. Will keep for several months.

BEAN CURD PUFFS (see TOFU PUFFS)

# BEAN SAUCES

## BEAN PASTE (SWEET RED)

Dark red color, thick, and quite sweet. Made from puréeing Chinese red beans, sugar, and shortening. Widely used in sweet pastries and sweet dishes. Sold in cans or by weight in Chinese pastry stores.

STORING: Will keep for weeks if refrigerated in covered jar.

## GROUND BEAN SAUCE

Also known as brown bean sauce or brown bean paste. Brown, thick, puréed sauce made from yellow soybeans, flour, salt and water; salty and pungent. Sold in cans.

STORING: Refrigerate in a covered jar; will keep for months.

## SICHUAN CHILI BEAN SAUCE

Orange-brown color, very salty, pungent, spicy, and hot. Used in Sichuan dishes. Available in 6-ounce cans or jars.

STORING: store as ground bean sauce.

## SICHUAN SWEET BEAN SAUCE

Labeled as sweet bean paste sometimes. Not sweet, but salty and pungent; tastes very much like ground bean sauce (which can be used as a substitute) Used in many Sichuan dishes. Available in 6-ounce cans or jars.

STORING: store as ground bean sauce.

## BEAN SPROUTS (WHITE)

Sprouts from mung beans, should be white, firm, and dry. Bad bean sprouts are brownish, limp, and watery because they are fermenting.

STORING: in refrigerator, use within 2 days.

## BEAN SPROUTS (GREEN)

Sprouts of snow peas; known as Taiwan bean sprouts, a newcomer, available only recently. They have green bodies and green heads, and are slightly longer than the white bean sprouts. They have a delicate, nutty flavor. A great addition to the Chinese vegetable family.

STORING: refrigerate in paper bag, will keep for about a week. Keep them dry; they rot easily after washing. Wash just before cooking.

## BIRDS' NESTS
(See recipe, Fu Yung Bird's Nest Soup.)
STORING: Will keep indefinitely.

## BOK CHOY
Means white vegetable in Chinese; a compact, leafy plant with wide white stalks and large ruffled green leaves. Pick the short and stout ones because they are sweeter and more tender. So it is better to buy many smaller heads than a few big ones. Discard the discolored leaves.
STORING: in refrigerator, will keep for about 5 days.

## BOK CHOY (GREEN)
Known as Shanghai bok choy or baby bok choy; look like the regular bok choy except their stalks as well as their leaves are pale green. Pick the smaller ones, because they are younger and sweeter.
STORING: as with bok choy (above).

## BROCCOLI (CHINESE)
The Chinese broccoli is similar to the Italian broccoli rape, which has a slightly bitter taste; but it is enhanced by cooking them with garlic, sugar or oyster sauce. Unlike the Western broccoli, the Chinese broccoli has very few flowers, but long and slender stalks. Strip and discard the large leaves and cut off a little at the end of each stem. The Chinese do not cut them into bite-sized pieces, but prefer to leave the stalk whole.

When you buy broccoli (no matter Chinese or Western), look at the end of each stalk, select those that are clear, without white centers, which indicate that they are woody and tough. Also, choose those that are perky and green. Old broccoli has brownish, droopy flowers.
STORING: refrigerate them in paper bag. Use within three days.

## CHINESE CABBAGE (NAPA)
Shaped like a short and stout celery; the Chinese call them Tientsin bok choy. They have wide, white stalks and light yellow leaves. It is crisp and mild and can be eaten raw. Choose the short and stout ones with pale yellow color, avoid the ones with green leaves.
STORING: in refrigerator, will keep for about 2 weeks.

## CAUL (LACE FAT)

Big sheets of fat that look like a net or lace, caul encases the inner organs of the pig; sold in Chinese or Italian meat stores.

STORING: Will keep for a few days in the refrigerator or for months in the freezer; thaw before use.

## CHICKEN BROTH (CLEAR)

If you prefer, make your own chicken broth. But many Chinese like to use College Inn or Swanson clear chicken broth. You can use straight or mix it with water.

## CHILI OIL (See SAUCES AND DIPS.)

## CHILI PEPPERS (dried)

Dried hot, peppers, orange-red, and the size of a small finger. Use with the seeds, which are essential for the hotness.

STORING: store in covered jar. Will keep for months.

## CHILI SAUCE

There is a variety of good chili sauce in the market. Some are made with garlic or black bean. They are used commonly as dip. Try them, and pick one you like best.

STORING: in covered jar in refrigerator; will keep for months.

## CHIVES, CHINESE (see page 217)

## CLOUD EARS (see MUSHROOMS)

## COCONUT MILK (unsweetened)

Also called coconut cream; thick cream extracted from fresh coconut meat. Imported from the Philippines.

STORING: leftovers can be frozen; will keep for months.

## CORIANDER (fresh)

Also called "Chinese parsley"; a very fragrant herb with long thin stalks and delicate leaves. Used as a seasoning and for garnishing. Sold in Chinese and Spanish grocery stores. Also known as "Spanish parsley" or cilantro.

STORING: wrap and refrigerate. Will keep about 4 days.

## CURRY PASTE (RED AND YELLOW)

Red curry paste is much hotter and spicer than the yellow. Buy the brands made in India or packed and bottled in India, such as the American Roland Food Company's curry paste.

STORING: will keep for months without refrigeration.

## DATES (CHINESE RED)

Chinese red dried dates, the size of small prunes; used in cooking.

STORING: Store in covered jar; will keep for years.

## EGGPLANT

A good eggplant has a firm body, shiny and smooth. An old one has a spongy body with discolored and wrinkled skin.

STORING: Keep refrigerated; use within 3 days.

## EGGS (PRESERVED)

Also known as thousand-year-old eggs. They are uncooked duck eggs coated with clay mixed with lime, ashes, and rice husks, then buried in an earthen pot for about three months. The egg whites become firm, amber-colored, and transparent, sometimes dotted with feather designs. The yolks turn dark green, firm but moist.

STORING: will keep a couple of weeks; no refrigeration needed.

## EGGS (SALTED)

Duck eggs steeped in salted water. The egg yolk should be bright orange and the white clear. If the white is cloudy and smells, throw it away. They are sold in boxes of six. Pick those that have clear white shells.

STORING: will keep at room temperature for two weeks.

## FIVE-FRAGRANCE POWDER

Mixture of five ground spices (star anise, clove, fennel, cinnamon, and peppercorns), cinnamon-colored, fragrant. Used sparingly to flavor food.

STORING: will keep indefinitely in a covered jar.

## FLOWER PEPPERCORN POWDER (See SAUCES AND DIPS)

## FLOWER PEPPERCORNS

Also called wild peppercorns; reddish-brown, gentle and delicate in hotness and scent. Must be roasted to release the fragrance.

STORING: will keep indefinitely in tightly covered jar.

## GINGER (fresh)

A very important seasoning in Chinese cooking, especially seafood. Eliminates fishy and gamy odors and adds flavor to meat, poultry, and seafood. Comes in a variety of shapes, like a thin potato covered with knobs. When it is young, the skin is smooth and has the color of a young potato; darker skin indicates an older root which is dry and fibrous. The meat is ivory in color and has a clear fresh smell as well as a hot and spicy taste. Always choose the one that is plump and smooth. Do not pick ginger that is dry and wrinkled. Its body will be dry and stringy.

Some old Chinese place slices of ginger root on the forehead to draw out bad air in the head (to cure headache).

STORING: will keep about a week without refrigeration.

## GINGER (SWEET RED IN SYRUP)

Ginger chunks dyed a red color, then Preserved in syrup. Sweet, hot, and crunchy. May be used in sweet and sour dishes for color or just eaten like candy. Sold by the bottle.

STORING: will keep indefinitely in jar at room temperature.

## GINGER JUICE

Not available in Chinese grocery stores. The simplest way to make it is to press a small chunk of fresh ginger root with a garlic press. Catch the juice in a small bowl. If you do not have a garlic press, just finely mince the ginger root.

## GINKGO NUTS

Nuts with hard, white shells. Available fresh or canned. Since fresh ones are often dried out inside or rotted, I suggest buying them canned.

STORING: cover with water and keep refrigerated. Will keep for a week. Frozen, they will keep for months.

## HOISIN SAUCE

Means "seafood sauce" in Chinese. Thick, brownish-red paste, spicy, salty, and moderately sweet; made from soybeans, water, garlic, chili, flour, and spices. Used in many dishes.

STORING: keeps for months refrigerated in covered jar.

## JELLYFISH SKIN

A sea organism (not the kind we see on beaches), dried, salted, and pressed into thin circles, about 14 to 16 inches in diameter. Crunchy and resilient, more texture than flavor. Must be rinsed and soaked before use. Used mostly in cold dishes. Sold by weight.

STORING: Will keep for months in refrigerator if salt is not removed. If already soaked, immerse in cold water, cover, and refrigerate. Change fresh water every two days. Will keep for weeks.

## LEEKS (See page 218)

## LETTUCE

"Lettuce" in Chinese sounds like the word for "growing wealth"; therefore, it is often included in Chinese New Year dinners, as a symbol of prosperity. Because waste matter is often used as fertilizer in China, we seldom eat lettuce raw; rather, we stir-fry it briefly (see page 15) . My first choice is iceberg lettuce, my second is romaine, for their crispness after being cooked. With iceberg lettuce, choose a head that is tight and pale green.

## LILY BUDS (DRIED)

Also known as golden needles or dried tiger lily buds. They are 2–3 inches long. The better kinds are still flexible, not brittle, and have a very pale gold color. Add delicate flavor in soup, poultry, meat, and fish.

STORING: Put in a sealed jar; will keep for months without refrigeration.

## LOTUS LEAVES

The leaves, fresh or dried, are primarily used to wrap and give a subtle flavor to food. They are available dried in some Chinese grocery stores.

## LOTUS SEEDS (DRIED)

Represent fertility and birth. Used in many dishes. Must be cooked.

STORING: will keep indefinitely in a jar.

## MANDARIN PANCAKES (See Peking Duck recipe, page 109)

## MUSTARD GREEN (PICKLED)

Also labeled as salted mustard greens, these are sold in barrels or in cans in Chinese grocery stores.

STORING: will keep for a few days in refrigerator or for months in the freezer.

## BITTER MELON (See recipe page 220)

## SILK MELON
Some Chinese markets call them Chinese okras. However, they do not taste at all like okra. They are giant in size—14-16 inches long and about 1½ inches in diameter, with tough, inedible, green skins and sharp edges. However, the flesh is smooth, silky and mildly sweet when cooked. Choose the young ones that are firm, heavy and break easily. Avoid the old ones that are light in weight, dry and tough.

STORING: In refrigerator will keep for about 4 days.

## WINTER MELON

Shape is between a watermelon and a pumpkin; green, frosty tough skin and soft white meat; mild and delicate in flavor. Sold fresh by weight, whole or in wedges.

STORING: Wrap with plastic wrap; will keep about 4 days in refrigerator.

# MUSHROOMS

## BUTTON MUSHROOMS (CANNED)
Identical to American button mushrooms canned in water. You may use the domestic or imported kind. Rinse before use.

STORING: store in refrigerator.

## CHINESE DRIED MUSHROOMS
Dried, black, aromatic, and luscious; sizes range from ½ inch to 2¼ inches in diameter. Used in innumerable ways. Must be soaked before use.

STORING: Will keep indefinitely in tightly covered container.

## CLOUD EARS
Also known as tree fungus or tree mushrooms; black, small, crinkled dried tree fungus. Must be soaked in hot water before use; will expand two to three times original size. They resemble a cluster of clouds or human ears; soft and resilient in texture, subtle and dainty in taste. Used to cook with chicken, meat, vegetables, or in soup. Sold by weight.

STORING: Will keep indefinitely in a covered jar at room temperature.

## STRAW MUSHROOMS (CANNED)
Also called grass mushrooms; very delicate, some small and some big, canned in water. Rinse before use.

STORING: store in refrigerator.

# NOODLES

## BEAN THREAD NOODLES

Also known as pea-starch noodles or cellophane noodles; wiry, hard, clear white noodles; made from mung beans. If used in soup, must be pre-soaked. They are very absorbent and become soft and translucent after soaking. Almost tasteless, but they easily absorb flavor of other ingredients. Should not be overcooked or they will become mushy. When deep-fried, no need to presoak; they pop up from oil like a snow-white nest. Sold in 2- or 6-ounce packages.

STORING: will keep indefinitely.

## FRESH RICE NOODLES (SHA HO NOODLES OR FEN)

Sha Ho in Chinese means "sand river." Made daily in noodle stores with finely ground rice powder and water. The dough is spread thinly over greased, metal trays and steamed to be set in ⅛-inch-thick white sheets. Then each sheet is rolled and cut into ½-inch-wide noodles. Used in soup or in stir-frying. Cook briefly; otherwise they become mushy. Sold by the sheet or by the pound. Available fresh in some Chinese noodle or bean curd stores.

STORING: Put in a plastic bag, they will keep in refrigerator for about 5 days.

## FRESH NOODLES

Made with flour and eggs, golden in color, elastic and usually thin. Sold by the pound.

STORING: will keep in refrigerator for about 5 days. Can be kept frozen for a couple of months.

## DRIED RICE NOODLES

Also labeled "dried rice sticks," they look almost like bean noodles, but are whiter and more brittle. Use them in stir-frying, soup, or deep-frying. For soup or stir-frying, they must be presoaked in hot tap water for about 15 minutes or until soft. There is no need to soak them if they are deep-fried. They pop up from the hot oil in a white nest.

STORING: will keep indefinitely without refrigeration.

## SHANGHAI NOODLES (fresh)

Made with flour without eggs, white in color, elastic, about ⅛-inch wide, sold by the pound.

STORING: can be frozen for a couple of months.

## TOFU NOODLES (GAN SI)

Also labeled as tofu shreds or bean curd sticks; fresh, thin, beige noodles, made of yellow soy beans; used in stir-frying; sold in package.

STORING: in refrigerator, will keep for a week or more.

# OILS

## PEANUT OIL, CORN OIL, AND VEGETABLE OIL

Chinese prefer to use peanut oil in the Orient, but I find corn oil is very good in the States. So use either peanut or corn oil for stir-fry cooking. For deep-frying, corn oil is the best choice, but vegetable oil will do, and it is more economical.

STORING: it can be reused many times. Strain it and keep it refrigerated. Discard the oil when it becomes dark and heavy with residues.

Oil used for cooking fish should be kept in a separate bottle. Reuse it for fish only. Keep refrigerated.

To remove odor from oil: heat the used oil to deep-fry temperature (375 degrees). Add 2 to 3 slices of fresh ginger root or raw peeled potato; fry until they turn golden. Then discard them; the oil will be refreshed.

## SESAME OIL

Savory, aromatic, topaz-colored oil made from roasted, white sesame seeds. Used sparingly to flavor food.

STORING: will keep indefinitely if refrigerated,

## OYSTER-FLAVORED SAUCE

A thick, caramel-colored sauce made from oyster extract, water, salt, and starch; salty, pungent, and tasty. Adds flavor to meat and poultry and is also used as a table condiment. There are many grades. The best kind is thinner and more runny than the inferior kind, which is usually too thick to pour and sometimes foamy.

STORING: cover and refrigerate. Will keep indefinitely.

## PEA SHOOT

These are the tender, dainty shoots of the snow peas, with a nutty flavor. Traditionally, they are a delicacy, served only on formal occasions, because of the scarcity. Now, they are sold in most of the Chinese grocery stores. Trim and discard the large leaves and stems. Use only the tender tips.

STORING: refrigerate in paper bag. Use within a week. Wash just before cooking.

## SNOW PEAS (fresh)

The Chinese also call them Holland peas. They supposedly originated in Holland. Choose pods that are soft and thin. These are young pods in which the peas have not yet matured. They are juicy, crisp, and sweet. Those that have thick pods and large peas with yellowish color are old.

STORING: keep in refrigerator, use within three days.

## PICKLES (SICHUAN)

Sometimes this pickle is labeled Sichuan Cabbage, Sichuan Jah Choy, or Sichuan vegetable. It comes in chunks in cans and is sold in Chinese food stores. It is hot, spicy, and salty, and must be rinsed before cooking.

STORING: do not rinse off salt and spices. Put in a tightly covered jar. This will keep for months in the refrigerator. It can also be frozen.

## PLUM SAUCE

Also known as duck sauce, it is a thick, chutney-like sauce, spicy, sweet, and sour, made from plums, ginger, apricots, chilies, vinegar, sugar, and water. Used as a table condiment for duck, fried wontons, egg rolls, or spring rolls. For thinner dip, dilute the whole can with sugar and water, see Plum Sauce Dip, page 314.

STORING: will keep for months refrigerated in a covered jar.

## PORK (CANTONESE BARBECUED)

Marinated pork chunks roasted on skewers; sweet, tender, and savory. Can be made at home (see page 126) or bought in Chinese grocery stores. Used in many dishes or eaten as cold meat.

STORING: wrap and refrigerate; will keep 4 to 5 days. May also be frozen.

## RICE CRUST
See page 237

## RICE (GLUTINOUS)
See page 236

## RICE POWDER
Powder ground from rice. Used in pastries and sweet dishes.
STORING: as with flour.

## RICE POWDER (GLUTINOUS)
Fine powder ground from white, glutinous rice; whiter than wheat flour. When cooked, becomes soft, sticky, and chewy. Used in making dumplings, sweet dishes, and pastries.
STORING: as with rice flour.

RICE STICKS (dried)
See Rice Noodles

SAUSAGE (CHINESE PORK)
Minced pork cured with seasonings, stuffed in casings, then tied in pairs to air-dry. Each link is 5–6 inches long and ½ inch in diameter. Red and white in color, savory and rich in taste. Used in stuffing, rice, soup, or steamed and served as a dish.
    STORING: wrap and refrigerate or hang in cool place; will keep for weeks.

SCALLIONS
Also known as spring onions; in a Chinese kitchen, scallions, fresh ginger root, and garlic are as essential as salt and pepper. The scallions are used like the American onion, which we call "foreign scallions". When we use scallions, we use not only the white part, but also some of the green part. But do pinch off the tired ends and discard the roots.
    STORING: keep refrigerated, use within one week.

SESAME SEEDS
Tiny seeds with nutty flavor; there are two varieties: black and white. Used in making oil, pastries, and dumplings.
    STORING: in covered jar, will keep for many months.

SHA CHA SAUCE
(See page 230)

SHAN ZHA BING
Also labeled as preserved plums, shan zha bing, or san jan cakes; made from sugar, plums, or apples, pressed into quarter-sized thin wafers. Red in color, sweet and sour in taste. Believed to enhance appetite; therefore, many old Chinese prefer children to eat shan zah bing rather than candies. Used in making sweet and sour sauce before ketchup became popular.
    STORING: in covered jar, will keep indefinitely.

SHRIMP (CHINESE DRIED)
Shelled and dried under the sun, they have a sharp flavor. They are used in small amounts for stuffing, with rice, or in soup. Best variety is light orange-pink and about 1 inch long. If color is dark and texture is powdery, they are no longer good.

STORING: will keep for months in a tightly covered jar without refrigeration.

## SHRIMP CHIPS

Thin, hard, quarter-size chips in assorted colors, made with shrimp, flour, and seasonings. Must be deep-fried to puff up and double in size; tasty and crisp. Eaten as a snack like potato chips or, used as a garnish for dishes.

STORING: will keep indefinitely. Need no refrigeration.

## SNOW PEAS (See PEAS)

## SOY BEAN NOODLES (See NOODLES)

## SOY BEAN SKINS (DRIED)

These yellow, paper-thin skins are dried but flexible. Some are 24 inches in diameter. They are the rich cream which floats on top of the soy bean milk. They are sold in packages in Chinese food stores.

STORING: refrigerate in plastic bag. Will keep for about a week.

# SOY SAUCES

Soy sauces are the most important seasoning in Chinese cooking. There are many varieties and grades. Thin or black, good or bad, domestic or imported, all are labeled "soy sauce" in English. Knowing their differences and using the right kind is the key to authentic, good-tasting dishes. The basic and frequently used soy sauces are black soy sauce and thin soy sauce. Others, such as fish-flavored soy, mushroom soy, and double black soy, are regional soy sauces for certain local dishes.

## BLACK SOY SAUCE

This is also known as dark soy sauce. It is made from soybeans, caramel, sugar, flour, salt, and water. Darker and heavier than thin soy sauce, it has a salty but slightly sweet taste. If you cannot read Chinese and don't know whether the bottle is black soy sauce or thin soy sauce, read the ingredients. If the ingredients contain sugar and caramel, it is black soy sauce; without them it is thin soy sauce. For stir-frying, I prefer the black soy sauce made by Amoy Canning Company. Soy sauce labeled "double dark soy sauce" is good for red cooking, but not as good for stir-frying: it is too heavy and sometimes too salty.

STORING: if it is not used very often, keep it in the refrigerator, and it will keep for months. If a white substance appears on the surface, the soy has turned bad; discard it.

## DOUBLE BLACK SOY SAUCE
Double black soy sauce, darker and heavier in taste than black soy sauce, is used in red cooking to add color and strength. The taste varies with the company that produces it. Some are slightly sweeter or saltier than others. I prefer the double black soy sauce made by Yuet Heung Yuen Company from Hong Kong. It is available in Chinese grocery stores.

STORING: store as black soy sauce.

## FISH-FLAVORED SOY SAUCE
Fish-flavored soy is a Southern soy, made with salt, water, and extract of fish. Its color is slightly lighter than the thin soy sauce. Use it as a dip or in dishes that require a fish flavor. It is available in Chinese grocery stores.

STORING: store as black soy sauce.

## MUSHROOM SOY SAUCE
Mushroom soy is very much like black soy sauce, but richer in taste and in color; it is made from soybean extract, flour, mushrooms, salt, and water. It may be used as a substitute for black soy sauce. The Pearl River Bridge brand from China is good. It is sold in Chinese grocery stores, especially those that carry goods from mainland China.

STORING: store as black soy sauce.

## THIN SOY SAUCE
Thin soy sauce, also known as light soy sauce, is made from soybeans, flour, salt, and water. It is topaz-colored, but thinner and saltier than black soy sauce.

STORING: store as black soy sauce.

## LITE SOY SAUCE (low sodium)
There are numbers of brands of this kind of soy sauce available in the market. They are about 40% less in salt than the regular soy sauces; therefore, they should not be used for preparing the recipes in this book. However, they are excellent for using as dips or as table condiments.

## SPRING ROLL SKINS (SHANGHAI)
Confusingly labeled as egg roll skins in America. Cooked, translucent crêpes, paper-thin and delicate, mostly handmade. Come in round or square sheets, 9 inches in diameter; made from thin flour batter or marshmallow-like dough adhered to a hot iron skillet. Used to wrap cooked meat, vegetables, seafood, or stuffed and then deep-fried. Will dissolve or turn mushy if put in soup. Sold in stacks by weight.

STORING: wrap and freeze. Will keep for months. Thaw at room temperature an hour or until soft.

## SICHUAN PICKLES
Sometimes labeled Sichuan cabbage or Sichuan vegetables, comes in chunks in cans. Hot, spicy, and salty; rinse before cooking.

STORING: do not rinse off salt and spices. Put in a tightly covered jar. Will keep for months in refrigerator. Also can be frozen.

## TANGERINE PEEL (DRIED)
Also known as old tangerine peel or mandarin orange peel; dried tangerine skin with coffee color and a condensed sweet fragrance. Used to flavor food.

STORING: keeps indefinitely in a tightly covered jar. The longer it is kept, the better it is.

## TARO
A potato-like starchy root with dusty, rough skin. Comes in many sizes and varieties. Can be slow-cooked with meat, deep-fried, steamed, or used in making pastry. The kind with white meat and purple, feathery grains is the best.

STORING: will keep about a week, if refrigerated.

## TOFU (BEAN CURD)
Made of soybeans, puréed, then pressed into brick-like cakes, 1 inch thick and 2 to 4 inches square. Smooth, fragile, custard-like, and ivory-colored. Tofu itself is bland in taste, but it quickly absorbs flavor from other ingredients with which it is cooked. As it is inexpensive and high in protein, tofu serves the purpose of meat and milk for many Chinese in addition to being used as a vegetable. Tofu is a nutritious and well-loved food. My grandmother used to say "Eat tofu everyday and your eyes will shine like the autumn moon; your skin will be smooth, and your hair soft and black." Available in Oriental grocery stores and many Western supermarkets. If you are buying those that are packed in boxes, pick the ones in which the water is clear and not cloudy. Avoid the tofu that is brownish and slimy.

STORING: in refrigerator, will keep for a week or more. If it is opened, cover with water and change water daily.

## TOFU, FIVE-FRAGRANCE
They are pressed soy bean cakes, seasoned with five-fragrance powder; hard and dark brown; slightly smoky in taste; available in Chinese grocery stores.

STORING: refrigerated, will keep for about a week.

## TOFU PUFFS (FRIED)
Golden color, fluffy and spongy, cushion–like, square cakes.
    STORING: store in plastic bag. Will keep for two weeks if refrigerated.

## TURNIP (CHINESE WHITE GIANT)
Shaped like a big sweet potato; has a white body and translucent skin. Mild in taste. Choose one that is firm and heavy. A good white turnip is solid, heavy, and firm. Inside it is moist, clear, and without white lines. An undesirable turnip is light, and the inside is dry and full of fancy designs. The Chinese describe an untrue mate as "Flower heart turnip," for he or she is light in heart and full of fancy desires. Will keep for a week in a refrigerator.

# VINEGARS

## CHINESE RED VINEGAR
Made from rice; has a clear color in the bottle but turns red within hours after bottle is opened. Used in cooking as well as in dips.
    STORING: store at room temperature; will keep indefinitely.

## CHINESE SWEET VINEGAR
Made from sugar and black vinegar; sweet, black, and pungent; also known as childbirth vinegar. Used primarily in cooking with ginger, pig's feet, and eggs. A nutritious, popular folk tonic (delicious too) of southern China; specially cooked and served to women after childbirth to help them regain strength (see recipe, page 135).
    STORING: at room temperature; will keep many months.

## VINEGAR (CHENKONG)
Chenkong (also Romanized as Chen-Chiang) is a large city in Kiangsu Province of China. This vinegar is dark brown, tangy, and spicy. With more strength and body than Chinese red vinegar. It is sold in Chinese grocery stores. No substitutes.
    STORING: will keep for months in refrigerator.

## WATER CHESTNUT POWDER
Lumpy, grayish flour made from water chestnuts. Used in making sweet pastries or as batter to coat deep-fried foods for crispness. Sold by weight.
    STORING: store as flour.

## WATER CHESTNUTS

The fresh variety are quarter-sized button-like bulbs, with deep purple skins. They grow in shallow, muddy water. When fresh and young, the meat is crystal white, sweet, juicy, and crisp. If old, they become starchy and less sweet. Must be skinned; eat fresh as fruit, or as vegetable cook with meat and poultry. Also can be glazed in sugar or ground into powder to make sweet pastry.

The canned variety are peeled and in water; crisp, but have lost sweetness in canning. Used as a vegetable; cook with meat and poultry.

STORING: let the mud stay on the skin to protect fresh water chestnuts from drying out; if refrigerated, will keep for 4 to 5 days. Or you may wash and peel them, put in a jar, cover with cold water, refrigerate, and change water every other day. Canned water chestnuts should be stored in the same way. Will keep for weeks. Freezing is not desirable; the meat becomes spongy.

## WHEAT STARCH

Wheat flour with gluten removed. Used in making dim sum. No substitutes.
STORING: store as flour.

## WINE (RICE WINE AND DRY SHERRY)

The purpose of using a small amount of wine in many dishes is not just for the flavor, but also to eliminate the odor in seafood, poultry, and meat. Rice wine is widely used by the Chinese in cooking. If it is not available, dry Sherry is the best substitute.

## SWEET WINE SAUCE (FERMENTED WINE RICE)

Glutinous rice fermented with wine balls. Sweet wine sauce is sold in jars; the rice is spongy and the sauce is sweet.
STORING: needs to be refrigerated; will keep for months.

## WONTON SKINS

Also known as shao-mai skins; 3½-inch squares, thinner than egg roll skins, but made with the same ingredients. Stuffed with shrimp, crab meat, meat, or vegetables, then cooked in broth, steamed, or deep-fried. Sold in packages.
STORING: will keep refrigerated for 4 to 5 days. Will keep frozen, sealed by the dozen in plastic wrap, for months. Thaw at room temperature for an hour or until soft.

YU CHOY (see BROCCOLI, CHINESE)

Yu Choy is one of the most delicious Chinese green vegetables. It has tiny yellow flowers, green leaves, and stems which are all delicious It has more flavor than bok choy and is also crisper. You can buy it in bundles in Chinese grocery stores.

STORING: keep in refrigerator; use within 4 days.

# Index